A Powerful Method for Elevating
Your Value and Relationships

BOUNDARY
BADASS

JAN YUHAS, M.A., MFT
JILLIAN YUHAS, M.A., MFT

For more information, visit www.boundarybadass.com

ISBN Paperback: 979-8-9888099-8-2

CONTENTS

PREFACE

About the Authors

Jan Yuhas, M.A., MFT, and Jillian Yuhas, M.A., MFT, inspire individuals to create remarkable relationships, elevate their value, and set boundaries like badasses. Their purpose is to provide the knowledge and skills needed to break free from feelings of powerlessness, ultimately allowing individuals to flourish in their relationships and their lives.

Being intuitive individuals has come with challenging life lessons for Jillian and Jan. In the past, they would speak up about their concerns when problems arose, yet their emotional expressions often resulted in temporary solutions that quickly fell short. Back then, they had no idea that their personal journey of self-discovery would ultimately become one of their most rewarding experiences, which they would later share with others. Tough times became turning points and even bigger blessings when they learned how to embrace their values to set healthy boundaries.

Setting boundaries became their calling after experiencing their needs being ignored in their personal relationships and clients pushing outside contractual agreements in their former entrepreneurial endeavors. In realizing this, they encountered others who also experienced similar situations in their relationships. The sisterly duo knew there had to be a better way to be heard, understood, and valued without enduring personal and professional losses. When the sisters discovered an effective communication method to overcome setbacks without creating a greater disconnect in their relationships, it allowed them to easily navigate difficult conversations on their journey of personal and professional development.

The mission behind the BOUNDARY BADASS METHOD is to inspire people to elevate their value and relationships. This method provides individuals with the framework to assertively express their authentic voice, honor their self-worth, fulfill their emotional needs, create valuable personal and professional relationships, and set boundaries like a badass. The BOUNDARY BADASS METHOD serves as a key to unlocking success in establishing and maintaining healthy relationships. By implementing this powerful approach, you gain techniques and strategies necessary to navigate the intricacies of interpersonal connections with self-assurance.

Boundaries are set to respect the relationship with oneself while simultaneously strengthening connections with others. When boundaries are set with good-natured individuals, they are usually met in good faith. However, not every individual encountered will be willing to respect your boundaries. Some individuals have deep-rooted personality complexities where their need for control and power takes precedence over the connection. If someone is unable to respect your boundary to the extent that your personal or professional life is threatened emotionally or physically, seeking professional support or physically removing oneself may be necessary.

The wisdom and guidance presented throughout the book is a result of the authors' Master of Arts in Marriage and Family Therapy, certifications in life coaching, mediation, micro-expressions, body language, deception detection, crisis counseling, and personal and professional experiences.

ONE

WHAT ARE BOUNDARIES

Have you ever found yourself biting your tongue or reacting out of frustration? And, once you do speak up, you have immediate regrets because of how the person negatively reacts to your wants and needs. If this sounds familiar, then you may feel like you are walking on eggshells to appease others, suppressing your feelings out of deeply rooted fears, or lashing out when you feel emotionally triggered and unsafe. Approaching relationship challenges by silencing your voice or outwardly expressing heightened emotion can lead to greater discord and unhealthy relational patterns where your needs are not met.

If you've ever experienced feelings of uncertainty and discomfort in your relationships, then this book will inspire you to feel confident in resolving relationship challenges and voicing your value. This book is for the person whose voice was shattered or underdeveloped in childhood. For the individuals whose voice has been denied for many years in unhealthy relationships. For the ones who are fearful of speaking up because their needs have been repeatedly ignored. For the person who has had their limits violated one too many times and feels powerless on how to command respect. For the person who is uncertain about how to respond to high-conflict or complex personality types out of fear of their reaction. For the individual who knows their worth but lacks clarity on how to best position their value for a desirable outcome. For those who are exhausted with not being heard, understood, valued, or respected. For anyone ready to feel powerful and build mutually beneficial relationships.

Although it may be uncomfortable, speaking up is the best way to be seen and heard. It can be daunting to express your needs and show vulnerability, but you have to ask yourself, *What is my inner peace worth?* Staying silent can lead to carrying the weight of emotional stressors and limiting beliefs, engaging in unhealthy relationship cycles, self-abandonment, and low self-esteem. As this happens, an individual begins to devalue their worth, creating an imbalance in the connection and affecting the overall health of the relationship and oneself.

Having healthy boundaries supports the foundation of your self-worth while authentically living according to your truth for personal alignment. Boundaries give you the ability to speak with confidence and conviction when a partner, colleague, family member, client, or friend violates your personal limits without hindering the connection. They enable you to get to the root of the disconnect and create a resolution that allows the relationship to effectively move forward with mutual respect.

Regardless of your personal or professional relationships, a positive voice of reason can inspire others to grow a relationship with you. It is important to remember that how you communicate your value is vital to your relationship success. As you embark on this self-discovery journey, you will quickly see how implementing the BOUNDARY BADASS METHOD will positively impact your relationships and lifestyle. Within minutes, you can turn uncomfortable conversations into remarkable moments of growth while feeling internally powerful. And most importantly, you will feel respected and valued.

To better understand the importance of BOUNDARIES and their purpose, we have created the following acronym for relationship B.O.U.N.D.A.R.I.E.S.

B. *Being Badass:* Aligning to your inner truth and speaking from your values to maintain self-respect and mutual respect with others.

O. *Owning Self-Worth*: Believing in yourself from a place of internal value and setting the standard for how you deserve to be treated.

U. *Understanding All Perspectives:* Having an open mind for understanding and respecting viewpoints or beliefs outside your own.

N. *Negotiating Differences:* Clarifying different perspectives, and when needed, negotiating back and forth until an amicable agreement meets the needs and goals of the relationship.

D. *Defining Values:* Providing clarity, certainty, and standards for personal alignment and fulfillment in your life and relationships.

A. *Asking for Alignment:* Establishing boundaries by asking, not demanding, a person to work with you and agreeing to a mutually beneficial plan to support the connection.

R. *Respecting Self and Others:* Allowing each individual to feel heard, understood, and valued.

I. *Implementing Integrity:* Maintaining trust and accountability by honoring one's word and boundaries.

E. *Executing Emotional Regulation:* Managing emotions helps prevent exacerbating discord and the displacement of heightened emotion onto a relationship.

S. *Setting Boundaries:* Voicing your value during unfavorable experiences will elevate your personal life and strengthen your relationships.

Setting boundaries is the integrity to respect ourselves, even when others are unable to see our value.

Boundaries versus Ultimatums

Boundaries and ultimatums are often misconstrued as interchangeable, yet they are the complete opposite of each other. Ultimatums come from ego-based thinking, where an individual attempts to exert control over another person through the demand of a specific consequence.

Demands are often seen as threats, such as, you must do x or y, or else this will happen. This increases tension due to focusing on the problem rather than seeking a solution to benefit the relationship. The individual on the receiving end of the ultimatum will feel less inclined to comply because they sense they are being controlled and have no voice in the outcome. These types of conversations can lead to a power struggle where the problem escalates, as neither individual is willing to see outside themselves to resolve the relationship differences.

On the contrary, boundaries are set using heart-centered thinking for self-respect and growth within the relationship to achieve a long-lasting, harmonious, and valuable connection. Boundaries are implemented by approaching the situation from a *we versus the relationship* problem, not a *me versus you* problem and by seeking a resolution that meets everyone's needs. When it comes to establishing boundaries, this involves negotiating each person's viewpoint, highlighting the importance of valuing the relationship over a singular perspective. This approach conveys that you highly regard the relationship and are committed to finding a mutual agreement that fulfills the needs of both parties. By engaging in this process, each person is given a voice in determining the boundary while maintaining mutual respect and understanding. Keep in mind, there will be times when unilateral personal boundaries are set for safety, such as but not limited to psychologically or physically harmful situations.

10 Differences between Relationship Boundaries and Ultimatums:

1. *Ultimatums:* Used to seek power and control over others.
   Boundaries: Used to regulate behaviors for safety and respect.
2. *Ultimatums:* Like walls, they block others out.
   Boundaries: Similar to gates; they keep out the bad but maintain the good.

3. *Ultimatums:* Expect immediate change in behaviors.
   Boundaries: Establish a plan of action for new and healthy behaviors.

4. *Ultimatums:* One-sided demands or threats that lead to disconnection.
   Boundaries: Requests for relationship alignment and for strengthening the connection.

5. *Ultimatums:* Hurt the relationship and create distrust.
   Boundaries: Elevate the relationship for growth and trustworthiness.

6. *Ultimatums:* Ego-based expectations and emotions that are projected onto the others.
   Boundaries: Heart-centered standards that encompass the values and needs of all parties.

7. *Ultimatums:* Rigid ideals from a unilateral perspective.
   Boundaries: Mutual agreements that bridge the gap between multiple perspectives.

8. *Ultimatums:* Create greater tension and conflict.
   Boundaries: Promote constructive resolution and mutual understanding.

9. *Ultimatums:* Self-driven and come from a *me* mindset.
   Boundaries: Mutually driven and come from a *we* mindset.

10. *Ultimatums:* Inflexible and used as coercion to intimidate others.
    Boundaries: A process of negotiation and occasional re-renegotiation to ensure that the evolving needs of the relationship are being met over time.

Honoring Boundaries

Establishing and respecting boundaries is a crucial foundation for cultivating healthy relationships. Boundaries reflect how you engage with yourself and others, playing a vital role in your personal and professional fulfillment. To fully benefit from boundaries, it is essential to honestly acknowledge your needs. This enables you to navigate conversations, make informed choices, and foster mutually beneficial connections. Whether setting boundaries is a new practice or a lifelong skill, maintaining consistency will result in improved implementation and successful outcomes.

As you evolve throughout your life cycles, taking responsibility to preserve your self-respect is necessary for receiving mutual respect from others. Honoring healthy boundaries within and outside your relationships will support your self-worth and value. If you decide to compromise your boundaries at any point, receiving what you deserve and desire from others will be challenging. Inconsistently honoring boundaries can undermine your integrity and create uncertainty about the stance and strength of your voice. On the other hand, consistently respecting your boundaries helps maintain your self-worth, allowing you to feel authentically empowered and elevating your relationships.

How do you know when your boundaries are being violated? You will feel it in your whole body like a fire alarm going off that will not stop blaring until you take action. The nervous system automatically reacts when something goes against your boundaries because it feels like harm, uncertainty, or negativity. Mentally you may think, *I feel unsafe*, while physically, you may experience a queasy stomach, your body temperature rising, or wanting to explode with anger. Your body may naturally enter into self-protection mode; however, that often yields zero results in resolving the problem. Instead, you will need to train your brain to *respond* to situations versus emotionally *react* (we will clarify exactly how to do this later in the book). Responding allows you to stay in your inner power, operating from logic and value to achieve the desired outcome. On the contrary, reacting is a response often emerging from emotion and ego, which only heightens the conflict. This eventually deteriorates your relationships and self-respect.

We Mindset versus Me Mindset

When setting boundaries, applying a *we* mindset is essential for creating healthy and balanced relationships. This mindset involves embracing a collaborative and empathetic approach, where both individuals actively participate in understanding each other's perspectives, needs, feelings, and boundaries. The goal is to find common ground, resolve conflict, and work together on finding solutions that accommodate everyone's well-being. By collectively looking at the bigger picture and recognizing the mutual benefits within the relationship, a *we* mindset fosters a sense of trust, respect, and connection.

On the other hand, a *me* mindset can hinder the progress of a relationship. When one person solely concentrates on their own needs, desires, and objectives without considering the other person's viewpoints, needs, or goals, it creates an imbalanced dynamic. This one-sided approach can lead to resentment, misunderstandings, and the breakdown of trust between the individuals involved.

However, it's important to recognize that there are times when applying a *me* mindset is necessary for self-respect. Honoring personal boundaries and prioritizing one's emotional and physical safety might require removing someone from your life if they repeatedly violate your boundaries or no longer add value to your life. In such instances, putting oneself first is crucial for maintaining self-respect and well-being.

Let the Journey Begin...

Whether you're embarking on a new journey of setting boundaries or have already been practicing this skill, we assure you that it will lead you down a transformative path of self-discovery. By investing in your personal growth, you become an invaluable asset in both your life and relationships. Establishing healthy boundaries serves to protect your emotional and physical well-being while cultivating meaningful connections with those who share your values. While voicing your value can feel unfamiliar at first, each boundary you set becomes a step toward reclaiming your inherent power and living authentically. Now, is the time to unleash the incredible strength within you and embrace your highest truth through the art of setting boundaries.

Authors' note: All stories are a reflection of real-life experiences, but they have been altered to protect confidentiality while conveying a psychological understanding of relational patterns and boundaries.

TWO
LIFE WITHOUT BOUNDARIES

The crowd stood up and gave her a standing ovation as she walked across the stage. Vivian had worked hard to earn her position as the new CEO of one of the largest investment banks in the world. She knew it would entail a lot of extra responsibilities, but earning the title meant everything to her.

Vivian had been a go-getter her whole life, but it often came with major sacrifices, like spending less time with her family. Damien, her husband, was her biggest fan and devotedly stood by her side. They greatly depended on each other despite the amount of emotional distance they felt at times in their marriage, but neither was going anywhere.

After her acceptance speech, Damien handed her a large bouquet of flowers and kissed her on the cheek. He couldn't have been prouder. But at the same time, he also felt envious of her. With her new financial success, Damien didn't know how he felt about his wife surpassing him professionally. He had always envisioned himself being the breadwinner in their household, but that was slowly slipping away.

The following night, Damien and Vivian went out for a celebratory dinner and began talking about how life was going to change.

Vivian said, "I most likely won't be home until seven or eight on weeknights until I get the hang of things. Do you think you can handle dinner for the kids?"

Damien sighed. "What choice do I have?"

Vivian paused. "I will help as much as I can. Are you not happy for me and for us?"

"Of course, I am, my love! I'm so proud of you. I'm not the best at the household stuff, but I can figure it out."

Vivian shook her head. "I have finally reached my dream job, and I'm not going to let you ruin it for me."

Damien immediately became defensive. "I'm not trying to ruin it, but it feels like I have to pick up your slack while you get to live the dream."

Vivian felt her face become flushed and her heart started to race. "Well, maybe after all these years you will finally realize how much I do for the family and how much I do to make you happy."

"I never said I didn't appreciate you."

Vivian threw her napkin down. "Then what is it? You don't like that the tables are now turned?"

Damien replied, "I don't know how I feel about all these changes. That's all."

Vivian said, "I'm not sure you have a choice. Clearly, you don't understand sacrificing for your family."

Both of them were completely silent the entire drive home from the restaurant. Neither one glanced over at the other, not even once. Vivian couldn't understand how one of the best moments of her life was being dampened by her husband's resistance to something simple, like household chores. Both got ready for bed and continued in silence. Vivian began replying to all her congratulatory emails from work colleagues while Damien immersed himself in a book. Soon, they dozed off to sleep without a kiss good night.

Vivian got up extra early the next day and prepped the kids' breakfast before heading out. She was ecstatic and couldn't wait to see her name across the door of her office, *Vivian Greenville, CEO*. She made her way around the office, greeting everyone, and then got to work. She felt unsure where to begin but knew she had big shoes to fill.

Vivian knew failure wasn't an option, which put a lot of pressure on her. Deep down she knew she wouldn't be able to face herself if she couldn't uphold the expectations of her duties. As much as she knew she deserved this job, she relentlessly questioned and second-guessed herself. Her whole life, she had wondered if she was ever good enough. She could hear her father's voice clearly when she didn't pass her math test at the age of seven. "Vivian, how dumb can you be to fail this test? You're an embarrassment to this family." From that day forward, it stuck in her head like a recording she could not shut off. She did whatever it took to make her dad happy. And, now she would do whatever it took to impress the board of directors at the investment bank. She threw herself into her work as if her life depended on it.

Vivian believed her promotion would also make her husband and children happier, but the stress in the household was rising. Damien was sulking around the house, and Vivian didn't know what to do to make things better. She thought making more money for the family would excite Damien, but she could see it was only causing friction between them.

Later that night after giving the kids a bath, Vivian said, "Damien, do you mind telling me why you're still upset?"

Damien muttered under his breath, "I'm not. Can you stop asking me?"

"Clearly you are. We have barely spoken in days, and I'm tired of being ignored."

Damien raised his voice. "Look, I don't want to talk about it. If I had something to say, I would. Now, drop it."

"We can't go on ignoring each other. What do you want to do about it?"

Damien aggressively replied, "I told you, nothing."

Vivian started to tremble while holding back her tears. "I can't stand the silence. We need to talk."

Vivian kept trying to talk to Damien, but she was getting nowhere.

She was starting to feel guilty for taking her new position. Vivian couldn't understand why he was so unsupportive. Vivian was starting to wonder if she should step down from her new dream job. The last thing she wanted was to destroy her marriage over her career. She truly felt stuck and didn't know how to make everyone happy, including herself.

Emotional triggers are your cue to take care of you and set boundaries

Insight

Even though Vivian had been fulfilled with her professional achievement, it triggered an internal discomfort in Damien. He no longer felt like a provider in the relationship, which led to him becoming emotionally distant and questioning his role within the family. When a couple experiences a change in dynamics, it can lead to power struggles in their relationship and consequently a loss of emotional intimacy.

During Vivian's celebratory dinner, Damien became frustrated with his new at-home responsibilities. As Vivian tried to address the tension between them, she received dismissive responses from Damien, creating an impasse. This led Vivian to become emotionally heightened, and she lashed out at her husband for his inability to support her on an emotional level. She resorted to giving him an ultimatum, forcing him to accept her terms without presenting options or negotiating a resolution. Only addressing her needs and telling Damien what to do showed signs of disrespect for her husband and their relationship. Vivian's demanding nature made Damien feel undervalued and triggered him to seek space away from her.

While Vivian continuously pressed her husband to talk, she showed a cyclical pattern of approval-seeking behavior that she had experienced with her father as a young child. Holding the belief of "not good enough" carried over into her marriage as an unresolved emotional wound. By avoiding her emotional wounds, she put an immense amount of pressure on herself to try and prove her worth to others and herself. When her husband became passive-aggressive about her success, Vivian questioned her new role and started to feel guilty. While no relationship is perfect, it is essential to understand how each partner's unresolved emotional wounds impact the health of a relationship. This is why healing relational trauma and setting boundaries is vital for resolving differences. In this case, the couple's lack of conflict resolution skills and couple boundaries made it challenging to have a constructive conversation and to create a mutually aligned plan for the family. *See Chapter 11 for emotional boundaries and Chapter 15 for couple boundaries.*

Poor Boundaries

Poor boundaries are the absence of well-defined limits of what is considered acceptable or unacceptable behavior within relationships. Living life without boundaries can leave you feeling confused, undervalued, or even taken for granted. Feeling powerless in your life or relationships can cause you to question your self-worth and feel mentally stuck, emotionally drained, or even physically ill. When we neglect to set boundaries, we inadvertently diminish our perceived value and self-worth in the eyes of others, as we are showing how we want to be treated. This can leave an individual in a vulnerable state and susceptible to unhealthy relationship experiences.

Someone who is fearful to set boundaries may find themselves in a perpetual cycle of people-pleasing or avoidant tendencies where they ensure others' happiness, often at the cost of their own well-being. For some, past experiences of trauma, abuse, or neglect may have a residual impact, making it challenging to assert boundaries to avoid experiencing the pain of rejection all over again. Not asserting boundaries is often a reflection of beliefs the person has internalized over time. Our belief system is a collection of thoughts and ideas that make sense to us based on how we perceive the world. Whether you were loved, pampered, neglected, enmeshed, or abused by a parent or caregiver, these interpersonal dynamics helped form your beliefs about yourself. Beliefs are generally shaped from infancy to age seven through childhood experiences in the home, but they may alter through profound life experiences that impact your mental or emotional state. These beliefs can also be developed through experiences with influential mentors, such as coaches, teachers, and camp counselors, or traumatic events, etc. Your beliefs affect your decision-making processes and whether you make choices that elevate your life or subconsciously hinder you from reaching your goals.

Similarly, boundaries that are poorly delivered can also yield zero results because they lack the clarity and assertiveness necessary for effective communication. When boundaries are unclear or inconsistently honored, people may not fully understand them, leading to misunderstandings, confusion, and violations. Additionally, if boundaries are communicated in a passive or non-assertive manner, they may be easily disregarded or ignored, undermining their purpose. Consequently, this can lead to communication breakdowns in relationships, as standards remain unmet and conflicts continue to arise. To achieve positive outcomes, it is crucial to communicate boundaries assertively, with clarity and consistency, ensuring that they are understood and respected by all parties involved.

Lastly, a lack of self-awareness can be a significant barrier to setting boundaries, as individuals may not even recognize their own needs and limits, making it challenging to communicate and uphold boundaries effectively. We will address these boundary-setting challenges further throughout each chapter so you can begin having healthier relationships and prioritize voicing your value.

Psychological Blind Spots

When it comes to decision-making processes, we can become our own worst enemy. We may fail to see the blind spots in our perceptions or behaviors, yet these blind spots can affect every aspect of our lives. Whether it's the tendency to hold yourself back out of a fear of failure, or an unconscious repeating of relationship patterns with different people, psychological blind spots have the potential to derail you from your goals.

Psychological blind spots can be present when there is a lack of emotional intelligence and self-awareness of one's personality traits and behaviors. If a person is operating according to their psychological blind spots, it is likely progress isn't being made toward their goals. This is because they may find it safer to deny these certain aspects about themselves than to accept them. Some unconscious patterns that may be present include viewing yourself differently than how others perceive you, responding to pain with sarcasm, finding yourself overreacting to benign comments, withdrawing when not in control, rationalizing controversial behaviors to make them consciously tolerable, or repeating cycles without progress. These patterns can lead to self-sabotaging relationships, as unfavorable choices continue to dictate actions you make in your relationships today.

To overcome our psychological blind spots, it is vital to develop greater self-awareness. By increasing one's understanding of personal thoughts and intentions in various situations, you can begin to identify the unhealthy patterns that may be hindering your growth. Being mindful and focusing on the present moment can help you strengthen your overall awareness. With time and implementation, you can gradually shift the unfavorable patterns that may be keeping you stagnant, ultimately making room for healthier thoughts and behaviors. In doing so, you can overcome your psychological blind spots and achieve greater fulfillment in all aspects of your life.

To Overcome Psychological Blind Spots, Ask Yourself the Following Questions:

- *What am I afraid to know?*
- *What is one thing I don't want to accept?*
- *What patterns keep showing up?*
- *What parts of myself am I denying?*
- *What goal in life do I desire that I am unable to reach?*
- *What assumptions am I making without evidence?*

Unresolved Emotional Wounds

Those who endured an unhealthy family dynamic growing up can feel perplexed on where to begin establishing healthy boundaries in their life. This is due to the parent-child relationship being unable to meet the child's needs, hindering the development of a healthy identity. In order for the child to escape or avoid experiencing ongoing uncomfortable feelings, such as anxiety, guilt, shame, and sadness, they develop defense mechanisms such as blaming others, people pleasing, or being overly optimistic to protect their ego from enduring pain. While defense mechanisms can be helpful in the short term by reducing immediate distress, they can also prevent individuals from confronting and resolving underlying emotional wounds. Instead of dealing with the deep-rooted pain, they may resort to wearing a mask as a way to cope with their feelings.

Carrying the weight of past painful memories or events can make it challenging to form healthy relationships or live a fulfilling lifestyle. As you encounter new life experiences and challenges, it can trigger a similar emotion based on a past event, keeping you in a continuous loop. Once this happens, you can become stuck in a dysfunctional pattern where you feel hostage to your past. Sometimes, this is an unconscious reaction because the pain has been dismissed for so long and/or the memories have been repressed. Emotional triggers will point you in the direction where healing is needed and put you on the path to set you free.

Trying to escape emotional pain in your life can lead to indirectly projecting onto others and creating greater emotional discord in your relationships and life. More importantly, when an individual neglects their emotional state around their emotional triggers or behavioral patterns, this can be a sign they are dismissing accountability for their unresolved emotions. Overall, a healthy relationship requires each person to take full responsibility for healing their unresolved emotional wounds so they don't create unhealthy cycles or relationship disconnects.

Unresolved Childhood Emotional Wounds That Impact Adult Relationships and Lives:

- **Wound of Rejection:** This develops during the first year of life when a parent or caregiver did not fully accept you, leaving you to feel dissatisfied with your personal identity. This relates to any time you cried or sought connection, and it was ignored by a parent, which made you feel unlovable. With this wound, an individual will wear a withdrawn mask to avoid getting too close to someone or to escape situations that could lead to rejection. Most often, this creates a sense of panic and unworthiness in the person experiencing feelings of past rejection.

  Traits of People Experiencing This Wound:
  - Anxiety or panic attacks during what would be considered everyday situations
  - Addictions and eating disorders to numb the pain
  - Obsessive thoughts or behaviors of perfectionism
  - Identity disturbances and dissatisfaction with self
  - Avoidance of people or places that ignite painful memories
  - Seeking approval or recognition from others

Overcoming Rejection: A person will need to work on taking risks and making independent decisions, boosting their confidence, developing their self-worth and identity, setting healthy boundaries, embracing emotional intimacy, and working through internalized fears or situations that lead to anxiousness.

- **Wound of Abandonment:** This forms between the first and third years of life in a relationship with a parent or caregiver who was unable to fulfill emotional needs, or was absent from parental responsibilities during early childhood development. This wound leads to a lack of independence and a sense of loneliness. An individual will wear a dependent mask to keep others close.

  Traits of People Experiencing This Wound:
  - Unexplained irrational fears of abandonment
  - Developing a victim mentality and creating chaos
  - Emotional dependence on others
  - Ongoing and unexplainable bouts of depression, sadness, or crying
  - Problems with decision-making or acting independently
  - Entering one relationship after the next out of fear of being alone
  - Often abandoning a relationship first, if they sense the other person pulling away

  Overcoming Abandonment: A person will need to work on feeling comfortable with being alone, boosting their confidence, developing their self-worth, learning to think independently, managing emotions and fears, setting healthy boundaries, and embracing trust within themselves and others.

- **Wound of Humiliation:** This occurs between the first and third years of life when a parent or caregiver prevented their child from experiencing joy around sensual or physical pleasure. A parent may have expressed disapproval of the child by publicly criticizing them in front of others. This can lead to feelings of shame and loss of freedom. An individual will wear a mask of masochism and seek out pain.

Traits of People Experiencing This Wound:

- Suppressing sensual desires and pleasure
- Fear of punishment due to the experience of excessive joy
- Pleasing others before honoring yourself
- Making people laugh through self-deprecation
- Constantly feeling unworthy, messy, or shameful
- Depending on others to identify their self-image due to low self-esteem

Overcoming Humiliation: A person will need to work on making independent decisions, expressing their needs and priorities, setting healthy boundaries, developing their self-worth and self-esteem, embracing freedom, and enjoying happiness and pleasure.

- **Wound of Betrayal:** This wound generally occurs between the second and fourth years of life when a parent is unable to provide adequate attention to meet a child's needs. A parent created a loss of trust, broken promises, or lies. An individual wears a controlling mask and experiences feelings of dissociation or denial.

Traits of People Experiencing This Wound:

- Striving for titles, special privileges, and superiority
- Lack of trust and confiding with those of the opposite sex
- Use of manipulation, controlling tactics, and telling lies
- Highly critical of others and self
- Inability to practice patience and quick to cut others off

- Difficulty respecting personal limits and space of others

Overcoming Betrayal: A person will need to work on being patient, learning to trust others and self, developing their self-worth, setting healthy boundaries, embracing heart-centered thinking, eliminating manipulation tactics, learning how to be alone, and delegating responsibilities to give up control.

- **Wound of Injustice:** This happens during the fourth and sixth year of life when a parent or caregiver showed coldness or insensitivity. An individual wears a mask of rigidity and gives the perception of living in a perfect world where there is no room for pain. They often display signs of aloofness and have little emotion toward others.

Traits of People Experiencing This Wound:

- Difficulties admitting problems and shows constant optimism
- Fear of losing control and needing to be perfect
- Inability to emotionally express feelings with self and in relationships
- Struggles to form fulfilling relationships due to injustice
- Great acceptance of pain and often aloof
- Resistant to accepting others' ways of thinking
- Inadequate communication due to rigid beliefs

Overcoming Injustice: A person will need to work on becoming more flexible in thinking and communication, setting healthy boundaries, developing trust with self and others, embracing emotional intimacy, working through fears of losing control, overcoming perfectionism, and finding acceptance with challenges.

Emotional Triggers

An emotional trigger is a thought, memory, or experience that has the power to evoke strong feelings or emotions within us. These triggers can be anything from being betrayed by someone you trust to feeling powerless when someone controls the conversation. Regardless of the source, these triggers can stir up our deepest emotions and memories. However, we can be completely unaware of how much they are affecting us on a subconscious level. Whether we want to accept it or not, emotional triggers greatly impact our internal beliefs and behaviors. Therefore, it is important to be aware of what triggers elicit your strongest reactions to better understand yourself and how to navigate situations when your limits have been crossed. Keep in mind that being aware of these triggers is the first step to healing unresolved wounds.

Emotional triggers can be complex and hard to identify, but understanding them is essential for developing healthy boundaries. If we stay in an emotionally reactive state, this can exacerbate fear and keep us from responding effectively to reduce discomfort and meet our needs. An individual who doesn't heal their triggers will continue in a cycle of heightened reactivity and operate from a trauma response. This inhibits the person from thriving as they are in a constant state of fight-or-flight survival mode. Rather than making impulsive decisions based on emotion, we want to shift to value-based decision-making. By identifying our triggers, we can uncover the underlying relationship values that are being neglected and unfulfilled. For example, feeling ignored may demonstrate a need for meaningful communication, while feeling disrespected may suggest setting a boundary for mutual respect. You will establish your values in Chapter 4.

Ultimately, recognizing and working through emotional triggers will help you heal past relational trauma, so you can move forward with your life in a confident and valuable way. You can learn more about emotionally reacting versus logically responding in Chapter 5. This is the beginning of becoming powerful and not letting your triggers control you.

Examples of Emotional Triggers:

- I feel excluded
- I feel judged
- I feel unloved
- I feel ignored
- I feel frustrated
- I feel rejected
- I feel betrayed
- I feel overwhelmed
- I feel hurt

- I feel powerless
- I feel blamed
- I feel lonely
- I feel forgotten
- I feel trapped
- I feel controlled
- I feel unworthy
- I feel used
- I feel blindsided

- I feel misunderstood
- I feel disrespected
- I feel unappreciated
- I feel unsafe
- I feel manipulated
- I feel disconnected
- I feel undervalued
- I feel confined
- I feel dismissed

Trauma Responses

There are four types of trauma responses people may use when experiencing an unwarranted situation that is emotionally triggering or physically threatening. Some individuals have learned these responses as a survival mechanism from early childhood trauma, toxic relationships, or severe adulthood trauma. When they feel threatened in an uncomfortable situation, they perceive the present experience as the same danger as a past experience, which leads to a cyclical emotional response. With each type of trauma response, the unhealthy version represents an emotional reaction to perceived danger. Conversely, the healthy version creates a logical response aimed at meeting one's needs and preventing further conflict in relationships while amicably resolving differences. Some individuals may have one or more trauma responses they developed as self-protection mechanisms. These self-protective responses shield the ego but can further disconnect an individual from their values.

The Four Types of Trauma Responses:

- **Fight Response:** The goal is to fight and protect oneself regardless of who gets hurt in the process.
  - Unhealthy response: You feel the need to immediately defend yourself by using bullying, demanding perfection from others, or controlling communication along with aggressive outbursts. Or, you may become physical by destroying property or throwing items. You are willing to pick fights at the cost of destroying the relationship to seek power and control.
  - Healthy response: You have the ability to establish a boundary, use assertive communication, advocate for yourself, become a strong leader, and create a safe environment when feeling discomfort to keep the relationship intact. You remain calm and collected regardless of the present stressor.
- **Flight Response:** The goal is to escape any burden or pain by leaving the situation.
  - Unhealthy response: You are in a constant state of fear, panicking, worrying, and micromanaging every little detail. You may have tendencies of perfectionism, obsessive thinking, or the need to stay busy at work. Or, you may avoid a conflictual situation altogether by traveling, moving, or fleeing. It prevents the relationship from evolving to the next level.
  - Healthy response: You find yourself setting boundaries when feeling emotionally flooded, have the courage to leave unhealthy relationships, are able to regulate emotions with self-soothing techniques, and properly assess danger when situations are no longer in your best interest. You respond versus react to the situation.

- **Freeze Response:** The goal is to self-preserve through dissociation.
  - ○ Unhealthy response: You find making decisions difficult, tend to self-isolate due to feeling emotionally or physically numb, detach from the situation or reality, have fears of achievement, and believe no action is low-risk. It hinders your ability to engage in healthy conversations to maintain the connection, as you are mentally checked out due to a loss of words.
  - ○ Healthy response: You have the ability to take action by pausing in the present moment and thinking of a solution before responding. You use mindfulness, exhibit self-awareness, and logically determine the best plan of action or boundary in the relationship. You remain open-minded during difficult times.
- **Fawn Response:** The goal is to appease people in order to dissolve any issues.
  - ○ Unhealthy response: You tend to stay in unhealthy relationships, willing to accept abusive behaviors at the cost of losing yourself. You place other people's needs above your own by being of service to them, have a fear of saying no, and are aware of other people's emotions yet neglect your own.
  - ○ Healthy response: You actively listen and have compassion for others. You objectively try to find a solution by setting a healthy boundary that will make everyone happy without compromising the relationship or your self-respect. You stand up for yourself and honor your self-worth.

Ego-Based Thinking Versus Heart-Centered Thinking

As much as human beings have an innate desire to connect with others, when they opt for ego-based thinking, they will likely find it hard to communicate and get their true needs met. People operating on emotions tend to create highs and lows in a relationship instead of stability and inner peace. Seeking control can have you mentally spinning because the fear of losing power is greater than honoring the relationship. This can lead to reactive behaviors that are destructive to the relationship and the outcome you truly desire. Additionally, one may displace futuristic thoughts on the connection in an attempt to control the narrative and avoid uncomfortable emotions at all costs. Ultimately, the ego can keep you from achieving your goals.

Individuals who choose to operate according to heart-centered thinking will approach life differently than those who use fear to dictate their life choices and goals. Heart-centered thinking individuals have the ability to respond with value, live in the present, find patience with the process of growth, honor their self-worth, and seek harmony within their relationships. They are willing to put their ego aside and face the uncomfortableness of disagreements in order to cultivate unity within the connection. When you confidently believe in yourself and fully accept who you are as an individual, you become unstoppable in your pursuit of happiness and success. Heart-centered people learn that boundaries are the key to achieving their needs and wants in relationships, even though it may not be initially easy.

Fears About Setting Boundaries:

- Fear of causing harm to others or the relationship
- Fear of vulnerability during uncomfortable conversations
- Fear of rejection or abandonment
- Fear of manipulation when voicing your boundaries

- Fear of conflict and greater discord
- Fear of judgment or being perceived as difficult
- Fear of losing control over a situation or relationship
- Fear of being seen as selfish or demanding
- Fear of change and disrupting the status quo
- Fear of failure that the boundary won't work

THREE

BECOME INVALUABLE

On Monday morning, the sunbeams glared through the curtains, waking up Benji at six-thirty. He rolled back over, hoping to get an extra five minutes of rest before jumping out of bed. He dreamt of snoozing away the day in his own comfort and avoiding all responsibility.

Benji bolted out the door to work. His passion for being an architect was more than just aesthetics. He truly loved being a part of his clients' lives and designing their dream homes. He had big hopes to one day start his own architecture firm with his brother. But, for now, he reported to his overbearing boss, which felt like walking on thin ice every time they talked. No matter what he said or did, he couldn't meet Mr. Tigsten's expectations. Even the slightest miss calculation on a draft led to blueprints being thrown across the room and Benji being told how incompetent he was at his job.

Despite their constantly clashing personalities, Benji was always the first to arrive at the office every morning. He made a point of brewing coffee for everyone before delving into his latest project. After pouring himself a cup, he returned to his desk, popping in his headphones and working tirelessly through the mid-afternoon hours. He found canceling out the office chatter kept him steadily focused on his goals while embracing the soothing sounds of piano music. There was something profoundly gratifying about creating his own oasis of serenity in the midst of a chaotic work environment.

While deeply entranced by the sounds of Chopin, Benji heard a knock on his office door. It was none other than Mr. Tigsten. He demanded Benji's blueprints be ready by four o'clock sharp. Benji sat there frozen wondering how he was going to meet the new deadline. The last email he had received on the project indicated he had another twenty-four hours to complete it. Benji began to panic, telling himself he was useless under pressure and that giving up was his only option. One thought led to another, which left him venting under his breath, "I will never be voted as the architect of the year if I have to finish projects according to absurd timelines."

Benji, known for his acute attention to detail, began to sink deep into his office chair. He began to ramble, "I am not smart enough. I'm a complete waste. My dreams of being an award-achieving architect are over. I will probably be fired."

Soon after, a flood of flashbacks began to cloud his thoughts. He started to replay memories of when he was fired from his first architect job. He had been featured in the local newspaper as the leading architect at the firm, only to be humiliated a week later when he was let go for a miscalculation. Benji never wanted to relive that day again. His heart was pounding fast all over again, and he was wondering what would happen if he did not finish his blueprint on time. The fear set in like a heavy thunderstorm. No matter how loud he cranked up the music to drown out his thoughts, his mind raced, leading him into a spiraling dark hole.

Benji began to feel physically ill as he wiped the sweat from his brow. He called his brother for encouragement; if anyone could get him out of this funk, it was him. But there was no answer. He felt helpless with nowhere to turn. He could not even fathom looking at his computer screen.

He thought, *If only I had the courage to stand up to Mr. Tigsten, I would give him a piece of my mind. Who does he think he is creating insane deadlines?* The longer Benji sat at his desk, the more he stirred with restlessness.

He decided to get up and grab another cup of coffee. He thought walking around the office would help him get out of his head, but he was still feeling overwhelmed after an hour. Deep down, he knew Mr. Tigsten had unrealistic expectations.

Benji tried to channel his artistic strength, but it was nearly impossible. He gazed up at the spinning ceiling fan and zoned out. By now, his procrastination and worrying were getting the best of him. When Mr. Tigsten came to check how the project was going, Benji blankly stared back with a complete loss for words.

The relationship with ourselves directly influences the quality of our relationships with others.

Insight

Benji found himself swimming in his thoughts, paralyzed by procrastination and unable to move forward out of fear of failure. Instead of taking on the challenge of finishing the project within the new deadline, he became wrapped up in the discomfort of his anxious thoughts. The minute he stopped trusting himself, he fell hostage to self-deprecating beliefs, such as "I am not smart enough" or "I'm a complete waste." He felt discouraged and was unable to complete the job due to being fixated on the time constraints versus embracing the project with fortitude. If Benji had maintained his self-confidence, this would have allowed him to adapt to the environmental changes more effectively without questioning or delaying his professional abilities. However, Benji carried the emotional burden from his previous job loss, which caused him to freeze in a moment of adversity.

When it came to the relationship between Benji and his boss, Mr. Tigsten, he felt powerless and fearful due to his boss's unpredictable, erratic nature. His boss lacked leadership skills when it came to encouraging Benji on how they could meet the new deadline. Instead, he became outraged and criticized his skillset, which only instilled more fear in Benji. Ultimately, Benji's inability to honor his authentic voice and set professional boundaries with his boss hindered his productivity.

While life changes are inevitable, being able to navigate obstacles without forgoing one's values is vital to reaching success. Even though circumstances may not be ideal, managing curveballs with confidence would have helped Benji overcome short-term emotions and achieve his end goal. Having a growth mindset and being aligned with one's values is the key to maintaining one's self-worth without attaching it to other people's choices of words, actions, or beliefs. *See Chapter 10 for personal boundaries and Chapter 23 for professional boundaries.*

Accepting Strengths and Shortcomings

Embracing our whole self empowers us to face unfavorable situations with invincibility. It entails fully accepting both our strengths and shortcomings, rather than cherry-picking certain aspects and denying others. When an individual engages in self-comparison or self-deprecation, they undermine their potential to thrive in life. While everyone encounters challenges in life, the key to success lies in transforming those shortcomings into strengths.

Overcoming shortcomings may present challenges along the way, but it is achievable through shifting our belief system and focusing on our goals and values. Those who struggle to embrace all aspects of themselves often feel stagnant, allowing perceived limiting beliefs, also known as shortcomings, to define their identity. Through evaluating these limiting beliefs, you can identify what holds you back from accepting yourself and forming healthy relationships with others. While personal challenges or negative thought patterns can weigh on your mind, accepting yourself will free you from self-criticism and allow you to see yourself in a positive light.

Seeing shortcomings as opportunities for growth enables individuals to conquer challenges and find self-acceptance. For example, let's say a person is shy and they fear large crowds. This individual may find socializing at events overwhelming and uncomfortable, wishing they were more outgoing. On the contrary, being shy may allow them to build deeper one-on-one relationships and thrive in intimate settings. As you can see, each personal attribute is open to interpretation, and how we perceive them determines whether we accept them as negative or positive traits. Remaining true to oneself involves embracing each unfavorable trait as unique and transforming it to one's advantage. Personal alignment lies in overcoming these obstacles while experiencing growth and fulfillment.

Fixed Mindset versus Growth Mindset

Having a fixed mindset or rigid, overly idealistic thinking patterns can hinder individuals from embracing their authentic selves and reaching their aspirations. Those with a fixed mindset tend to close themselves off to perspectives that challenge their beliefs or expectations. When confronted with questions or opposing viewpoints, they may quickly give up on their goals or relationships because confronting their beliefs becomes a threat to their self-image. This type of mindset limits one's ability to strive forward toward their goals, as their approach becomes inflexible, one-sided, and driven by the fear of uncertainty or failure. Instead of embracing self-acceptance and others, they fixate on perfection or unrealistic ideals, sabotaging their growth and personal fulfillment.

Fixed Mindset Thinking:

- Focuses on the problem
- Believes new efforts are pointless and unnecessary
- Thinks they know best based on intelligence

- Avoids challenges and gives up easily
- Ignores constructive feedback and perceives it as criticism
- Feels threatened by the success of others
- Blames others for their setbacks or shortcomings

Individuals with a growth mindset or realistic thinking patterns fully embrace themselves rather than succumb to self-criticism, compartmentalization, or fixating on their perceived shortcomings. Growth-oriented individuals actively listen to outside perspectives and are open to valuing these viewpoints as opportunities for learning. When faced with setbacks, they have a willingness to explore new strategies and understand that taking risks is better than remaining stuck in unproductive patterns. Finding ways to trust the process and remain resilient when experiencing adversity empowers them to pursue their goals with confidence. A growth-minded person continuously invests in personal development and seeks opportunities that promote growth in both their lives and relationships. By having a positive mental attitude, they unlock their potential for continuous self-actualization.

Growth Mindset Thinking:

- Focuses on a solution
- Believes intelligence is developed over time
- Recognizes effort as the path to self-mastery
- Accepts mistakes and failures as part of learning
- Embraces challenges as opportunities for growth
- Welcomes feedback from others
- Views others' successes as inspirational

The difference between having a fixed mindset and a growth mindset can significantly impact reaching desired goals. For instance, consider a situation where a person with a fixed mindset feels afraid of speaking on stage. They might simply dismiss the opportunity, believing it's too uncomfortable for them. In contrast, an individual with a growth mindset would embrace the challenge despite their fears and find creative ways to connect with the audience comfortably without avoiding the situation entirely. A growth-minded person might explore alternative approaches to tackle the speaking opportunity. They may choose to break the large group into smaller ones, present virtually, or even hire the guidance of a public speaking coach to conquer their fears. By considering different approaches, they achieve their goal while remaining true to themselves through self-mastery and personal growth.

Self-Image Mindset Exercise

How you perceive yourself will define how you feel internally or appear externally to others in the outside world. Embracing self-love allows you to create a healthy self-image and cultivate an unshakable self-worth. Your feelings, beliefs, and perceptions all reflect your defined self-image and how it has been shaped over time. However, your identity can be subject to distortion from factors such as emotional wounds, childhood experiences, parental attitudes, relationships with others, or environmental influences. These factors can lead to painful consequences in your current lifestyle, such as job loss, divorce or break-up, financial stressors, parenting obstacles, relationship disputes, or the avoidance of life fulfillment. It's crucial to recognize that these limiting beliefs are often rooted in fear and shouldn't dictate your potential for new experiences.

To overcome these limitations, it's essential to challenge your beliefs and reflect on what might be holding you back from achieving your goals. How you value yourself in your personal and professional relationships is a direct reflection of your self-image. For instance, if you believe you're unworthy of love, you might sabotage potential relationships, cling to toxic ones, or avoid pursuing meaningful connections altogether. Understanding the relationship with yourself can give you deeper introspection as to what hinders you from reaching your fulfillment.

While your self-image primarily stems from your internal perception, your external appearance also contributes significantly to feeling at ease with your identity. Your physical well-being involves adopting a holistic wellness lifestyle, encompassing nutritious eating, a regular fitness regimen, and comprehensive self-care. Embracing the mind-body connection early on facilitates a smoother path to attracting your desires in life and confronting challenges with unwavering determination. When you believe in yourself, you can achieve anything you set your heart and mind to.

It's essential to complete the exercise below before you move forward, as it can clarify any limiting beliefs that may be hindering your life and relationships.

A. Write five INTERNAL traits you find unfavorable about yourself. These are traits you can manage. Examples: Codependency, Anxiousness, Seeking External Validation from Others

    1._____

    2._____

    3._____

    4._____

    5._____

B. Write five EXTERNAL traits you find unfavorable about yourself. These are traits you cannot change. Examples: Height, Eye Color, Birthmarks

    1._____

    2._____

    3._____

4._____

5._____

C. How can you see each INTERNAL unfavorable trait in a healthy way? Example: Codependency – "I enjoy feeling connected to people in my life."

1._____

2._____

3._____

4._____

5._____

D. How can you see each EXTERNAL unfavorable trait in a healthy way? Example: Height – "My petite stature allows for comfort on airplanes."

1._____

2._____

3._____

4._____

5._____

E. Write down five limiting beliefs you have about yourself. Example: "I'm not good enough," or "I'm a procrastinator."

1._____

2._____

3._____

4._____

5._____

F. Rewrite your limiting beliefs into positive affirmations. Example: "I'm not good enough" becomes "I am worthy of a healthy relationship." "I'm a procrastinator" becomes "I am great at working under pressure."

1._____

2._____

3._____

4._____

5._____

G. What would you be able to accomplish in life if you believed your positive affirmations? Example: "I will have a healthy relationship with a loving partner," or "I will be successful."

1._____

2._____

3._____

4._____

5._____

Implementing Positive Affirmations

When challenging limiting beliefs, implementing positive affirmations can help shift these self-defeating thoughts. If a limiting belief has served a purpose over a significant amount of time, it may take longer to break this unhealthy pattern. Affirmations can be used to connect with yourself by rewiring these limiting beliefs into beneficial ones, which can motivate you to reach your life goals, reduce stress, improve your self-esteem, and increase lifestyle enjoyment.

Affirmations are crucial to designing your life story because they can help you embrace self-acceptance. You can view affirmations as a mental exercise for your mind, similar to how you use physical exercise for your body. The more you implement them in your daily practice, the more positive results you will see. The most significant benefit of affirmations is that they allow you to focus on the present moment. This is where you can find your higher power in creating inner peace and mental strength.

When Rewriting Limiting Beliefs, Ask Yourself These Questions:

- How does this belief impact my life?
- What evidence supports or contradicts this limiting belief?
- Is this belief self-deprecating or self-appreciating?

Benefits of Using Affirmations:

- Elevates daily mood and motivation
- Provides focus and clarity toward goals
- Improves self-esteem and confidence
- Helps overcome obstacles and life challenges
- Heals from traumatic experiences
- Supports authenticity
- Increases mental stamina
- Eliminates anxiousness and stress
- Maintains a positive mindset
- Boosts resilience
- Achieves self-acceptance
- Improves sleep quality and inner peace

Creating Positive Affirmations:

There are several ways you can create positive affirmations. You can write affirmations in a daily journal, jot them down in notes on your phone, or recite them out loud while standing in front of the mirror every morning before you start your day. It is necessary to physically write or recite them each day according to the positive beliefs you are working toward to reap the benefits.

Guidelines for Affirmations:

- Start with the words "I am," "I believe," or "I will"
- Keep the affirmation in the present tense
- Use a positive tone
- Keep it concise with ten words or less
- Make it specific to goals that are achievable and realistic
- Make them for yourself, not others

Examples of Limiting Beliefs:

- "I will never be successful. I am a failure."
- "Nobody respects me."
- "Life is so hard. I am giving up."
- "I will never be accepted in my industry."
- "I feel like I am not good enough."

Examples of Positive Affirmations:

- "I am worthy of success."
- "I believe I deserve a healthy relationship."
- "I will be patient with myself."
- "I am a leader and will continue to strive forward."
- "I am enough just the way I am."

Self-Worth

Self-worth is a personal evaluation you give yourself, playing a primary role in how you perceive your value and navigate your relationships and life. It encompasses a collection of beliefs about how you see yourself, the standards you set, the values you uphold, and your ability to maintain self-respect. Individuals who recognize their inherent value establish a high standard for how they deserve to be treated and refuse to settle for anything less. Those with unwavering self-worth possess a blend of humility, confidence, and an invincible mindset that elicits respect from others.

While every individual deserves love and respect, there are instances when a person may fail to extend that same kindness to themselves, instead settling for less than they deserve. One might accept mistreatment from others, compromise their skills in jobs beneath their capabilities, or accept life's limitations as is. However, the truth is that every person is worthy of pursuing their desires and dreams. Past experiences, such as the loss of relationships, employment setbacks, or a challenging upbringing, do not diminish an individual's inherent value. The transformation begins when we recognize our worth, set healthy boundaries, and witness the profound positive impact it has on our lives and the respect we receive from others. By believing we deserve better, we attract healthier relationships, better opportunities, and more extraordinary experiences.

Defining self-worth is an internal process unique to each individual. It is influenced by life experiences, personal achievements, the strength of our character, and the expansion of our skills and knowledge. Crucially, this evaluation should not rely on external variables like appearance, wealth, or a relationship, as such aspects are transient and may change unexpectedly. Seeking instant gratification or external validation can lead to an unhealthy relationship with ourselves and mask our true self-worth. To truly understand our value, we need to look within, appreciating the unique qualities that make us who we are and recognizing that our worth extends far beyond external circumstances. Owning our value is not about proving our worth to others; it's about attracting the right people into our lives who can appreciate us. Embracing this understanding enables us to build a solid foundation of self-worth and cultivate a deep connection with ourselves, leading to a more fulfilling and empowering life journey.

Self-Love

Your self-worth is deeply intertwined with the love and care you give yourself each day. While self-care involves the physical aspects of nurturing your body through healthy habits, like working out or nutrition, self-love embraces the emotional and mental aspects of nourishing your mind and heart, like breathwork and journaling. A common challenge individuals face when struggling to love themselves is self-abandonment. Self-abandonment is the inability to develop a healthy relationship with oneself due to the ongoing habit of ignoring or suppressing one's needs. This emotional experience can make life seem overwhelming, confusing, and unfulfilling, along with bouts of feeling unlovable or unworthy. Neglecting one's emotional or physical needs can lead to seeking external validation, engaging in emotionally reckless behaviors, self-destructive tendencies, neediness, and feelings of worthlessness. As a result, this can lead to imbalances in relationships with others.

When someone lacks self-love, it is often traced back to early developmental experiences. Whether individuals were pampered or neglected by their parents, the outcome tends to be the same – conditional love. If parents were unable to fulfill their child's emotional or physical needs or failed to teach them how to meet their own needs, then it can cause them to self-abandon themselves today. While pampering may appear to fulfill a child's needs, it can actually hinder the emotional development of self-regulation, confidence, and internal worth, as they are constantly shielded from discomfort.

Emotions serve as psychological and physiological cues for us to take care of ourselves when we encounter discomfort or pain. Avoiding or suppressing specific emotions can lead to unfavorable consequences in other areas of life. Suppressed emotions rarely resolve themselves on their own and may manifest in relationships, daily habits, mood, overall health, work performance, or aspirations. Effectively processing emotions when they arise makes it easier to achieve happiness, inner peace, and fulfillment in life. Taking responsibility for our emotional state empowers us to rely less on others for the love we may seek and to feel more secure in life. By nurturing self-love and mastering emotional well-being, you can experience emotional freedom and build healthier relationships with yourself and others.

Cultivating a healthy connection with yourself not only equips you with better self-awareness but also lays the foundation for establishing healthy boundaries in your relationships. By prioritizing your needs and filling your emotional reserve with self-love, you're better positioned to navigate challenges and face them with courage and strength. Devoting regular time to yourself provides opportunities to recharge, rejuvenate, and maintain focus on your goals. Whether it's fifteen minutes or an hour a day, depending on your schedule, dedicating time to your well-being helps you progress towards becoming a healthier individual, which in turn enhances your value and relationships.

Self-Love Exercises:

- Journaling
- Meditating
- Breathing exercises
- Reciting positive affirmations
- Prioritizing yourself first
- Establishing self-reflection time
- Owning your inner voice
- Finding forgiveness
- Engaging in creative hobbies
- Setting boundaries

Choosing Happiness

You are the creator of your inner world and what brings you happiness. While it's not a constant state of euphoria, you can still be happy on days that bring unwelcome emotions. Happiness is not something that can be bought through tangible goods or found within another person. It's the result of your daily choices that fuel your heart, life purpose, and align with your values and goals.

Happiness can be challenging to define, as everyone has their own idea of what it means to be happy. However, there are some commonalities that the happiest people share, such as confidence and an optimistic outlook on life. They tend to approach each day with resilience and quickly bounce back from setbacks. Happy people also have a strong support system and invest in nurturing their closest relationships. They are grateful for the simple things, such as fresh air, sunshine, clothing, and meals on the table. They prioritize what genuinely matters and adds value to their lives.

Contrary to choosing gratitude, some individuals may adopt a scarcity mindset. They may think things like, *If only I had more wealth, a bigger social circle, a healthy relationship, better skin, a luxury car, etc., then I would be happier.* Believing external validation or greater resources will lead to lasting happiness is a fleeting illusion. These externally driven highs will fade away the minute the immediate gratification wears off. While external factors may offer temporary pleasure, they do not provide sustainable, long-term happiness.

Ultimately, happiness is a choice, not an end goal. If there are limiting beliefs holding you back from being happy or from achieving satisfaction in life, then shifting your mindset will help you uncover how to create a happy place in your present life. It can be challenging and uncomfortable to revisit past experiences that shaped you, but staying complacent and unhappy today will not serve you well either. So, you have to ask yourself, *What is my happiness worth?*

Ways to Increase Happiness:

- Setting short-term and long-term goals
- Focusing on positive emotions
- Enjoying the present moment
- Maintaining a healthy routine
- Nurturing your self-love
- Practicing gratitude
- Going after your passions and interests
- Pursuing your purpose
- Valuing meaningful relationships
- Being optimistic and resilient

Journal Exercise

Unresolved emotional wounds and triggers can lead to overthinking, anxiousness, depression, and even exacerbating one's fears. Journaling is a great healing technique that allows you to take unsettling thoughts and put them onto paper to reduce stress, calm your mind, and release pent-up emotions. It can help you reflect on your feelings, gain clarity around emotional triggers, and let go of the emotions weighing you down. Journaling doesn't have to be a strenuous activity. Even just five minutes a day can improve your mental and emotional health, strengthen self-awareness, discover your inner voice, bring your goals to fruition, and elevate the quality of your relationships.

Tips for Effective Journaling:

- Write any time of the day that works for you, but be sure to schedule it
- Use a technique that best suits your writing style, long or short form

- Choose the best outlet for writing or typing, such as paper, phone, or computer
- Start small, even if its five minutes a day
- Stay consistent with the process each day to reap the benefits
- Pick an environment that is a safe and calm space
- Make your journaling a personal message
- Keep it private to remain open and honest with yourself
- Have journal prompts on hand when you aren't sure what to write about
- Look for the lessons and blessings instead of getting stuck on problems
- Use graphics, arrows, colors, and sketches if you are more of a visual person

FOUR

IDENTIFY YOUR VALUE SYSTEM

Showing up at the lake cabin three hours late for the annual summer kickoff festivities was no surprise to his friends. Owen was well-known by his boating buddies as "Mr. Entertainer." He took great pleasure in making extravagant entrances and being the center of attention.

This year, Owen blindsided everyone by bringing a couple of girl-friends to the exclusive guys' fishing trip. Although his friends were taken back, they knew Owen had a one-track mind of doing things his way. His friends all had a saying, "He pulled another Owen."

As it turns out, the plans for a laid-back weekend of grilling out, boating, and fishing immediately took a detour. Suddenly, it became a full-throttle weekend of karaoke, jet skiing, and hot tubbing all night long. It wasn't that his buddies didn't enjoy having the ladies around; it just created a different atmosphere than they had all agreed on.

Owen was a man who lived life by the seat of his pants and didn't think of anything other than the thrill of the moment. He owned and operated a private investigative agency with his father, so seeking intensity was in his blood. Even though Owen and his father did not have the best relationship growing up, they still managed to work together. Over time, when Owen became co-owner of the company with his father, he finally felt like he had a voice in the business. But he quickly learned that was not the case. Owen and his father would often clash when it came to onboarding new clients, which would usually end in a silent stand-off between them.

Owen's father wasn't easy to please. He was bitterly cold, short-tempered, and highly critical of Owen. Owen couldn't catch a break from his dad, even on his best days. If he didn't work a full day on a client's case, then his dad would look at him with disappointment and swipe him from the project immediately.

But this wasn't new to Owen. He had been dealing with this his whole life. Even as a kid, if he didn't get out of bed on time for school, his dad would scold him and call him lazy. And, when he played hockey, if Owen didn't score a goal during the game, his father would tell him to try harder and threaten to stop paying for him to play. Nothing Owen did met his father's expectations despite how hard he tried. He continuously felt like a letdown, and not much had changed in their father-son relationship at the agency.

When Owen had enough of his father's criticism, he would rebel to escape the weight of his heavy feelings. His latest rampage led him to the car dealership, where he impulsively purchased a new sports car. The rush of driving at incredibly high speeds, even reaching one hundred and fifty miles per hour, brought him a sense of freedom. However, deep down, Owen was aware that this behavior was pushing him to the brink of losing control. Even if the high only lasted for five minutes, the excitement of feeling powerful consumed him and provided relief from his emotional turmoil.

Adrenaline wasn't Owen's only escape. He would go out partying every night to numb the pain, hoping it would eventually go away. Owen would overconsume alcohol only to wake up feeling worse, then do it all over again after listening to his father at the office all day. His friends noticed the minute he began to spiral because he would disappear for days on end and not call anyone back. Owen became so unpredictable that he ended his two-year romantic relationship out of the blue.

Despite Owen's outward appearance of enjoying life when he was out and about, at home, he couldn't let go of the overwhelming feelings of self-pity and despair. He wondered why life was a never-ending uphill battle day after day. While he sat at home, aimlessly flipping through television shows, dark thoughts would rush over him.

Owen desired his freedom with little responsibility, yet his father's command held him captive, leaving him feeling like a helpless child all over again. He felt internally conflicted working with his father and would reach for any substance in sight that would help him forget the day. It was the only way he knew how to drown out his thoughts of resentment toward the one man he looked up to.

The week after the fishing trip, Owen started to deeply regret leaving his girlfriend. When television and alcohol became mundane, he endlessly sought her forgiveness and attention. He became consumed with excessively calling her and sending flowers with little notes, expressing how much he missed her. He was determined to win her back.

Boundaries lead to growth; expectations lead to disappointment.

Insight

Owen's life was a constant pattern of impulsive decisions. He craved the emotional high from adrenaline rushes but abandoned himself when it came down to his emotional needs. Being disconnected from his values and suppressing his unresolved wounds left him seeking external gratification by escaping through materialism, substance use, and people in his life.

Owen's lifelong discontentment was rooted in the troubled relationship he shared with his father. Throughout his upbringing, he faced the constant scrutiny of his emotionally distant father, which left him feeling rejected and undeserving of love. The absence of emotional support and parental encouragement hindered his ability to cultivate a strong sense of self-worth. When a child receives conditional love, they grow up thinking they aren't worthy of receiving healthy love or achieving success.

Feeling voiceless around his father, Owen attempted to seek power in other ways rather than set family boundaries. From driving fast cars to abruptly leaving his girlfriend, he was projecting how powerless he internally felt. When Owen's emotions became too much to bear, he would react with a flight trauma response to escape his emotions. Owen was trying to avoid the pain he felt from his father, but it was only causing him more harm in the end. When someone rejects an individual before they can be rejected, this is a sign of a maladaptive coping technique. They have a fear of being hurt so they keep people at arm's length out of self-protection and emotional safety rather than expressing their needs for security. Ultimately, this person may end up self-sabotaging their life goals or relationships due to their lack of self-love and deep-rooted fears that override their value.

In addition to Owen struggling with his romantic and family relationships, he was also inconsiderate of his friends. Owen was self-consumed with his personal needs and agenda rather than what was mutually agreed upon for their guys' fishing trip. Showing up hours late with a couple of girlfriends was a clear indication Owen lacked personal integrity and disregarded mutual respect within his friendships.

Owen's constant need for external gratification and control turned into an unhealthy cycle of self-abandonment. A person who struggles to have a healthy relationship with themselves will continue to face challenges in their connections due to the inability to honor their values and set boundaries. When someone continuously makes impulsive decisions without thinking about the consequences of their actions, life can become more challenging as opposed to making hard decisions upfront for a much more fulfilling and easier life down the road. *See Chapter 10 for personal boundaries, Chapter 13 for friend boundaries, and Chapter 17 for family boundaries.*

Next, you are going to discover how relationship values are key to being respected and creating alignment in your life and relationships.

Relationship Values Meet Your Emotional Needs

Our emotional needs play a significant role in our lives, as we all yearn to feel loved, understood, respected, and valued. When our needs are not met, we can experience feelings of isolation or a disconnect in our relationships. Connecting with our relationship values becomes the most effective way to address and fulfill our emotional needs. These values act as an internal compass, guiding our intentions and behaviors toward achieving fulfillment and happiness.

However, navigating life decisions and choosing healthy people to surround ourselves with can be challenging, particularly if we are unsure of our own value system and beliefs. Embracing individuals into our inner world without having clarity of their values can lead to discord and uncertainty in our relationships. When our boundaries are violated, it serves as a clear sign that someone is not in alignment with our value system and may not be able to meet our needs within the relationship.

Identifying your values empowers you to make conscious decisions about who adds value to your life, who may disregard your limits, and where you need to redefine relationships to maintain healthy interactions. Honoring your values grants you the ultimate freedom to speak up for yourself and ask for what you truly deserve in your relationships and interactions with others. By embracing and upholding your values, you can establish meaningful connections with individuals who share similar beliefs, leading to more harmonious relationships in your life.

Connection versus External Validation

It's natural to seek out connections and form genuine relationships that provide us with a sense of belonging and purpose. Authentic relationships feel raw and real because they promote a sense of vulnerability and transparency between individuals. When we feel connected, we fully accept each other for who we are, fostering shared expressions and mutual understanding.

The process of building connections involves heart-centered conversations, where individuals engage in a balanced and rhythmic pattern of similar topics without monopolizing the conversation. They relate to one another through shared experiences, find common interests, and embrace differences with an open mind. This allows genuine connections to evolve naturally without the pressure of personal agendas or unrealistic expectations. The ultimate factor to successful relationships lies in having a *we* mindset, where individuals value and appreciate each other's contributions rather than solely focusing on their own needs.

Sometimes when forming new relationships, an individual may unintentionally seek external validation even though they wholeheartedly desire a genuine connection. External validation occurs when you look to others to tell you who you are, accept you into their world, or seek approval on whether you're doing things right in their eyes at the expense of your self-worth. This approach can hinder the development of healthy relationships as it prevents you from speaking your authentic truth. When engaging in conversations, these individuals tend to stay on the surface with topics, solely talk about their experiences, and shy away from being vulnerable or transparent about their feelings. This can lead to individuals feeling disappointed as genuine people will pick up on surface-level engagement and will think twice before spending time with someone who has *me* mindset. Individuals who evaluate their self-worth based on external opinions and validation rather than embracing their inherent value can lead to developing unhealthy relationships. On the contrary, if someone admires you for your success or appearance, while you may feel instantaneously validated, this sensation is often short-lived and creates a disingenuous connection.

Relationship Intelligence

Relationship intelligence skills come from a collective comprehension of emotional intelligence, a we mindset, healthy boundaries, and constructive communication. At times, relationships can be complex, confusing, or even downright combative if we lack the proper relationship skills to effectively manage differences. When facing challenging personalities or controversial situations, it is essential to see outside your perspective to further understand the other person's needs before being able to create alignment with them. Seeing the bigger picture will also be beneficial to positioning valuable solutions and meeting your own emotional needs.

One of the main components of relationship intelligence skills is emotional intelligence, which consists of four quadrants. Each aspect allows you to understand and manage your emotions, empathize with others' emotions, recognize body language cues, resolve conflict constructively, and grow interpersonal relationships with others. Developing emotional intelligence is vital to reaching both personal and professional relationship goals.

The Four Components of Emotional Intelligence:

- **Self-Awareness:** Being conscious of your emotions and behaviors and how they directly impact your life choices and relationships
- **Social Awareness:** Reading others' emotions, actively listening, and caring about what people are experiencing on a personal or collective level
- **Self-Management:** Having emotional regulation allows you to align according to your values while pursuing goals and opportunities with the ability to be flexible and overcome setbacks
- **Relationship Management:** Implementing conflict resolution skills and strengthening your connections by empathizing

with others' feelings and effectively communicating your own feelings for the greater good of the relationship

Healthy versus Unhealthy Relationships

It can be difficult to determine if a relationship is healthy or unhealthy without the self-awareness of your relational patterns or experiences. If you grew up in a home where unhealthy relationship behaviors were modeled, this can distort the perception and understanding of what a healthy relationship feels like. While some behaviors may seem normal to one person, they may seem completely foreign or unhealthy to another person. Values can bring you clarity by determining what is healthy or unhealthy in your relationships and what will create a mutually beneficial alignment.

Signs of a Healthy Relationship:

- Communicate in a constructive manner
- Show mutual respect and appreciation
- Be open to considering alternative viewpoints
- Build mutual integrity and trust
- Offer emotional support and acceptance without judgment
- Share honest feelings and goals
- Spend quality time together
- Respect the need for privacy and personal space
- Uphold personal and relationship boundaries
- Maintain a balance of giving and receiving
- Discuss important matters with mutual consideration
- Acknowledge mistakes and accept responsibility
- Resolve relationship issues in a timely manner

Signs of an Unhealthy Relationship:

- Attempt to control the other person or connection
- Disregard established boundaries
- Avoid discussing important issues
- Experience an imbalance in giving and receiving
- Deflect or avoid responsibilities within the relationship
- Feel goals and values aren't respected
- Neglect spending quality time together
- Use manipulative language or tactics
- Avoid sharing honest feelings
- Suffer from an addiction
- Place the responsibility for their emotions on the other person
- Feel anxious or withdrawn in the presence of the other person
- Encounter difficulties in resolving conflicts
- Engage in physical, emotional, or sexual abuse
- Lack of trust and integrity in the relationship

Relationship Values Exercise

Relationship values serve as the foundation of one's core beliefs that lead to fulfillment in both your life and your relationships. They act as a roadmap, guiding you to honor your self-worth while communicating your needs logically and respectfully. When you express your needs based on these values, you increase the likelihood of being heard and understood. While it may be instinctive to communicate from an emotional standpoint, doing so can sometimes yield unfavorable responses, as others may not share the same emotions or perspectives. Solely communicating from a place of emotion can lead to misinterpretations and minimize the importance of your message. On the other hand, values are universally recognized and comprehended, making them a more effective means of communication. Ultimately, values are your voice of reason during moments of confusion, conflict, or connection.

To create a clear path in your life, it's essential to choose your top five relationship values to live by each day. These values should represent what you stand for, fostering personal alignment and healthy relationships. Honoring these values through daily actions is crucial, as we can only ask for the values that we ourselves are committed to embodying. Living by your values enhances your internal self-worth and integrity and enables you to identify when someone has violated your boundaries. Conversely, stepping away from your values can impede personal and professional growth and cause rifts in your relationships.

If you find it challenging to identify or narrow down your top five values, reflecting on past experiences, relationships, or childhood memories where your needs weren't met or you felt triggered can provide valuable insights. These experiences help shape the values you honor when building new relationships or redefining existing ones. For instance, an unhealthy relationship where you experienced betrayal might lead you to value trust and loyalty. Similarly, being lied to may instill a strong appreciation for honesty. Furthermore, the absence of emotional support from a parent might lead you to highly value communication in your current relationships. When at least three out of your five relationship values align with those of another person, it serves as a promising indicator of the potential for a long-lasting and meaningful relationship.

Examples of Relationship Values:

- Communication
- Integrity
- Open-Mindedness
- Growth

- Loyalty
- Authenticity
- Positivity
- Transparency

- Honesty
- Commitment
- Trustworthiness
- Kindness

- Mutual Respect
- Family
- Teamwork
- Personal Space
- Mutual Partnership
- Community
- Success
- Time
- Empathy
- Accountability
- Privacy
- Leadership
- Health
- Connection
- Work-Life Balance
- Patience
- Financial Responsibility
- Collaboration
- Consistency
- Freedom
- Intimacy

Depending on the type of relationship, personal or professional, you may have slightly different value systems. For example, you may value time or teamwork with your work colleagues but find this less critical in your personal relationships. And, in your personal relationships, you may value intimacy and communication, whereas at work, it's less important to you. Additionally, your values will not waver based on what others value, as they are solely true to you and your beliefs.

What are your top five personal relationship values?

1._____

2._____

3._____

4._____

5._____

What are your top five professional relationship values?

1._____

2._____

3._____

4._____

5._____

Once you have identified your values, you will want to incorporate them into your day-to-day interactions with yourself and others to create alignment with your authentic truth. The more you are aligned with your values, the easier it is to set boundaries in your relationships. To complete this exercise, write down three value statements each day that reflect your values. You will want to continue this exercise until your values become innate behaviors in how you present yourself and engage with others.

Examples of Value Statements:

- *Trustworthy:* I made plans to grab dinner with a friend and kept my word.

- *Communication:* I was open with my co-worker about delegating tasks to meet a tight deadline.

- *Integrity:* I told my partner I would help out with the chores on Saturday morning so we could spend quality time together that evening. I finished by noon.

FIVE

UNCOVER THROUGH DISCOVERY

In late September, when the leaves were starting to turn, Sammy eagerly persuaded Jon to go on a spontaneous week-long adventure. Their excitement began to overflow as they couldn't wait to escape into the mountains to hike and camp. This getaway was precisely the downtime they craved from their ambitious careers and round-the-clock schedules. Jon worked back-breaking hours as a surgeon, while Sammy was the head sales manager of a technology company. Dedicated to their professions, they struggled to get away from their demands to find quality time together. Cherishing their independence often meant pushing their relationship to the backburner when work was demanding.

Spending little time together meant less time for arguing, but Sammy and Jon soon discovered that was not the case. Occasionally, they found themselves bickering over the small things, like whose turn it was to unload the dishwasher. These arguments lingered for days, while the sink piled up with dirty dishes. They were both stubborn to their core and neither were willing to budge on their stance.

The standoffs started to weigh heavily on Sammy, who sensed that the spark in their marriage was fading fast. Many evenings she would come home from work and cry out of frustration and hopelessness about not knowing how to turn their relationship around. She was depending on their camping trip to rekindle the romance in their marriage. She was tired of feeling like roommates.

As Sammy got the suitcase out of the top of the closet, she found an old note that Jon had put inside the suitcase from her last business trip. She missed the little things that Jon used to do for her. She wondered where the old Jon, who she had fallen in love with, had gone. As she crammed their clothes into a suitcase, she hummed to the music playing in the background. She wanted to get everything packed, from flannels and hiking boots to swimsuits, before Jon came home from the hospital.

They had agreed they would leave at three o'clock to start their fourteen-hour drive. Sammy was unsure what they needed at the campsite, as that was more Jon's wheelhouse. But she set out the tent, a mini grill, fire starters, sleeping bags, and other essentials that came to mind. She finished checking everything off her list.

Jon arrived home from work an hour later than he had anticipated. He rushed and tossed everything into the back of their SUV, assuming Sammy had packed everything they would need. Three hours into their drive, Sammy started going over things in her head and had a gut feeling that something was left behind.

When they stopped for fuel, Jon did a quick inventory of their belongings and realized they had forgotten essential items for camping: the cooler, a pot for boiling water, and a tarp for the ground. Just as Sammy returned with snacks in hand, Jon's temper got the best of him and he shouted at Sammy. He blamed her for the oversight in not packing the additional campsite items.

"We talked about the camping gear we would need several times. I really do not understand how you neglected to put these items on the list. These things are common sense for a camping trip."

Sammy was annoyed. "Why would you expect me to know everything we need? I have never been camping in my life. You constantly blame me when something goes wrong, and I am getting tired of it. I thought we both agreed to make a list."

Jon sighed and rubbed his temples. "I didn't make a list! Now we have to go out of our way to buy new equipment. You know how much I despise wasting money."

"Oh, so you expected me to be responsible for everything when I've never been camping? Sounds so typical of you."

They jumped back into the SUV and took off in total silence. Sammy turned up the music to mentally tune Jon out. They traveled for the next few hours with neither of them making eye contact or exchanging words. As they continued to drive into the night, Jon's eyes began to burn with exhaustion. He asked Sammy to take over for a while, as he needed a break. They pulled over at a rest stop to stretch and use the restrooms. When they got back into the truck, Sammy decided to clear the air with Jon. The tension brewing between them was giving her a headache and she couldn't take it any longer.

"You know, Jon, the whole point of this trip is for us to get away from stress and spend some quality time together. Yet, all we are doing is fighting."

Jon replied, "I do not want to spend the next week fighting with you. Can we agree to disagree on what happened?"

Sammy turned on the ignition. "Whatever."

"Can you not have an attitude about this? I am trying to move on from this argument that has been completely blown out of proportion."

Sammy was annoyed and pushed down on the gas pedal. "That is what you always do. Just move on and act like nothing happened to avoid accountability. This is why nothing will ever get resolved, and these arguments will keep happening.

Jon raised his voice. "Enough! Let's move on. Why is that so hard for you?"

Sammy remained silent.

They continued driving until they reached another rest stop. Both extremely tired from driving, they grabbed dinner and decided it was no longer worth fighting about. They made a promise to enjoy their trip and shoved another fight behind closed doors.

Boundaries are the courage to voice your value during times of adversity.

Insight

Jon and Sammy had experienced an impasse in their communication channels when items were left behind for their camping trip. Each assumed the other knew what to pack and neglected to clarify whether or not they were on the same page. Their lack of assertive communication skills negatively impacted their trip and led to greater discord and misunderstandings. Both Jon and Sammy resorted to blame-shifting rather than accepting responsibility for their communication blunders. It became a power struggle of *me versus you*, rather than *we versus the relationship problem*. Using accusatory language continuously added fuel to the fire and created an emotional disconnect between them. When this happens, not only does each person lower their value, but it also makes it challenging to have trust and find an amicable resolution.

To make matters worse, emotions were heightened throughout their conversations, which hindered their ability to understand each other. Being in a heightened emotionally reactive state and resorting to the silent treatment prevented them from getting to the root of the issue. When someone cannot see perspectives outside of their own or ask for what they need, it can be challenging to remain connected. During their discussion, both showed an unwillingness to compromise for the greater good of their relationship, operating from a fixed mindset and a lack of teamwork.

If Sammy and Jon continued their current relational patterns without developing conflict resolution skills and implementing healthy boundaries, over time, it would create a greater divide. A relationship can only withstand a limited amount of ongoing conflict before one or both individuals feel emotionally neglected and undervalued. Omitting emotional or couple boundaries led to continuous discord between

Sammy and Jon. *See Chapter 11 for emotional boundaries and Chapter 15 for couple boundaries.*

Now, let's get into one of the most important components of setting boundaries that would've resolved Sammy and Jon's miscommunication.

Discovery Questions

When resolving disconnects or strengthening your relationships, it is important to be curious and seek clarification of the other person's viewpoints by using open-ended discovery questions. In modern-times, it has become common to talk at someone by making statements rather than talk to each other by asking questions and building connection. A person who talks at you is having a one-sided conversation, often seeking what they need from you without considering the relationship. Whereas, talking to someone creates an open dialogue for an exchange of information and connection while prioritizing the relationship. Implementing discovery questions in your conversations can help you gather information and gain insight into an individual's perspective or behavior for greater alignment. Using this style of questions prevents us from making assumptions or internalizing another person's behaviors or beliefs, which can lead to further misunderstandings. Discovery questions will help save you time, prevent overthinking, reduce confusion, diffuse conflict, and diminish emotional distress during the exploration process to build connection.

One of the biggest communication blunders to avoid is "why" questions. The reason we want to avoid asking "why" questions is because they might be perceived as judgmental towards someone's perspective, instead of genuinely seeking to understand the reasoning behind their beliefs or behaviors. "Why" questions can make the receiver feel voiceless, attacked, or defensive, or they can lead to exiting the conversation altogether. "Why would you say that?" "Why would you do that?" or "Why do you think you're right?" are types of questions that can cause frustration or anger, escalating conflict rather than bridging the gap between differences or uncovering vital information.

Before setting a boundary, it will be essential to learn how to implement discovery questions in your conversations for healthy rapport and engagement. After all, without assessing the full picture of an individual's belief or behavior, it will be nearly impossible to gain the benefit of boundaries. As a result, if a boundary is set too soon without the discovery process, it may falter due to the inability to get to the root of the disconnect. By asking discovery questions, we can gain greater clarity of the relationship disconnect, pinpoint potential roadblocks, find common ground, and indirectly guide the conversation to a resolution.

Examples of Discovery Questions:

- Where
  - Where would you like to go for dinner?
  - Where do you want to meet?
  - Where are the keys to the car?

- What
  - What do you mean?
  - What time does the event start?
  - What is your perspective on (x)?

- How
  - How come you're late?
  - How come we are unable to meet the deadline?
  - How are you feeling today?

- Tell me more about
  - Tell me more about your favorite memory.
  - Tell me more about your experience, so I can better understand you.
  - Tell me more about your thoughts on (x).

- Who
  - Who did you meet at the conference?
  - Who is invited to the celebration?
  - Who is cooking dinner tonight?
- Help me understand
  - Help me understand how come we haven't been on a date in a while?
  - Help me understand what is needed to increase productivity?
  - Help me understand how come you don't trust me?
- When
  - When can we talk about our financial budget?
  - When do you want to go to the grocery store?
  - When can we talk about what happened last night?
- Can
  - Can you share more details about this project?
  - Can you not interrupt me when I'm talking?
  - Can we schedule a family vacation this summer?

Emotionally Reacting versus Logically Responding

Reacting refers to an immediate, automatic response to a situation, often without much thought or consideration of the outcome. When it comes to relationships and life, it's easy to get caught in the heat of the moment and react to triggers. Emotionally reacting too quickly can jeopardize one's worth, the relationship, or the goal due to heightened emotions being projected onto the connection. Emotional reactions can lead to feeling powerless or voiceless because one's emotional needs aren't being met. When an individual is in a reactive state, it can function as a coping mechanism against stress or trauma, aiming to avoid discomfort, fears, or uneasy emotions. The body may signal cues you are being emotionally triggered through perspiration, panic, emotional withdrawal, persistent overthinking, the urge to escape, rapid heartbeat, headaches, or muscle tension. Unfortunately, this approach can hinder conflict resolution during times of discord because there's a lack of values in place.

To prevent unfavorable emotional reactions, it's best to create some distance from the situation, enabling you to evaluate and assess before deciding how you want to proceed forward. This allows you to reflect with deeper understanding and self-awareness, so you do not say or do something you may later regret. Practicing the power of pause or using discovery questions can give you time to process your emotions and regulate them before engaging further in the conversation. The power-of-pause technique can be applied through methods like mentally counting to ten before responding, taking intentional deep breaths, writing in a journal, going for a walk, or temporarily excusing yourself from the conversation to revisit it later. A sign that you've returned to your emotional baseline is when you experience composure and calmness, accompanied by a steady heartbeat and a feeling of mindful balance. Implementing self-soothing exercises empowers you to communicate from a place of inner strength and self-worth, rather than reacting from heightened emotions.

Responding involves a thoughtful and strategic approach to communication, taking into careful consideration the benefits and consequences of your actions as a result of your reply. This approach enables you to voice your value, break down the other person's defensive mechanisms, foster healthy engagement, and collaborate towards finding solutions. When you are able to emotionally regulate, this allows you to share thoughts, feelings, and needs while maintaining a sense of confidence and personal power.

When engaging in open conversations, the selection of words holds significant weight over the outcome. Opting to respond rather than react when addressing a disconnect ensures that you can navigate these differences while upholding mutual respect, without feeling guilt or a sense of powerlessness. Your authentic voice, paired with heart-centered thinking, stands as your most powerful resource for addressing and reconciling a disconnect within the relationship. However, if you find yourself slipping into a reactive state, it serves as an indicator that you've veered away from your authentic truth and are now entering a state of emotion rather than value.

Emotional Reaction versus Logical Response:

- Emotional Reaction: Withdrawing or shutting down.
  Logical Response: Communicate your needs openly and honestly. Share what's bothering you and express your desire for understanding or personal space.

- Emotional Reaction: Attacking or using aggressive behavior
  Logical Response: Remove yourself from the situation to collect your thoughts and emotions. Return to the conversation when you can communicate effectively and assertively.

- Emotional Reaction: Becoming defensive or blaming.
  Logical Response: Seek to understand the other person's perspective and communicate your own thoughts, needs, or values. Address the disconnect by finding mutual alignment.

- Emotional Reaction: Making demands or ultimatums.
  Logical Response: Set healthy boundaries. Communicate your needs and limits clearly, allowing room for negotiation and collaboration.

- Emotional Reaction: Emotional flooding or long-winded tangents.
  Logical Response: Practice concise communication. Focus on expressing your thoughts and concerns confidently to be heard and understood.

- Emotional Reaction: Seeking validation or instant gratification.
  Logical Response: Express your long-term goals and desires.

Use your values as a guiding roadmap to build a genuine connection.

- Emotional Reaction: Over-explaining or pleasing behavior.
  Logical Response: Pause and stick to the facts. Provide thoughtful responses without oversharing unnecessary information.

- Emotional Reaction: Numbing or escaping discomfort.
  Logical Response: Allow yourself to feel and process your emotions by choosing a self-love activity to connect with yourself.

- Emotional Reaction: Catastrophizing thoughts or anxiousness.
  Logical Response: Reflect on what you can control in the situation. Focus on taking constructive actions that align with your goals and values.

- Emotional Reaction: Deflecting or avoiding responsibility.
  Logical Response: Take accountability for your part in the situation. Acknowledge your role and work towards a collaborative resolution.

If you take a closer look at Sammy and Jon's conversation earlier in the chapter, they became emotionally reactive when planning and packing for their camping trip. Neither of them asked discovery questions to understand where the miscommunication occurred or how the camping gear was left behind.

Dialogue One between Sammy and Jon from the story would look like the following if they had used discovery questions and emotional regulation:

Jon: "How come I can't find the tarp, pot, or cooler in the back?"

Sammy: "I put everything in the SUV that was on my list. What was on your list?"

Jon: "I didn't make one. I thought we were making a master list when we talked about it. I guess these items got left behind. Can you search for a camping store while I load this stuff back in?"

Sammy: "Sure. How about next time we go through the list together before leaving?"

In this example, as Jon and Sammy used constructive communication, the emotional tension between them began to lessen, allowing them to find a solution. The use of insightful discovery questions helped them better understand each other's viewpoints and behaviors without being accusatory, leading them to a resolution. Additionally, it kept them from blaming each other or emotionally flooding the other person, which generally leads to an impasse or a cycle of repeated relational problems.

Discovery Questions Exercise

Now that you have an understanding of discovery questions, it's your turn to begin using them in conversations where you want to create connection, gain clarity, reduce conflict, or guide the conversation to a resolution. Discovery questions apply to all relationships, personal and professional, to sustain healthy engagement. Having patience will be essential, as learning new ways of responding can take practice before it becomes an innate behavior. Try implementing discovery questions in the situations below to begin developing your skill set.

Example: You received a last-minute calendar invite for a meeting at 5 p.m. from your boss, but you have a wellness appointment scheduled for 5:15 p.m. later that day.

Discovery Question: I received the notification for today's meeting. I have a wellness appointment at 5:15 p.m. that can't be rescheduled. Can I get a recap in the morning?

Conversation 1:

Scenario: Your friend shows up thirty minutes late to a dinner reservation.

Write one example of a discovery question you would like to ask:

_____

_____

_____

_____

Conversation 2:

Scenario: You are running out the door for an appointment and your parent shows up unexpectedly at your home.

Write one example of a discovery question you would like to ask:

_____

_____

_____

_____

Conversation 3:

Scenario: Your partner consistently refuses to help keep the house clean.

Write one example of a discovery question you would like to ask:

_____

_____

_____

_____

SIX
BOUNDARY VIOLATIONS

The alarm was set for 6:15 a.m., but Grant was already out of bed and sitting in the breakfast nook watching the news while Christine made coffee. Christine asked Grant if he would prefer his usual eggs and bacon or pancakes with homemade blueberry syrup. He opted for pancakes, a sign he was going to be in a cheerful mood. As Grant finished breakfast, he headed out to the barn to feed the chickens and horses.

Christine and Grant had been married for twenty-five years. However, things weren't always peachy in their marriage.

Long before they tied the knot, Grant had developed a jealous streak. During Grant and Christine's first month of dating, Norman, Christine's ex, tried to intervene to get Christine back. He wasn't over her and didn't like that she was now dating Grant. Christine continued to entertain Norman's phone calls as friends, but she never crossed the line in her eyes. This became a sore spot in Christine and Grant's relationship, as Grant couldn't let it go. He wanted to trust Christine, but it bothered him that she was still so friendly with Norman.

Even though Christine hadn't shown any signs of betrayal, Grant often made remarks when she went off to play golf at the country club with her girlfriends. He would say, "Have fun, but don't have too much without me." Grant was passionately committed to Christine, and the mere thought of losing her to another man would have internally shattered him to pieces. And to make matters worse, the country club was full of single bachelors, including Norman, whom Grant wasn't fond of.

It was the first Saturday of the golf season. Christine jumped out of bed with excitement as she couldn't wait to get out on the course. Christine was meeting up with her old college crew for a round of nine holes and lunch.

Before she left that morning to meet her friends, Grant called.

"Good luck, and tell the ladies I said hello. Can you please not hang out with Norman if he's at the club?"

Christine sighed. "You know I don't want to date anyone but you. He and I are old news. Where is this coming from?"

"You're very social," Grant said. "And he's flirtatious with you."

Christine rolled her eyes. "I can't control how he is, but I will respect your request. What's wrong with being social?"

"Nothing. I'm afraid something will happen. I value being able to trust each other. Can we agree not to hang out with our exes?"

Christine reluctantly agreed. "Sure, but there is nothing to worry about. This is kind of absurd. And I don't make plans to hang out with him alone. I will see you after golf around one."

Christine, a free spirit, was annoyed with Grant and his overprotectiveness. But she loved him and stood by him despite their differences in personalities. As she hung up the phone, she looked down at her watch. She needed to get moving, as she despised being late for tee-off.

After their round of golf, the ladies ran into a few of the guys in the dining room. The gentlemen asked if they could join them for lunch. Christine and her girlfriends said they didn't mind, so they sat down at their table.

Earlier that morning over the phone, Christine had told Grant she would come by his place at one o'clock when she finished her round, but now it was almost two in the afternoon. Christine knew Grant was probably growing suspicious as to why she hadn't arrived yet. As

Christine ate her cobb salad, Grant unexpectedly walked into the dining room of the country club. The look on his face said it all, and Christine's stomach dropped. He was infuriated because Norman was dining at the table.

Christine immediately asked the waitress to bring her a to-go box. She knew if she continued to have lunch with her friends or asked Grant to join them, it was only going to make matters worse. Even though Christine didn't think she was betraying the relationship, she had confirmed that she would keep her distance from Norman out of respect for Grant.

Many years passed, and Christine and Grant decided to hang up their golf cleats and country club membership. They were now living on their farm in the countryside, yet they enjoyed gathering with their old golf friends from time to time. Every summer, they hosted an annual cookout to catch up. They extended the invitation to all of their neighbors.

As Grant came in from feeding the animals, Christine was working on the guest invites for their upcoming cookout. She mentioned inviting their new neighbor, Norman, who recently purchased a ranch about half a mile down the road. Of course, Grant was flooded with old memories the minute he received the news.

"Here we go again." Grant sat down to take off his boots.

Christine looked over at Grant. "We have been married for twenty-five years. How come you are still not over him? Can we let it go?"

Grant stood up and mumbled under his breath. "If you had honored what we agreed upon years ago, we wouldn't be talking about this. But do what you want."

"I made a mistake in the past, but I can't change it. I have let it go, and I hope you can too. Can you be a good neighbor?"

Boundaries aren't meant to control others. They are an opportunity to connect.

Insight

Grant and Christine's relationship patterns started during their first month of dating when a trust issue arose between them. With Norman intervening in their relationship, this triggered Grant's fear of rejection, causing him to become insecure in the relationship. To feel safe, Grant set a boundary with Christine asking her to no longer hang out with Norman at the country club. However, Christine, being social and outgoing, couldn't understand Grant's perspective.

Christine found Grant's fears unnecessary, yet she blindly agreed to Grant's boundary without voicing her value or perspective on what trust meant to her. Agreeing to a boundary to appease another person without negotiating the differences can lead to repeated violations for the boundary setter. While Christine valued trust, she violated Grant's boundary when Norman joined her and her friends for lunch. Neglecting to establish mutual alignment on the value of trust created greater distrust between Grant and Christine. This hindered their ability to form emotional security in their relationship, which led to ongoing resentment between Christine and Grant.

If Grant and Christine had approached the situation by defining what trust meant to each of them and their limits, they could have avoided this twenty-five-year-long fight altogether with healthy couple boundaries. The isolated and old incident at the country club impacted their conversations off and on throughout their entire marriage, as they were never able to get to the root of the disconnect. Establishing healthy boundaries requires a discovery process to align the beliefs of both individuals involved within the relationship, fostering a sense of unity centered around shared values. When each person has a voice in the agreement, the boundary is more likely to be honored and respected. *See Chapter 15 for couple boundaries.*

Boundary Violations

A boundary violation occurs when an individual crosses your personal limit that has already been established in the connection. A breach of a boundary can cause harm and instill feelings of uneasiness or disrespect. Sometimes, a person may violate boundaries due to poor negotiation skills, unhealthy relationship patterns, unresolved trauma, resistance to learning a new behavior, or personality complexities. Those with personality complexities, may disregard your boundaries because they hold beliefs such as *your feelings are irrelevant, accept me as I am,* or *my needs are more important than yours.*

Boundary violations can arise from either intentional actions or accidental behaviors. It's important not to immediately assume ill intentions, as the person might be unaware of their innate behaviors that lead to disregarding the boundary. Nevertheless, if a violation takes place and you address it, yet the other person continues to disregard the boundary, it can indicate there is a deeper issue related to this person's desire for control. This behavior might stem from a sense of powerlessness within the relationship dynamic or a belief in their own superiority, rather than a willingness to uphold the mutual respect that supports the relationship's needs.

When it comes to addressing violations, the individual responsible for setting the boundary may find it necessary to reestablish the initial boundary or to set a new one altogether for greater alignment. This process requires prioritizing values over emotions, ensuring that the boundary is effectively communicated and well received. Learning new communication skills takes time and coincides with noticeable changes in the dynamic of the relationship. For many, it can feel relatable to learning to eat with your non-dominant hand after habitually using your dominant hand for many years. However, being consistent becomes essential when embarking on the journey of setting boundaries, as it paves the way for elevating personal growth and development.

When boundary violations go unaddressed, it can lead to unhealthy relationship patterns and a lack of self-respect. Staying silent and letting violations slip under the rug leads to indirectly accepting poor behaviors and an imbalance in the connection. When you neglect to advocate your self-worth, you are letting the other person know it's okay to treat you in a way that violates your value. The ultimate responsibility lies within us to maintain and uphold our boundaries, as they serve to protect our emotional and physical well-being. By demonstrating self-respect and treating others with respect, we effectively communicate our value and teach others how we wish to be treated. This highlights the significance of operating from a place of heart-centered thinking when establishing boundaries, as it enables us to prioritize our own needs and ensure that our boundaries are honored and respected.

Relational Cycles

Holding onto emotional wounds can lead to harboring negative emotions and recurring cycles in relationships. Carrying the weight of past painful events and not getting to the root of the misalignment can make it challenging to maintain a healthy connection. As an individual encounters new experiences or challenges, it can trigger a similar emotional response based on a past event. Sometimes, this is an unconscious reaction because the pain has been dismissed for so long, the memories have been repressed, or a boundary wasn't set during the initial violation.

When an individual neglects their emotional state around personal triggers or behavioral patterns, this can be a sign they are dismissing responsibility for their emotions. Trying to escape emotional pain can lead to placing blame on others or expecting others to be responsible for someone else's past actions. This creates unhealthy relationship patterns and repeated wound cycles because the deeper need is unmet. Overall, a healthy relationship requires each person to take full responsibility for healing emotional wounds so they don't dampen the connection and create unhealthy cycles for years to come.

Violations with Challenging Personalities

Setting boundaries with challenging personality types can be an uphill battle. It may feel like your needs are being dismissed or blatantly ignored. These individuals will resist boundaries because they operate in a *me mindset* and struggle to see outside themselves. It doesn't mean your boundary isn't necessary or should be ignored. It may mean this is where the line of respect ends in this connection, and it needs to be redefined for your own well-being. Certain individuals may continuously provoke you and refuse to be held accountable for their actions. When a person refuses to acknowledge their actions, it can become toxic to the emotional and mental health of everyone involved. This is where healing emotional triggers becomes a source of power when interacting with this type of individual; doing this no longer gives them control over your emotional state.

Complex personality types are known to change the narrative of the situation to create confusion regarding the boundary. They will attempt to use manipulation tactics to alter the dialogue or incident in their favor. This can make you second-guess your recollection of the event, where they are no longer in violation. If these patterns persist, it may even lead to self-doubt, where you feel powerless or even guilty for bringing it up. This is when you'll want to stay outside the direct source of conflict or power struggle and take a big-picture approach by addressing the disconnect. For instance, "I can see that we might have differing perspectives," "It appears that we may remember the events differently," or "It seems like we're not on the same page." This prevents you from feeling responsible for their emotions or perspective, allowing you to gain further insight into the disconnect. Proceeding forward with discovery questions will help you gain further insight into the facts or uncover underlying intentions. Once you have established clarity, then you can choose to set a boundary or redefine the relationship if this person is unable to respect you and the relationship.

Redefining Relationships

When an individual disregards your boundaries consistently, this often means the relationship will need to be redefined or dissolved. Your self-esteem doesn't have to plummet at the cost of sustaining the relationship. Sometimes, individuals cannot remove a particular person from their life because they rely on the relationship to support their financial well-being, share children together, care for or live with a parent, or have a business arrangement. When these circumstances arise and there is no longer respect but the relationship cannot be dissolved, redefining the relationship will best support your mental health.

Redefining the relationship may look like spending less time with this person, limiting communication to email, working in privacy, creating your own family gatherings, or moving to a new safe space or location. Redefining a relationship can be different for everyone, and each person will need to consider all variables involved based on the relationship type.

Examples of Boundary Violations:

- Ignoring mutually respectful requests
- Canceling commitments last minute
- Calling and texting excessively
- Being manipulated, gaslit, or coerced to comply
- Staying silent when mistreated
- Creating expectations or ultimatums
- Keeping people in your life who cause more harm than good
- Saying yes to appease others
- Denying your needs, standards, values, and authentic truth
- Forgoing work-life-love balance
- Dismissing time constraints and deadlines

- Invading personal or physical space
- Forcing emotions or beliefs onto others
- Projecting unresolved emotional wounds
- Dismissing consent for sexual intimacy or touching
- Working past professional work hours
- Betraying one's trust
- Criticizing opposing perspectives
- Engaging in unhealthy lifestyle habits
- Disregarding verbal or written agreements
- Avoiding financial responsibilities
- Neglecting to return communication
- Using resources or funds without reimbursement
- Humiliating others publicly
- Accessing others' private information

SEVEN

COMMUNICATION
CULTIVATES CONNECTION

Three weeks had passed in the blink of an eye since Jenna and Kristen's previous conversation. Lost in the whirlwind of their chaotic work schedules, neither had realized just how long it had been since they'd last spoken. Both tirelessly navigated their busy lives, often darting between television sets. Kristen's expertise as a sought-after hair stylist for commercial projects kept her swamped, while Jenna's meticulous work as a set designer commanded her full attention.

Despite their professional endeavors, their friendship never skipped a beat. Jenna messaged Kristen to make plans, seamlessly picking up where they had left off weeks earlier. During their conversation, they decided to meet up for dinner the following Wednesday. While they didn't nail down the location, they both agreed they were long overdue and couldn't wait to see each other.

However, the next day, Jenna received some life-altering news. She had successfully landed a new job on a television series that was set to be filmed on a tropical island four thousand miles away. Over the past year, she had put in the hours to become a household name in the industry, and this opportunity felt like her well-deserved big break. Excitement flowed through her veins as she eagerly shared the news with her family. But the one person she wanted to tell in person was Kristen. Jenna's heart filled with joy and anticipation as she envisioned surprising her friend with the incredible news during dinner.

The one person who wasn't thrilled about her new job opportunity was Jenna's partner, Craig. She was going to be relocating for a few months on the island. This would be the longest they had ever been apart after meeting on set a year ago. Jenna reassured Craig it would go by quickly and how important the project was for her career.

Over the weekend, Jenna got a call from the television studio about an impromptu meeting next Wednesday evening to go over the schedule. She immediately confirmed without hesitation.

The night before their dinner plans, Kristen sent a text to Jenna.

Hey! Where are we meeting tomorrow and what time works for you? Can't wait to catch up, and I have so much to share with you!

Jenna immediately replied, *Omg! You're not going to believe this!! I landed my first destination job.*

Wow, I'm so happy for you! We have so much to talk about.

Jenna apologetically wrote back. *Sorry, I need to cancel dinner. I have to meet with the team tomorrow night to go over the details of the television series.*

Wait, you're canceling? I kept my schedule blocked off since we made plans. When did you find out about the show?

Jenna started to bite her nails. *I knew last week and couldn't wait to share it with you. But my producer reached out on Saturday to meet up and confirm details. I'm really sorry.*

Kristen paused with frustration. *I wish you had told me sooner like a good friend. I've had so many client requests for appointments and didn't book them. But don't worry about my time. I'll figure it out like I always do.*

Jenna immediately sent another text. *Please don't be mad. I really am sorry. You know how much I love you.*

It's fine.

A month later, Jenna walked off the plane and arrived at her charming apartment near the television set. She video-called Craig, wanting to assure him of her safe arrival, and gave him a quick virtual tour of her place. The conversation was brief, as Jenna's call time the next morning was at five o'clock, which demanded she get to bed early. She was battling jet lag and could barely keep her eyes open.

As the days blurred together on set, Jenna found herself fatigued from long work hours. The tight schedule left little room for downtime, and she would often return to her apartment only to crash on her bed. The significant time difference between the island and back at home made it challenging to maintain communication with Craig. Their conversations became scarce, and Jenna's exhaustion compounded the difficulty of trying to stay connected.

Craig started growing increasingly frustrated with Jenna's lack of effort, as he felt her slipping away. He continuously attempted to video call her every night, but the calls went unanswered. This deeply upset him, leading Craig to wonder if something was wrong between them. The emotional rollercoaster started to take a toll on Craig. He impulsively shut off his phone to keep himself from incessantly checking to see if she had texted or called back.

Effective communication is the bridge between confusion and clarity.

Insight

While Jenna's professional ambitions became a top priority in her life, she started to take her closest relationships for granted due to her poor work-life-love balance. When it came to Jenna's communication style with her friend, Kristen, and her partner, Craig, she operated from a *me* mindset, solely consumed with her needs and work schedule. She pushed her friendship to the wayside without any regard for Kristen's time or their plans. This left Kristen feeling undervalued by Jenna's last-minute cancellation. Kristen passive-aggressively expressed her frustrations with Jenna but didn't set a boundary regarding her value of time. Forgoing assertive communication, Kristen indirectly undervalued herself. This could have given Jenna the impression that it was okay to cancel last minute in the future without regard for the friendship.

Jenna's communication with Craig had also started to deteriorate when she didn't return his calls, showing a lack of mutual respect for their relationship. Craig emotionally reacted by resorting to silence and shutting off his phone rather than addressing the disconnect with Jenna. Prior to her departure, the couple neglected to establish a communication plan to sustain their connection. This would have supported each partner's need to feel secure in their relationship while spending time apart. Their physical distance quickly turned into a growing emotional disconnect. Plus, given their different time zones and work schedules, neither partner was prepared on how they would keep their communication channels open. Disregarding healthy couple boundaries or communication boundaries in their relationship left Craig feeling insignificant and wondering where he stood in Jenna's life.

As Jenna's career started to evolve, she became even more self-focused and undervalued her support system. When a person neglects their support system due to their professional endeavors, it can damage their interpersonal relationships. This can be an indication they are neglecting their values, lacking personal integrity, or avoiding emotional intimacy. Success in any profession or relationship requires healthy lines of communication and mutual respect to sustain the connection. *See Chapter 13 for friend boundaries, Chapter 15 for couple boundaries, and Chapter 27 for time boundaries.*

Next, you will learn healthy communication skills and gain insight into how valuable they are to your relationships.

Five Cs of Communication

When cultivating remarkable relationships, it is best to use the five Cs of communication. The five Cs provide the optimal delivery and sharing of information for building rapport and addressing relationship concerns respectfully and effectively. Communication skills strengthen your connections, help resolve discord, and prevent misunderstandings for greater alignment.

- **Calm:** Upholding a calm demeanor can make all the difference in a conversation and how well the other person receives your message. By keeping a calm composure, it allows you to think rationally and clearly about the message you want to deliver without reacting. Statistically, 10 % of conflicts are due to differences in opinion and 90% are due to the heightened tone of voice.

- **Concise:** Keeping messages brief and factorial will help eliminate misunderstandings during conflict or engagement. It helps reduce confusion and tension and diminishes emotional flooding through long-winded messages. It's important to say what you mean and mean what you say in the least number of words to be heard and understood.

- **Constructive:** Using constructive communication allows for healthy dialogue to take place when differences arise. Staying positive during moments of adversity creates stronger cohesion, mutual satisfaction, and potential solutions. It is not about right or wrong or whose perspective is better. It's a *we versus the relationship* problem, not a *me versus you* problem.

- **Consistent:** Maintaining interpersonal relationships requires consistent communication. Consistency will vary from person to person as well as the type of relationship dynamic. While you may talk to a significant other or family member every day, you may only speak to work colleagues or friends on a weekly or monthly basis. Establishing a rhythmic flow will be essential to sustaining healthy, trustworthy, and evolving connections.

- **Confidence:** Being a confident communicator means remaining loyal to one's values. Confident communicators have the ability to convey their messages clearly, concisely, and with unwavering conviction. They actively listen and respond appropriately, showcasing their integrity and self-worth through their body language, composed demeanor, and communication style. This involves effectively and assertively sharing ideas, thoughts, and emotions during interpersonal interactions.

Active Listening

The skill of active listening is one of the most significant communication techniques for building connections. Active listening is a conscious choice that allows us to effectively listen and engage with others, understand messages being conveyed, as well as provide thoughtful feedback. In comparison, passive hearing is the act of processing sounds without considering the meaning behind the words being spoken. It is similar to listening to a song without recognizing the meaning of the lyrics. The intent of passive listening is often used by a person who is only waiting to have their turn to speak while ignoring deeper insight into the other person's message. Passive hearing hinders the connection, creates confusion, and prevents the ability to genuinely relate to one another.

When it comes to active listening, paraphrasing statements can validate the speaker's inner voice and confirm their message was heard correctly, as communication can easily be misinterpreted based on one's belief system. The use of reaffirming statements also lets someone know their message was received, such as "I see," "I understand," "Thank you for sharing," or "I hear you." Acknowledging someone's message does not imply you agree with their statement, but you can understand their perspective. Validating outside perspective not only fosters open communication but also builds trust and strengthens the relationship. When individuals feel heard and understood, they are more likely to approach uneasy conversations more calmly.

In times of confusion, it is wise to seek additional clarity by asking discovery questions when you suspect a potential misunderstanding or lack of comprehension of another person's viewpoint. Neglecting to inquire further about a person's perspective or statement can lead to misguided assumptions or misconceptions.

The best communicators, negotiators, leaders, and problem-solvers are all excellent active listeners, which allows them to gain insight and maintain an open mind for building powerful connections. In high-conflict situations, great communicators utilize the power of active listening as their superpower. By attentively tuning into the speaker's message, they can effectively guide the conversation toward a mutually beneficial outcome. Without listening to every word spoken, we can't form alignments or achieve resolutions to relationship disconnects.

Nonverbal Communication

While verbal communication is essential to delivering a message, non-verbal body language cues are even more crucial to communication and your relationship success. Ninety-three percent of communication being exchanged between the speaker and the responder is delivered through nonverbal communication. Only 7% is delivered through the actual words being said. When it comes to nonverbal communication, body language accounts for 55%, and tone of voice accounts for 38%.

Being observant of body language is key to gaining valuable insights into someone's expression and thought, regardless of what is being spoken. Subtle cues like eye contact and arm gestures often signal when it is appropriate for you to contribute to the conversation. These subconscious cues and facial expressions enable you to read the emotional responses and build trust within the relationship dynamic.

For example, if a listener crosses their arms or consistently gazes off in a different direction, they may resist to connecting even if they verbally express interest. On the contrary, if the listener's arms are open with appropriate eye contact, they may be receptive to creating deeper engagement. Generally, when a person's verbal and nonverbal cues are congruent, they are genuinely telling the truth. Conversely, if their nonverbal cues are incongruent with what they are stating, this usually is a telltale sign they are being deceitful. However, it is best practice to use discovery questions to fully assess the information being delivered instead of reading body language as factorial evidence. (Note: nonverbal communication is open to interpretation based on a person's mannerisms in their natural state, the topic of conversation, comfortability, and environment.)

Additionally, nonverbal cues in communication can be universally understood across many diverse cultures. A simple smile or handshake can convey acceptance and kindness, even when two individuals do not share a common language. However, it is important to note that nonverbal cues can be subject to various interpretations across different cultures. It becomes crucial to carefully consider these interpretations, taking into account varying practices and norms. For instance, while direct eye contact may be perceived as disrespectful in one culture, it can be seen as a sign of positive engagement in another. In such situations, relying on your intuition and being mindful of your surroundings and cultural norms is often the best approach.

Communication Styles

There are five types of communication styles that people use in their relationships. The most appropriate style for building remarkable relationships is assertive communication. Even if someone learned an unfavorable interpersonal communication skill growing up, they can adjust their communication style to effectively benefit their life and relationships today. No matter the situation, discovery questions and healthy boundaries will help you navigate each of these communication styles.

- **Assertive Communication** is the most effective and positive style of communication when it comes to having healthy relationships, both personally and professionally. This style of communication is calm, composed, and constructive without the use of aggression or manipulative tactics that would infringe the rights of others. Assertive speakers are confident and openly express their opinions and feelings, can resolve interpersonal conflict, take accountability for their choices, set healthy boundaries, and uphold respect for themselves and others.

  Assertive Communicators Do the Following:

  o Communicate with social and emotional awareness to influence positive engagement for mutual respect within the relationship.

  o Use a medium pitch tone of voice, have an open posture, maintain appropriate amounts of eye contact, and display respect for physical space.

  o Cause others to feel respected, offer clarity about where they stand in the connection, create comfort for addressing concerns, and foster trust.

- **Submissive Communication** is used by people who tend to avoid expressing their feelings or opinions, deflect from identifying their needs, and refrain from conflict at all costs. Those who use a submissive communication style generally place the needs of others above their own to prevent the loss of a connection, as they tend to depend on others for validation. When this occurs, it's a clear indication there is a lack of healthy boundaries in place. A submissive individual is unlikely to experience healthy relationships or advance their connections because people do not take them seriously. Those who constantly say yes to others at the expense of their own emotional needs tend to feel guilty when they say no. People who use submissive communication can feel taken advantage of in their relationships.

Submissive Communicators Do the Following:

○ Communicate to seek approval from others by overcompensating and undervaluing one's worth.

○ Use a soft tone of voice, often are withdrawn or have downward head tilting, avoid prolonged eye contact, and maintain physical distance when communicating with others.

○ Cause others to feel frustrated, waste people's time, create disengagement, or can be seen as pushovers to others.

• **Aggressive Communication** is when a person expresses feelings or opinions to seek power over the other person or topic of conversation. An aggressive communicator focuses on "winning," even if it is at the expense of someone else or ultimately sabotaging the relationship altogether. The individual believes they are entitled to receive what is important to them before trying to work with the other person, and they often lack boundaries. Their unpredictable intimidation is about gaining control in the relationship, which is counterproductive to both people being heard and understood. People do not respond well to aggression and will disengage even at the expense of the relationship.

Aggressive Communicators Do the Following:

○ Communicate with aggression to try and "win" in every situation, even though it can backfire and sabotage relationships.

○ Use a high-pitched tone of voice, display ultra-masculine posture, convey angry facial expression, and overstep one's personal space with a lack of spatial awareness.

○ Cause people to feel hurt, afraid, resentful, humiliated, and make others feel a lack of respect toward them.

- **Passive-Aggressive Communication** is when a person acts passively on the surface but feels bouts of aggression behind the scenes. This individual may feel resentful or powerless in the relationship because their emotional needs aren't being met due to poor boundaries. When this occurs, they can seek revenge through backhanded compliments or rude comments in an attempt to punish a person because their feelings are hurt, or they aren't getting their way. A passive-aggressive communicator can find it thrill-seeking when the person they resent experiences a personal disadvantage because it makes them feel powerful in their own life. Ultimately, they lack the ability to show vulnerability and are complex, which creates an impasse in working through relationship discord.

  Passive-Aggressive Communicators Do the Following:

  - Communicate to gain power through indirect, backhanded strategies, and seek revenge for perceived insults.
  - Use a kind yet sarcastic tone of voice, rest their hand on a hip when speaking, frequently display politeness intertwined with disrespectful body language, and can stand too close in proximity.
  - Cause people to feel confused, resentful, angry, and hurt.

- **Manipulative Communication** is when a person is controlling and calculated to gain power through the exploitation of others for their own advantage. Their spoken words tend to conceal their true intentions, avoid responsibility, or cause confusion and doubt through manipulation tactics. They may even use artificial tears to get people to feel sorry for them while dismissing any form of boundaries. This individual often feels internally powerless and will take great strides to patronize others to reach their goals, even at the expense of damaging the relationship.

Manipulative Communicators Do the Following:

○ Communicate to gain control by sulking and using underlying messages of deceit, only to potentially destroy the relationship after their goal is achieved.

○ Use a high pitch, envious tone of voice, display prolonged intense eye contact, or exhibit a pouting facial expression.

○ Cause people to feel irritated, frustrated, guilty, exploited, untrustworthy, and uncertain about where they stand with this person.

Communication boundaries are prevalent in every relationship and can help you with each type of communicator. Throughout each of the following boundary chapters, you will discover communication boundaries.

Types of Communication Boundaries

• Sharing availability for personal and professional communication

• Establishing the frequency of communication

• Choosing a platform for communication

• Addressing lack of communication or failure to respond

• Shutting down inappropriate, abusive, disparaging, or defamatory comments

• Speaking up to honor self-worth and values

• Maintaining constructive communication

• Requesting space when discussions become emotionally intense

• Honoring the privacy of confidential information

• Being transparent about perspectives, beliefs, or feelings

• Excusing oneself when nonverbal communication feels threatening

- Creating a safe word for uncomfortable situations
- Listening when others are speaking
- Being open-minded to other's viewpoints
- Respecting different communication and attachment styles

EIGHT

TRUST IS A MUST

Eloise looked down at her phone and saw her mother, Rosalynn, was calling. It was their weekly call where Eloise sat quietly and listened to her mother tell her about everything she was doing wrong in life. Even though Eloise had gotten used to her mother's outlandish remarks for the past thirty-eight years, her compulsive need to have things be her way irked Eloise. As Eloise hung up the phone, she felt emotionally drained and numb. Rosalynn aggressively interrogated Eloise about what she wore to work that day and whether she paid her bills on time. Whenever Eloise went the extra mile to assure her mother life was picture perfect, her stomach sank because she knew she was lying to avoid her mother's long lectures.

Eloise wasn't happy but she couldn't pinpoint why she felt unfulfilled. If her mother only knew the truth, she would be knocking down her door telling her to try harder and to stop feeling sorry for herself. Eloise was sick of being nagged, even though she knew it was her mother's way of showing she cared. Many days she felt utterly lost and didn't know who to turn to when she needed someone the most.

As her spirits plummeted, she got online and started shopping for new shoes. While she scrolled through images, she impulsively selected three new pairs to put into her shopping cart for check-out. Although people rarely commented on her heels, Eloise remained loyal in adhering to her mother's voice in her head, believing that looking her best was paramount.

When Eloise walked through the office door, she was immediately greeted with a towering stack of tasks on her desk. The pile never seemed to shrink, as Eloise was constantly going out of her way to help her colleagues at the office. This usually left Eloise working overtime at night trying to catch up, but often left her feeling overwhelmed and stressed. Climbing her way up in the company was something she dreamed about because she knew how proud her mother would be.

As Wednesday unfolded, Eloise found herself leaving the office frazzled and burnt out. She had plans to meet up with her partner for a much-needed happy hour. However, he wanted to try something other than their usual spot, which Eloise wasn't too thrilled about. She clung to the comfort of their usual place and requested they go there. As they sat down at their table, Eloise took charge and ordered food for both of them. Wyatt often caved to what Eloise wanted because it was easier than disappointing her. As they savored their appetizers, Wyatt sat there in silence. Eloise immediately grew worried and started asking what was wrong because he wasn't being his usual talkative self. Wyatt reassured her that nothing was wrong, but Eloise knew something was off in her gut.

Eloise called her mom the next day to tell her Wyatt was acting strange.

"Hey, Mom, can we talk? I feel like something is bothering Wyatt, but he keeps saying everything is fine."

Rosalynn gasped. "What did you do this time? I'm sure you said something since he's not speaking to you."

Eloise immediately regretted calling her mom. "Mom! Why do you always assume I did something wrong? I told you I didn't do anything. He is being weird. What should I do? Gosh! Can't you be helpful for once?"

"Eloise, I don't understand why you're getting mad at me. I've always supported you. You know that. Maybe he is just having a bad day.

I don't know. But it sounds like you need to make him a nice dinner and treat him better."

"Make him dinner? I make him nice dinners all the time. That isn't the issue."

Rosalynn nonchalantly said, "Well, I'm not sure sweetheart. You do have a habit of picking the wrong guys. Maybe you need to move on and find someone better. I never really liked Wyatt anyways. You guys are complete opposites."

Eloise looked down at her nails in disgust. "You're right. I am bad at choosing partners. Maybe I'll break up with him tomorrow."

Rosalynn smiled. "I love how you're still my little go-getter. You never cease to amaze me, as I know you will make the best decision."

Eloise got off the phone and curled up in a ball on the couch. She didn't want to end things with Wyatt, but maybe her mom was right. In the back of her mind, she thought they were perfect together, but now she started to second-guess herself. Eloise was left confused about whether or not to trust her mother's advice.

A relationship without trust is bound to bust.

Insight

Eloise's relationship with her mother was far from nurturing. Her mother, Rosalynn, thrived on controlling Eloise's life decisions even into adulthood. Her mother constantly criticized and disapproved of Eloise's choices, from how she dressed daily to the partners she dated. When a parent is highly critical, they are often displacing their own shortcomings onto their child due to their inability to take responsibility for their emotions or thoughts. They see their child as an extension of themselves and expect their child to live up to their so-called perfect standards. Because Rosalynn repeatedly belittled Eloise's decisions, Eloise second-guessed whether she knew what was in her best interest. This left her feeling unsatisfied in life. Instead, she constantly sought her mother's approval to make sure was doing the right thing.

When it came to Eloise's relationships, they were transactional rather than genuine, which can be a sign of poor boundaries and low self-esteem. She developed relationships based on control, mirroring the relationship she shared with her mother, which left her feeling unworthy. She would go out of her way by overextending herself, focusing on her appearance and achievements in hopes of receiving recognition at the office. This led to her neglecting and undervaluing herself while constantly being at the service of others. When someone undervalues who they are, it can prevent them from knowing their personal limits, neglecting to set healthy boundaries, and failing to trust their own decision-making.

When it came to Eloise's romantic relationship, she chose a partner who she could have control over to protect herself from getting hurt. The minute she felt a shift in the relationship, rather than resolving the disconnect, she was quick to conclude that it was best to leave him before he had the chance to leave her. This is a sign of an unresolved emotional wound. Choosing a partner where one person feels superior over the other creates an imbalance and leads to a lack of fulfillment. Rather than being vulnerable and valuable in her connection, she chose to mask her feelings because she was disconnected from her values. Opening herself up to others had often resulted in negative outcomes, leaving her feeling exposed and fearful. Consequently, she developed a tendency to prioritize external validation over a genuine connection, fearing that trusting herself and others would only lead to disappointment. Her mother's influence had stifled the growth of her inner voice, robbing her of the ability to trust her instincts and inhibiting her from forming deep connections with others. *See Chapter 10 for personal boundaries, Chapter 11 for emotional boundaries, Chapter 15 for couple boundaries, and Chapter 17 for family boundaries.*

Trusting Yourself

Building trust in a relationship begins with being able to trust yourself first and foremost. Self-trust gives you confidence and clarity with each choice you make and the ability to find resilience when facing adversity. It instills an unwavering belief in your capabilities to transform challenging situations into triumphant victories while pursuing your goals. The more self-awareness and self-acceptance you embody, the more self-trust is cultivated.

If you are struggling to trust your choices, then it can be an uphill battle to build trustworthy relationships. The root cause of distrust can come from various life experiences. Perhaps, you had a tumultuous childhood where a parent was absent, an ex-partner was deceitful, or a friend abruptly cut you off out of the blue. Such instances of broken trust, if left unaddressed, can prevent desirable outcomes in present or future relationships. When an individual allows the past mistakes of others to influence their current relationships, then they are giving power to their past experiences over their fulfillment and happiness today. This not only does an injustice to the individual but also to their new relationships. The process of healing these lingering and suppressed emotions is pivotal to strengthening self-trust.

Embracing new opportunities and actively seeking personal growth can serve as the catalyst for strengthening self-confidence. When faced with critical life decisions or a sense of stagnation, your values act as a guiding roadmap, directing you towards choices that harmonize with your long-term aspirations and contribute to your overall well-being. By taking small daily risks, you can begin the journey of transforming your belief system and cultivating trust, even in the face of unfamiliar situations. Trusting your ability to make healthy choices that align with your life goals empowers you to navigate challenges with poise and to embark on a fulfilling and purposeful journey.

Trusting the Process

Trusting the process can be a taxing experience when striving toward goals, especially if the outcome remains uncertain. If you find yourself attempting to exert excessive control over the process or others, it can impede your progress and lead to disappointment when things don't align with your ideal vision. However, the only way to truly discover what lies ahead is to take a leap of faith, believing that things will ultimately unfold in the best possible way. It doesn't mean stop planning and preparing, but when you are open-minded to opportunities, it will allow you to be present in the here and now. The present moment is where we reap our greatest joy and can create remarkable relationships

When faced with uncertainty, having patience and self-trust will allow things to evolve naturally. While it can feel like a wave of emotions to trust the process, allowing fears to override your goals can leave you feeling dissatisfied. In the end, letting go of control gives you more emotional freedom and inner peace. As difficult as it can be, embracing flexibility, forgiveness, and self-assurance will be essential until the desired goal is achieved.

Key Factors to Building Trust:

- Communicating with transparency
- Having integrity with your word
- Being responsible and accountable
- Honoring mutual respect
- Being humble, genuine, and authentic
- Showing vulnerability
- Letting go of control, expectations, and ultimatums
- Spending quality time with self or others
- Having compassion and understanding
- Honoring values and boundaries
- Being consistent

Rebuilding Broken Trust in Relationships

When someone breaks your trust, it can feel like the foundation of the relationship has collapsed. You may struggle with intense emotions and question whether or not you can find forgiveness for their actions. Keep in mind, their behaviors are primarily a reflection of their internal beliefs and unresolved wounds, and less about you personally. Most often, when trust has been damaged, misaligned values are present in the relationship. A full assessment of the relationship dynamic, behavioral patterns, and personality traits will give you clarity as to whether the trust can be rebuilt.

The first step to rebuilding trust with someone begins by communicating how their behavior made you feel and its impact on the connection. This honors your inner voice and self-worth, providing a guide on what you need to rebuild trust and sustain the relationship long-term. On the contrary, if you have broken someone's trust and are seeking forgiveness, it's crucial to be honest with yourself and to take accountability for your actions. Being transparent and showing remorse can begin healing the connection, if given the opportunity.

Rebuilding trust requires open communication to assess where the differences lie between your value systems or viewpoints. This will allow you to bridge the gap and realign the relationship for growth. While it can feel uncomfortable, valuing the relationship shows you are committed to rebuilding the trust between the two of you. After redefining each person's needs and boundaries, an accountability plan will need to be implemented to move forward in the connection. Remember that healing takes time and patience, even with a plan, as the person who feels betrayed may struggle to overcome the distrust. It will be up to the person who betrayed the relationship to show they can be trusted again through their actions.

Actionable Steps to Rebuilding Trust:

- Acknowledging responsibility for actions
- Apologizing for untrustworthy behaviors
- Assessing the disconnect within the relationship
- Asking for forgiveness
- Showing empathy and understanding
- Realigning the connection through healthy boundaries
- Following through with a mutually agreed action plan

NINE
BOUNDARY BADASS METHOD

Identical twins Dahlia and Demi grew up in the backwoods of a quaint, rural town of nine hundred people. Life had its own pace, slow and steady. From riding horses through the oak trees to picking wildflowers along the side of the road, the sisters were rarely short of free-spirited adventures. Their upbringing and home life felt tranquil, but they were in for quite the wild ride when they set out for an experience that would forever change their lives.

Late one summer, Demi and Dahlia decided to leave their small-town life after high school graduation. Stuck like glue, the sisterly duo packed their bags and headed for a fast-paced city several hours away from home, venturing into uncharted territory. Together, they naively approached the unknowns of their new surroundings and quickly realized that there would be a ton of changes to digest and experience all at once. At times, trying to find their way felt like searching for the missing piece of a jigsaw puzzle in a city of three million strangers. Slowly, they got used to the hustle and bustle of the city, even though it felt slightly out of their comfort zone and different from their upbringing. Little by little, they traded running through flower fields under the stars for gallivanting beneath the bright city lights.

Not long after settling in the big city, the sisters had their first eye-opening experience. While they quickly made several new friends, they were unaware of the true nature of those they had welcomed into their lives. Soon enough, Demi and Dahlia realized that some of their new connections held values entirely different from their own, which left them feeling a bit uneasy. They were thrown into culture shock. The integrity and trust they sought proved to be almost nonexistent, causing them lots of frustration and leading them to rely on each other for support.

Over time, Demi and Dahlia eventually found their footing and discovered their fascination with the world of psychology and mediation. Driven by their genuine desire to make a positive impact, they eagerly volunteered as crisis counselors. Fully immersed in their interests, the sisters recognized their intuitive ability to understand the complexities of interpersonal dynamics. They dedicated their time by extending a compassionate heart and an empathetic ear to teenagers who had found themselves in desperate situations, having run away from their homes.

Through their work as crisis counselors, Demi and Dahlia were able to refine and master their conflict resolution skills. Their role was to bridge the gap between the teenager's perspective and their parents, ultimately finding a resolution that would make the teen feel safe enough to return home. They collaboratively addressed the needs of everyone involved and aimed for a mutually beneficial outcome. Demi and Dahlia's remarkable capacity to connect with others and guide them through life's turbulent waters revealed a profound purpose within them. By offering hope and practical solutions to those struggling with life challenges, they discovered a path that filled their heart with joy and led to their next adventure.

Their volunteering experience inspired them to pursue their graduate studies, where they committed themselves to strengthening their understanding of interpersonal psychology. With valuable insights from their prior work with families, they aspired to uncover the deeper roots of relationship patterns and behaviors. It was an exciting time in their lives, filled with unlimited possibilities, and everything flowed with endless potential. Little did they know at the time, that the road ahead wouldn't be so smooth and would become a pivotal turning point in their journey.

This turning point ended up being two years later. After returning from a long weekend away, Dahlia sensed that something was off with her significant other. She confided in Demi that they had gotten into a disagreement about him constantly questioning her, but he wasn't willing to talk it out. Despite Dahlia's best efforts to talk through things, he resorted to making harsh and critical remarks about the sisters' entrepreneurial endeavors, avoiding any discussion of their relationship issue. In an outburst of anger, he told Dahlia their business would fail and she would never be successful. For Dahlia, it shattered the harmonious connection she had known for the past five years, and it felt like her world was wrapped in storm clouds. She began to feel undervalued in the relationship, wondering where things had gone wrong and uncertain about how to resolve them.

Shortly after, Demi hit a rough patch in her relationship too, leaving her feeling uneasy and confused. Even though their significant others greatly differed in personality, both partners were reluctant to be open and vulnerable about their feelings. The sisters would stay up late into the night talking about their relationships, stuck thinking how all the emotion-based techniques they had learned in graduate school weren't helping them feel truly heard in their romantic relationships. Their hearts were fully invested, yet they were at a loss for words on how to get their emotional needs met, which they knew they deserved. It felt like the door had been slammed shut, and nothing could break through to their significant others. They remained optimistic that there must be a better solution to resolving their differences with their significant others, but they couldn't figure it out. Their resilience kept them searching for answers, no matter how difficult the journey.

Time passed and Demi's relationship with her significant other appeared to be on the upswing. They even began discussing the possibility of getting engaged, and he took her to look at rings. However, when Demi tried to bring up the next step in their relationship, he shut down completely, refusing to discuss the matter further. The more Demi tried to get him to open up, the more he withdrew, eventually leaving their home abruptly. To make matters worse, she discovered that he had put in his resignation at work, leaving her blindsided about their future together. This was not the man she had fallen in love with over the past six years, and she was left stunned without answers.

Meanwhile, Dahlia found herself burdened by the ongoing struggles in her relationship. She was exhausted from not feeling heard by her significant other, despite her efforts to address the challenges. It felt like she was talking to a brick wall, as he thrived on the control of always having things his way. As time went on, his attention became solely fixated on his professional accomplishments, completely ignoring the emotional distance in their relationship. The warmth that had once filled their home had faded away, leaving Dahlia feeling a deep sense of distress. She couldn't help but wonder if there was even the faintest glimmer of hope remaining.

As much as Dahlia and Demi loved their significant others, they knew their relationships had become disconnected when their partners could no longer meet their needs. They had tried to express their feelings, but despite their attempts, nothing ever seemed to significantly change. It became clear to Dahlia and Demi that they needed to prioritize their own self-worth and well-being, even if that meant walking away from their long-term relationships. It was one of the hardest decisions in their lives, but they knew it would ultimately be for the best. They both believed they deserved to be in relationships where they felt heard, respected, and valued – something their parents had ingrained in them at an early age. And while it was hard to leave, they were excited to embark on a new journey of self-discovery and growth.

Life carried on, and Dahlia and Demi remained committed to staying true to their values, despite the unknowns ahead of them. They turned tough times into triumph and channeled their energy into their business goals, determined to build something truly worthwhile and valuable. One day, while chatting at their office, they began to reflect on their past relationships and their connection as twins. The sisters started connecting the dots on how they had successfully managed client relations through professional boundaries and built a reputable company by applying their strong family values. As they continued talking, they realized that both of them had consistently taken each other into account when making decisions in business or life, especially when those decisions had an impact on the other. They wondered if their values and a *we* mindset were the keys to overcoming all relationship obstacles, but they still couldn't pinpoint it.

Since emotion-based modalities had fallen short in resolving differences with their past romantic partners, they knew they had a real dilemma. Sitting with a problem wasn't in their nature, and they had to do something about it. As they exchanged stories back and forth, they came to a profound realization and had their light bulb moment. The values they had prioritized in their business relationships – integrity, communication, and mutual respect – were the same qualities that had been lacking in their past partnerships and friendships. Almost instantly, the sisters discovered that by shifting their communication approach to a value-based framework, they could achieve greater alignment in both their personal and professional relationships. Their values would serve as a voice of reason for resolving differences and creating mutual respect. This aha moment took the sisters from feeling powerless to powerful, ultimately fulfilling their purpose.

Today, Dahlia and Demi have cultivated mutually beneficial relationships in every aspect of their lives by embracing the transformative power of the BOUNDARY BADASS METHOD. Although they have encountered lots of obstacles along their journey, their experiences served as valuable lessons that propelled them toward uncovering the fundamental principles of interpersonal relationships. Through their own personal growth and development, it inspired them to create a truly valuable method that is both powerful and universally applicable to a wide range of relationship challenges.

Authors' note: The story above is a glimpse into our life journey over the past two decades. While specific details have been excluded to protect the confidentiality of others, these life experiences were the purpose behind this book and our mission. For the past ten years, we have been implementing and coaching the BOUNDARY BADASS METHOD, both personally and professionally, to elevate our relationships and those of others.

Values are the voice of reason to be heard and understood in relationships.

Insight

Growing up in a small town instilled us with strong values, but we soon discovered that not everyone we encountered shared them. The culture shock of moving from a rural town of nine hundred people to a metropolitan city of three million was a massive adjustment, along with the challenge of navigating new relationships where mutual respect fell short. Despite life's challenges, we supported each other through tough times, and this gave us the resilience to step out of our comfort zone. However, we quickly discovered that being overly compassionate left us needing to develop stronger boundaries where we were valued and mutually respected.

When it came to expressing our feelings during times of discomfort in our adult interpersonal relationships, we felt powerless. Simply voicing our feelings, as we had learned through emotion-based techniques and our upbringing, unsuccessfully provided practical solutions for real-life relationship challenges. Our extensive knowledge and advanced graduate degrees in the field of psychology had proven to be a double-edged sword, primarily due to our deep understanding of individuals and the absence of proactive techniques to establish healthy boundaries.

While we valued assertive communication, integrity, and mutual respect, our past significant others lacked these values, along with active listening. They became emotionally reactive and closed off from getting to the root of the disconnect. One partner resorted to stonewalling while the other used highly critical language to deflect from emotional responsibility. Despite both of us having a shared desire for resolution and reconnection, the misalignment in communication styles led to a greater disconnect and formed challenges in seeking mutual understanding. Additionally, each of our significant others went through career changes that took precedence over prioritizing the relationship's needs, lacking a work-life-love balance.

As much as we wanted our relationships with friends and significant others to evolve, we knew it took a *we* mindset to achieve mutually beneficial relationships. As identical twins, this concept was ingrained into us during childhood. We came to appreciate the importance of taking each other's values and viewpoints into account when making collective decisions that could affect one another. While we grew up with a *we* mindset, we soon discovered that this wasn't consistently shared by those we invited into our lives.

Despite of our extensive knowledge of interpersonal psychology and our capacity to understand others, we discovered something was lacking in effectively voicing our value and resolving relationship disconnects. Motivated by our own self-development journey, we vowed never to feel powerless again in our relationships. We poured our energy into elevating our personal value rather than seeking what others could not see. We transformed our painful experiences into a greater purpose while achieving inner power. With our unwavering determination, we created a powerful method to cultivate healthy relationships for ourselves and others across all aspects of life.

Our values became the ultimate relationship roadmap for identifying unhealthy behaviors and creating alignment through setting boundaries. Only when we reflected on our approach to managing business relationships did we realize our method could be universally applied to all types of relationships. We honed in on our assertive communication style, opted for a value-based technique during times of relationship distress, and skillfully negotiated differences without jeopardizing the connection, all while upholding respect. This transformative realization of blending interpersonal psychology and conflict resolution skills marked a pivotal turning point in our relationships and laid the foundation for the development of our BOUNDARY BADASS METHOD.

Presently, when confronted with a disconnect in an interpersonal relationship, we respond with value rather than emotion. We approach difficult conversations with a holistic perspective, recognizing the potential to strengthen our relationships. With grace and confidence, we assert our inherent value, identifying that the behaviors of others are a reflection of their inner beliefs and do not define our true selves. We view these unfavorable instances as opportunities to gain a deeper understanding of their perspectives and to bridge the gap between differences for greater alignment. Throughout our journey, the more we understood ourselves, our needs, and our boundaries, the better equipped we became to navigate and negotiate interactions with others.

The imbalance of mutual respect we experienced in our past interpersonal relationships became the driving force in discovering our life purpose and transforming modern-day relationships. On our journey, we continue to inspire others to recognize their own power through creating remarkable personal and professional relationships, owning their self-worth, expressing their value, and setting boundaries like a badass.

Boundary Badass

Being a *Boundary Badass* means having self-respect and exuding profound confidence when speaking. You are willing to voice your authentic truth in an honest, humble, and respectful manner, while unapologetically standing up for your beliefs and values. The essence of your inherent power does not come from external forces but from personal value alignment. You are open-minded to the thoughts of others without internalizing their behaviors as an opposition, and instead seeing them as an opportunity to understand perspectives outside your own. When experiencing adversity, you stand firm with integrity and have an unshakeable commitment to your value. Ultimately, a *Boundary Badass* believes respect is given yet knows when to set a boundary if respect isn't reciprocated.

Critical Inner Voice

The critical inner voice, also known as a false narrative, focuses on feelings of inadequacy and an individual's inability to believe in themselves. It can lead to self-destructive behaviors and feelings of powerlessness when attempting to set and maintain healthy boundaries. These self-deprecating thoughts can hinder the ability to maintain positive thinking and implement problem-solving skills. This can lead to self-criticism, devaluation, distrust, guilt, self-blame, self-sabotage, or harboring resentment toward oneself and others. Such experiences arise due to a misalignment with one's values, unaddressed emotional wounds, or lack of self-acceptance. Being self-critical is the act of denying yourself what you truly deserve and desire.

The inner critic may sound like, *I am unlovable, I am not good enough,* or *I am behind in life and not where I want to be.* If a person repeats these limiting beliefs daily in their thoughts, they will continuously feel stuck in an everlasting cycle and won't be able to move forward toward their goals. Ruminating negative beliefs can trigger mood changes, create an inability to form or maintain healthy relationships, and self-sabotage one's happiness in life.

Remaining stuck in a cycle of self-sabotage may give the impression of having control over one's decisions or relationships, but it often results in an undesirable outcome that feels safer. Self-sabotage is a coping mechanism that creates an illusion of control, making it easier to predict how one will feel emotionally, mentally, or physically in various situations. As a result, when faced with unfamiliar opportunities, one may consciously or unconsciously make counterintuitive decisions that feel more predictable rather than trusting the process of exploring unknown feelings or circumstances. Over time, self-sabotage can negatively impact one's personal and relationship goals.

When an individual continues to criticize and judge themselves, they are operating from a fixed mindset that prevents them from seeing possible opportunities or the growth they have already achieved. The best way to transform the critical inner voice is to find alignment with your values and heal any unresolved emotional wounds. This will allow you to shift your focus from the negative to the positive.

Authentic Inner Voice

Having a strong inner voice filled with positive self-talk plays a crucial role in setting and maintaining boundaries. When individuals possess this inner strength, it empowers them to stay true to themselves and to prioritize their values and goals above all else. By nurturing one's authentic inner voice of self-guidance and intuition, individuals can develop effective strategies to establish boundaries in their personal and professional lives. When you truly believe *I am worthy of love*, *I am successful*, or *I trust myself*, you gain the confidence needed to pursue your heart's desires without being swayed by setbacks, external pressures, or societal expectations.

Our authentic voice enables us to communicate with compassion, honesty, and courage, aligning our words and actions with our core values. This alignment helps us maintain our integrity while having the ability to self-reflect and achieve continual growth. In essence, a strong inner voice of self-acceptance serves as a foundation for creating and upholding healthy boundaries in all aspects of life.

"You" versus "I" Statements

As a boundary setter, taking ownership of your needs is crucial to achieving a desirable outcome. While it can feel innate to point the finger or shift blame when feeling emotionally triggered, you are stepping away from the power of your authentic inner voice. Using "You" statements, such as "You are so selfish and only think about yourself," can feel like a personal attack on the receiver's character, potentially exacerbating the conflict and hindering a resolution of the relationship problem. Accusatory language can cause the receiver to become resentful, defensive, or withdrawn because they no longer feel emotionally safe and believe their character is in jeopardy. This creates a disconnect in the connection and prevents reaching a mutual understanding and resolution. Simultaneously, using "You" statements can reduce the value of your position or perspective because the receiver will focus on the disrespect rather than the greater message of the unwarranted behavior. As a result, "You" statements prevent alignment and hinder relationship growth, resulting in a power struggle.

On the other hand, using "I" statements, such as "I feel undervalued when our relationship is not a priority," honors your self-worth and standards and encourages each person to take responsibility for their part in the relationship issue. Although it may be challenging to use "I" statements, especially in the midst of a heated moment, they can greatly impact the success of your relationships and getting your needs met. Using assertive communication, like "I" statements, promotes positive engagement and rapport, increasing the likelihood of effectively resolving differences and feeling heard. Additionally, it fosters clarity and enables deeper understanding without attacking the other person's character. This approach also reduces defensiveness and creates a neutral environment, preventing misunderstandings or inaccurate assumptions so a resolution can be reached.

Examples of "You" vs. "I" Statements:

Avoid: "You never listen to me."
Try: "I don't feel heard right now."
Avoid: "You are dismissing my perspective."
Try: "I'm not feeling understood."
Avoid: "You are controlling."
Try: "I need some space."
Avoid: "You never help out."
Try: "I don't feel appreciated."

Asking versus Demanding

When setting boundaries, asking someone to work with you from a value-based perspective will promote mutual respect in your relationships and help to meet your needs. However, the manner in which you present a request can significantly influence the response you receive. By approaching the situation with a *we* mindset, you create an environment that encourages a shared commitment to achieving a common goal that benefits the relationship. Requesting alignment shows respect for the other person and your willingness to consider their feelings, perspectives, and needs, in addition to your own. This approach is more likely to yield a positive response because both individuals have a voice in negotiating a resolution that honors the relationship boundary. It's important to remember that you are not negotiating your personal worth but rather working together to find common ground that upholds the value and integrity of the relationship.

Conversely, demanding to have your needs met without considering the other person's needs, feelings, or perspectives can come across as aggressive, controlling, or entitled. This lack of regard for the relationship or the other person's viewpoint can hinder finding common ground. When an individual makes unilateral demands or gives ultimatums, the short-term result may fulfill one's desires, but it often leads to resistance or resentment from the other person. Demands that solely prioritize one person's needs or expectations can be seen as a threat, disregarding the relationship's overall health. When individuals feel coerced or compelled to comply, they may question the intentions of the other person or even repel the relationship altogether. Such power imbalances can leave one feeling voiceless in the decision-making process and may result in ongoing, long-term conflicts, which are detrimental to the relationship's success. This underscores the distinction between setting personal boundaries for self-care and establishing relationship boundaries for growth. When no one is at risk for harm, an open discussion becomes the path to mutually beneficial resolutions and alignment within the relationship.

The Difference between Asking versus Demanding:

Demanding: "Don't call me after 9 p.m."
Asking: "Can we find a time to talk before 9 p.m. tomorrow?"
Demanding: "Stop leaving clothes in the washing machine."
Asking: "How come the clothes were left
in the washing machine overnight?"

Negotiating a Plan of Action

Once a boundary has been set, establishing a detailed action plan for implementing new healthy behaviors becomes crucial to achieving alignment in the relationship. This may require an exchange of perspectives until the terms of the plan are mutually agreed upon. While compromise and collaboration may be necessary, it's important to note that neither individual should devalue their self-worth. This will require a *we* mindset to navigate differences and uncover common ground, ensuring all individuals receive mutual respect.

During the negotiation process, if emotion becomes heightened, it may be best to take a temporary timeout to regulate emotions. The purpose of the timeout is not to ignore the issue but to acknowledge that one or more individuals are unable to have a constructive conversation at that time to form a mutually agreeable plan. Before taking personal space, it's important to establish a time for when you will regroup to address the relationship disconnect. This can vary from one relationship dynamic to the next; however, it is best to find a resolution within twenty-four to seventy-two hours.

After a plan of action has been established, if one or more individuals are unwilling to show accountability for their part of the agreement, then reassessing the boundary may be needed to gain further insight into the disconnect. Additionally, relationship dynamics can shift with time, resulting in the potential need to create new boundaries or redefine the relationship to honor your self-respect.

Benefits of Setting Boundaries:

- Provides inner peace, self-respect, and mutual respect
- Helps everyone feel heard and understood
- Creates connection for greater fulfillment
- Supports emotional and physical needs
- Elevates the relationship for growth
- Honors self-worth and value
- Reduces fears and worries
- Improves assertive communication
- Minimizes conflict in relationships
- Boosts confidence and self-esteem
- Increases empathy and compassion
- Attracts healthy people
- Lessens stressors and uncertainty

- Instills trust in self and the relationship
- Prevents resentment and misunderstandings
- Improves decision-making
- Supports short-term and long-term goals
- Builds resilience and responsibility
- Establishes work-life-love balance

Boundary Badass Exercise

Implementing the BOUNDARY BADASS METHOD begins with assessing the relationship disconnect or behavior (not the person) without assuming you have all the information to understand the situation. When you assess the situation, you are clarifying where the problem exists and what led to feeling emotionally triggered. Assessing the relationship disconnect or unfavorable behavior can be accomplished by using discovery questions, like in Chapter 5. If you neglect to assess the disconnect, it will be almost impossible to get to the root of the relationship issue, making it challenging to find a resolution or to set a boundary. After you have assessed the behavior, you'll want to decide which value has been crossed – this is the opposite of the emotional trigger. Being aligned with your values will make it easier to recognize relationship disconnects and unfavorable behaviors to set healthy boundaries for self-respect and mutual respect. If you need to clarify your values, refer to Chapter 4. After setting a boundary and requesting alignment in the relationship, it becomes crucial to engage in negotiation to achieve a mutually beneficial resolution that takes into account each person's perspective of the relationship value. Once an agreement is reached, each person will need to maintain the integrity of the boundary to cultivate a healthy relationship dynamic.

Boundaries are communicated using "I" and "We" statements (avoid using the words "You" and "Me"). "You" statements can come across as accusatory, where the other person feels judged for their beliefs or behaviors rather than communicating what doesn't feel good to you. "I" statements allow you to take ownership and honor what you need to thrive in the relationship. "We" statements show you have respect for yourself and the relationship collectively.

Below, you will find examples of how to set personal and professional boundaries in your relationships. Each boundary is an organized structure of three sentences, making up part of the BOUNDARY BADASS METHOD. Where there are parentheses, you will want to fill in the information based on the emotional trigger or disconnect, the behaviors you find disrespectful or unfavorable, the relationship value you desire to be met, and the request for relationship alignment. Using the acronym ASAP will help you remember to set a boundary as soon as possible when experiencing a disconnect or violation. ASAP also clarifies each action you need to take when setting a boundary: Assess the situation. Set a boundary. Agree to a mutually beneficial plan. Proceed with accountability.

Are you ready to go from feeling powerless to a *Boundary Badass*? Let's start with the value-based structure below.

Three-Sentence Boundary Structure:
Personal Boundary: I feel/think (*emotional trigger or thoughts*) when (*the behavior you find disrespectful or unfavorable*). I value (*relationship value - opposite of the trigger*). How can we (*request for relationship alignment*)?

Professional Boundary: It seems/appears (*identify the disconnect and depersonalize it*) when (*the behavior you find disrespectful or unproductive*). I value (*relationship value - opposite of the disconnect*). How can we (*request for relationship alignment*)?

Examples of Personal Relationship Boundaries:

- I feel disconnected when we don't go on dates. I value quality time. How can we spend more time together?

- I feel blindsided when parts of the story are left out. I value transparency. How can we work on open communication with each other?

- I feel disrespected when my career goals are criticized. I value mutual respect. How can we support each other's career aspirations?

Examples of Professional Relationship Boundaries:

- It appears missing deadlines is becoming a pattern when working on team projects. I value time management. What strategies can we utilize to complete the team projects on time?

- It seems we are on two different pages when it comes to managing the company's finances. I value financial responsibility. When can we schedule a time to create a monthly budget?

- It appears there was a miscommunication when scheduling the client's appointment. I value collaboration. Can we reschedule the client's appointment on a day that works for both of us?

Follow the ASAP steps for implementing the BOUNDARY BADASS METHOD:

Step 1. **Assess** *the situation with discovery questions*

Step 2. **Set** *a boundary using a relationship value*

Step 3. **Agree** *to a mutually beneficial plan*

Step 4. **Proceed** *with accountability*

It is essential to follow each step below when setting boundaries in your relationships.

Assess the disconnect in the relationship or unfavorable behavior through the use of discovery questions. This can provide greater clarity regarding the disrespectful behavior and prevent any misunderstandings prior to setting a boundary.

Set a boundary after clarifying the root of the relationship disconnect. To do this, identify the emotional trigger or disconnect associated with the unfavorable behavior. Then, determine which of your relationship values has been compromised in the connection to establish a boundary. The value will be the opposite of the emotional trigger or disconnect in the relationship. By utilizing relationship values, you can confidently facilitate a constructive conversation and request alignment for mutual respect within the relationship.

Agree to a mutually beneficial plan that introduces new healthy behaviors and provides support to all individuals involved. This plan may involve negotiating perspectives until a common ground is achieved that honors the shared relationship value. The goal is to ensure everyone feels valued and respected within the terms of the mutual agreement.

Proceed forward with the mutual plan. This entails all individuals taking responsibility for upholding the agreed-upon boundary. By implementing this plan, the relationship can evolve and a healthier dynamic can be established for mutual respect.

Below is an example of applying the BOUNDARY BADASS METHOD to uphold the value of mutual respect.

Scenario: A friend cancels dinner plans thirty minutes prior to the reservation.

Step 1: **Assess** *with Discovery Questions*
> Boundary Setter: How come you're canceling at the last minute?
> Boundary Receiver: Something came up, and I can't make it.

Step 2: **Set** *a Boundary*
> Boundary Setter: I feel frustrated when our plans are canceled last minute. I value mutual respect. How can we be more mindful of each other's time?

Step 3: **Agree** *to a Mutual Plan Using "I" Statements and Discovery Questions*
> Boundary Receiver: I understand and will be more mindful next time. I will text you later to reschedule.

Boundary Setter: Thanks. Can you give me advance notice next time if you need to cancel?

Boundary Receiver: Sure, but this was last minute. I didn't intend on canceling tonight.

Boundary Setter: Okay, I understand. But I could have made other plans if I had known earlier in the day.

Boundary Receiver: Next time, let's confirm plans by lunch. How does that sound?

Boundary Setter: That works for me!

Step 4: **Proceed** *with Accountability*

Boundary Setter: (Two weeks later at noon) Hey, I'm looking forward to the concert tonight. What time are we meeting?

Boundary Receiver: Right after work at my place. How about 5 o'clock?

Boundary Setter: Great, I will be there.

Practice Setting Boundaries

Using your relationship values established in Chapter 4, practice writing out personal and professional boundaries. You will want to implement the three-sentence boundary structure in Step 2 of the BOUNDARY BADASS METHOD. Use current or past situations in your life where your personal limits have been violated by others to inspire the boundaries you write below.

1. Write a boundary using a relationship value:

_____

_____

_____

_____

2. Write a boundary using a relationship value:

_____

_____

_____

_____

3. Write a boundary using a relationship value:

_____

_____

_____

_____

4. Write a boundary using a relationship value:

_____

_____

_____

_____

5. Write a boundary using a relationship value:

_____

_____

_____

_____

Authors' note: Depending on the types of relationships you are finding challenges with, you may find some subsequent chapters more pertinent than others. The idea is for you to have a reference guide for when challenges arise so the relationship disconnect can be resolved effectively and efficiently.

TEN
PERSONAL BOUNDARIES

Exhausted from her long day at work, Mikaela stumbled through the front door and collapsed onto the couch. She was beyond spent and couldn't even take off her shoes or change out of her scrubs. Depleted with fatigue, she fell into a deep sleep for two hours.

As the head prenatal nurse at the children's hospital, Mikaela was always on her feet. She was working twelve-hour shifts back-to-back, which didn't leave much room for personal time. Lately, she had become the go-to nurse to pick up the extra shifts when fellow nurses called off. She didn't have it in her heart to tell her boss no, even though the grueling hours were becoming too much to bear.

On the way home from her shift, she stopped by the nursing home to visit her grandmother. She did her best to make it there at least three days a week, no matter how tired she was. They played cards, sometimes rolled dice, and talked about their days over a soothing cup of peppermint tea. On other nights when she didn't have to stay late at the hospital, she would rush home to make dinner for her and her fiancé.

She took great pleasure in caring for others, as it gave her a profound sense of fulfillment. In fact, the more responsibilities she had, the more it fueled her purpose. Her smile was infectious, and she could turn any gloomy day into radiant sunshine.

One morning, she received an unexpected call from her best friend, Susan, who had fainted at work. After accidentally splitting her head open on her desk, she was rushed to the hospital where Mikaela was on call. The emergency room doctor told Susan she would need to stay in the hospital overnight to ensure she had no abnormal swelling.

Being a single mother, Susan needed someone to pick up her daughter, Isabella, from daycare. Mikaela felt terrible for Susan since she didn't have any family nearby to help out. She agreed to pick up Isabella and keep her overnight. However, Mikaela wasn't going to be off work until six o'clock, and the daycare closed at five o'clock. She had to come up with a creative plan quickly. Mikaela started to feel regretfully overwhelmed after she offered to help. She knew she was overcommitting herself, but she also knew this was why her friends trusted her so much. She knew she couldn't say no to Susan, especially during an emergency.

Mikaela called her fiancé, Bryan, to see if he could pick up Isabella and watch her until she got home from work. Thankfully, he was able to pick her up, taking the immense amount of pressure off Mikaela's day. While on her afternoon work break, she swung by Susan's hospital room to let her know Isabella would be picked up and not to worry.

As Mikaela's nursing shift was ending, she made one last round to all the newborns in the neonatal unit. Everything was calm as Mikaela made her exit to rush home. When she got in the car, she began pondering what to make for dinner. She could not remember the last time she cooked for a child. She also knew Bryan was not about to eat macaroni and cheese for dinner.

While at home, Isabella was busy coloring a rainbow for her mom, and Mikaela mustered up the last bit of energy she had left in her and began to cook dinner. She decided to whip up grilled chicken with a side of crispy sweet potato fries. In the midst of cooking, an intense throbbing sensation gripped her back, making it hard to catch her breath. Mikaela had been battling a slipped disc for the past year. She knew she needed to rest, but it was impossible with the current circumstances. Bryan noticed her in pain and offered to cook, but Mikaela insisted he keep Isabella content with coloring. When she couldn't bear the pain anymore, she reluctantly walked away from the stove and poured herself a glass of wine in hopes of alleviating her agonizing pain.

After dinner, she threw the dishes in the dishwasher and swiftly wiped down the counters. She looked at the clock and realized she needed to give Isabella a bubble bath before it got too late. Once Isabella was ready for bed, Mikaela made a cozy pillow fort in the living room for her to sleep in. Isabella eyes magically lit up and she couldn't wait to sleep in it all night.

As they settled into the fort, Mikaela struggled to keep her weary eyes open. She had just finished her second glass of wine, hoping it would melt the stress away. Mikaela began to reading Isabella's bedtime stories and noticed halfway through that Isabella had fallen asleep. Mikaela quietly covered her up with a fuzzy blanket and headed back to the kitchen.

She grabbed one last glass of wine before heading off to bed. She was starting to find herself in the same daily predicament of pure exhaustion. It had become a distant memory since she had relaxed with a good book or even went to her weekly meditation class. She had zero time for herself, and the stress was starting to show in the creases of her face as she looked in the mirror while brushing her teeth. She had finally hit her breaking point and could no longer handle being pulled from all angles.

Our integrity is defined by the power of our boundaries.

Insight

Mikaela had a warmhearted personality and would go above and beyond for anyone in her life. She was highly devoted and thrived on her purpose of feeling needed by others. Bound by her people-pleasing tendencies, Mikaela found herself continuously prioritizing the needs of others, often at the expense of her own well-being. Despite the mounting challenges in her life, she wore a permanent smile, concealing the overwhelming sense of dissatisfaction that consumed her. The immense internal pressure to keep everyone happy compelled her to suppress her own emotions and self-care, seeking relief from alcohol as a means of self-medication.

When individuals resort to numbing their pain or escaping their feelings through self-medication, it becomes increasingly difficult to discover healthier solutions that honor their authentic truth and self-worth. In Mikaela's case, she struggled to break free from the cycle of self-abandonment. While she served as the dependable go-to person for everyone in her life, her inner world remained unfulfilled. Unbeknownst to those around her, she was neglecting the most crucial relationship of all – the one she had with herself.

Despite showing she had everything together on the surface, Mikaela's relationships had become blurred. She found herself disconnected from her own needs, compromising her values, and failing to assert herself in her relationships. The imbalance became increasingly apparent in her connections, as she indirectly invited others to consume her time without consideration of her limits. The absence of boundaries within herself and her relationships left her feeling depleted, as she was being pulled in a million different directions. Resulting in an internal conflict, it left her silently coping with the fear of letting others down, perpetuating a sense of unease.

Definition of Personal Boundaries

Personal boundaries are self-imposed limits and standards that individuals set for themselves, and with others, based on their self-worth. Personal boundaries pertain to emotional, physical, mental, or spiritual aspects and are influenced by an individual's values. Sometimes, an individual has boundaries that are not apparent to others but serve to meet their personal needs within their lifestyle.

People Pleasing

Being a giver is valuable for cultivating meaningful relationships. However, it is important to consider the extent of one's giving, as healthy relationships thrive on a balance of giving and receiving. If you find yourself consistently prioritizing the needs of others while receiving little in return, it becomes crucial to pause and reflect on whether the other person shares a similar level of investment in the relationship. At the same time, maintaining healthy relationships requires effort from both individuals, as an imbalance can prove detrimental to the emotional well-being of the perpetual giver. Additionally, holding a strong desire to be liked by everyone can lead to relying on the approval of others, thus placing one's self-worth in the hands of external sources.

If you find yourself continuously bending over backward for people in your life, or if you believe you're responsible for others' emotions, it will most likely give you the opposite response you desire in your relationships. Persistent givers in relationships can be taken advantage of, as they often overextend themselves to appease others. They may feel guilty for needing time alone or saying no to a loved one out of fear of creating conflict or loss of connection.

At the same time, consistently saying yes can be perceived as an open invitation for manipulative individuals who view it as an opportunity to exploit the people-pleaser in the relationship. It can create an unhealthy pattern of being unfulfilled in your connections and feeling emotionally exhausted from not having your needs met. Eventually, the relationship dynamic becomes dysfunctional, and the people-pleaser can begin to question their sense of self. Placing people on a pedestal can leave you feeling undervalued, unworthy, or unappreciated by others. This is a sign that personal boundaries are nonexistent, as limits haven't been established to honor your value.

Ask Yourself:

- What am I gaining by overextending myself?
- How do I feel when I am the only one giving?
- Can they meet my relationship values?
- What do I need to continue this relationship so it feels good to me?
- What's holding me back from setting a boundary?
- What am I afraid will happen if I address the lack of mutual respect?

Avoidance

Individuals who tend to avoid uncomfortable conversations often lack setting personal boundaries. They feel apprehensive that if they do set a boundary, it won't turn out in their favor. An avoidant may experience anxiety about the direction of the conversation, have concerns a desirable outcome will not be achieved, or fear the reaction of the other's person response. When a person shows signs of avoidance, they are typically thinking of every possible outcome of how it will go wrong, or they want to shove it under the rug hoping it will disappear on its own.

When a person continues to disregard the real issue, they neglect themselves, which is detrimental to their emotional health. However, most avoidants will not think about it this way because they believe escaping is easier than overcoming the obstacle. Suppressing your emotions and desires can perpetuate negative thoughts and behaviors that impact different areas of your life. While avoidants may come off as detached on the surface, this is usually a sign of avoiding discomfort that keeps them in an unhealthy holding pattern and prevents them from resolving relationship issues. Avoidant tendencies may also indicate low self-esteem and a fear of having their viewpoints rejected when faced with differences in a relationship.

Ask Yourself:

- What am I gaining by avoiding the problem?
- How do I feel when an unresolved issue is consistently brought up?
- How is avoiding the issue impacting my life?
- What do I need to continue this relationship so it feels good to me?
- What's holding me back from setting a boundary?
- What am I afraid will happen if I address the problem?

Self-Abandonment

Self-abandonment is the neglect of one's physical, emotional, spiritual, and mental needs. It can be seen as devaluing the self and prioritizing someone else's desires and needs over your own, such as people-pleasing or avoiding. When an individual denies their basic needs or inner voice, they feel stuck because they experience feelings of unworthiness. This leads to abandoning their personal and professional growth due to underlying fears or experiencing failure if they were to try something new. An individual who continuously disregards their needs can engage in unhealthy habits such as overthinking, escaping responsibilities, avoiding conflict, self-criticizing, or self-blaming.

Individuals who have adopted these unhealthy patterns as a way to cope with dysfunctional upbringings tend to have unrealistic expectations of others and find themselves in relationships that aren't mutually beneficial. This cycle of self-destructive patterns may lead to suppressing emotions, escaping through substances or addictive behaviors, feeling voiceless or powerless, remaining disconnected from values, or lacking internal trust.

Staying silent or forgoing personal boundaries will keep anyone feeling undervalued and unappreciated in their relationships. While others will not automatically be able to read your mind or be aware of your needs, it is your responsibility to openly communicate what you value. By voicing your beliefs and standards, people learn how to interact with you to form better alignment. This also allows you to create valuable relationships that feel good or to let go of those who cannot show mutual respect.

Signs of Self-Abandonment:

- Codependent on people or substances
- Perfectionism and procrastination
- Self-criticism and judgment
- Neglecting to honor one's values
- Failing to set healthy boundaries
- Ignoring one's emotional and physical needs
- Inability to trust oneself and others
- Exhibiting people-pleasing or avoidance tendencies
- Seeking external validation from others
- Disconnecting from the authentic self
- Comparing self to others
- Placing others on a pedestal

Standards versus Expectations

It is often misconstrued that standards and expectations have similar meanings, yet they can produce vastly different outcomes. Expectations are beliefs or demands projected onto a relationship, where the other person is expected to adhere to conditions and validate the *me* mindset of the person who set the expectation. Expectations, like ultimatums, show little respect for the relationship or the other person's viewpoints, as they are fear-driven and used to control the future outcome. An individual with unrealistic expectations will continue to face disappointment in their relationships because the receiver is often unaware of the expectation being projected onto them.

On the other hand, setting standards comes from a place of value on how you desire to be respected. It clarifies what behaviors are acceptable or unacceptable for the connection to continue while maintaining self-respect. Standards, like values, create a level of quality in the relationship that meets both individuals' needs so the relationship can thrive in unity. For instance, setting a standard for open and honest communication means that each individual agrees to be truthful and forthcoming in the connection. Standards help maintain mutual respect, ensure that boundaries are respected, and provide a framework for addressing issues and conflicts within the relationship. A *we* mindset can help you build greater understanding and trust, which are essential for maintaining a healthy relationship.

Types of Personal Boundaries

- Maintaining daily self-care and self-love exercises
- Loaning possessions to trustworthy individuals
- Speaking up when something feels uncomfortable
- Living in alignment with your values

- Asking for help when needed

- Having mutually beneficial relationships

- Finding balance between love, work, and social

- Honoring personal and professional commitments

- Declining social invites or politely excusing oneself

- Spending within financial budget and means

- Establishing personal and physical space

- Creating time for personal hobbies or interests

- Setting time limits on engaging with specific individuals

- Expressing standards and needs

- Maintaining professional work hours

- Being mindful of social media, television, and electronic usage

- Using passwords or security features for privacy

- Keeping tidy living quarters

- Being conscious of food and beverage choices

Example of the Boundary Badass Method for Personal Boundaries

ASAP: *A*ssess with discovery questions, *S*et a boundary, *A*gree to a mutual plan, and Proceed with accountability

Step 1: ***Assess*** *with Discovery Questions*

> Boundary Setter: Can we talk about compensation for overtime hours?
>
> Boundary Receiver: Yes, what questions do you have?

Step 2: ***Set*** *a Boundary*

> Boundary Setter: I feel undervalued when asked to work overtime without additional compensation. I value time. How can we determine the pay rate for hours worked beyond the weekly requirement?

Step 3: **Agree** *to a Mutual Plan Using "I" Statements and Discovery Questions*

Boundary Receiver: I wasn't aware you were working overtime hours. Can you share your shift schedule from the past month?

Boundary Setter: I can send it to you later today. Out of curiosity, what is the pay rate for overtime hours?

Boundary Receiver: We compensate time-and-a-half for overtime hours.

Boundary Setter: Great! When will my paycheck reflect the overtime compensation?

Boundary Receiver: I will submit your overtime hours to the payroll department once I receive them. It will appear on the following month's paycheck.

Boundary Setter: Okay. Thank you.

Step 4: **Proceed** *with Accountability*

Boundary Receiver: (The following month) I received my paycheck. Thank you for compensating me for the overtime hours.

Boundary Setter: You're welcome. Thank you for being a dedicated nurse and picking up extra shifts.

Boundary Receiver: I'm happy to help.

Examples of Discovery Questions and Personal Boundaries

Discovery Questions:

- How come I'm financially responsible for paying all the bills?
- What is on the grocery store list?
- Can we skip going out this weekend?

Personal Boundaries:

- I feel undervalued when I am solely responsible for covering all the household expenses. I value mutual respect. Can we establish a monthly plan and allocate our shared expenses?

- I think we have different food preferences when grocery shopping. I value health. How can we incorporate healthier choices?
- I feel exhausted when we go out every weekend. I value personal space. How about we go out next weekend?

ELEVEN
EMOTIONAL BOUNDARIES

Ethan called Nora, his girlfriend of five years, to express that he no longer saw her as his long-term partner. He felt they were on different pages when it came to their relationship goals.

Upon receiving the news, tears streamed down Nora's face as she felt utterly shocked. She had no idea where Ethan was coming from and began scrolling through old text messages looking for clues that Ethan was unhappy. Nora knew he had been somewhat distant, but she didn't think it would come to this.

Nora had planned out her entire life with Ethan, but that all changed in a split second. The thought of not having him by her side devasted her, as she confided in him on everything. Anytime Nora had a bad day, which was more often than not, she would call Ethan mid-meltdown, and he'd have to convince her everything would be okay before getting off the phone. Eventually, this weighed on Ethan, as he felt dragged down from taking care of Nora's problems. But Nora couldn't believe he would end things over it, especially since she would do the same for him. She felt deeply betrayed and hurt.

Nora laid in bed for a week straight with a box of tissues next to her. She didn't have the strength to eat or shower. She explained to her boss what had happened, and they agreed she could take personal leave and collect herself before returning to work the following week. As the days passed, she replayed the last few months over and over in her head, but nothing felt off to her.

While self-isolated at home, Nora called her best friend Poppy. Poppy was stunned by the news and asked Nora if she needed anything.

Nora sobbed. "Yes, can you come over after work?"

"Of course, babe. Do you want me to bring you anything?"

Nora paused and tried to gather her thoughts. "Can you bring me some soup? I haven't eaten today."

Poppy replied, "No problem. I'll grab us some soup and salads, then head over at six."

Nora was relieved that she would have company. "Thank you. You're a lifesaver!"

Nora watched movies to pass the time until Poppy got there, but everything reminded her of Ethan. Whether it was a romantic love story or a drama-filled film, she would find a reason to connect the movie back to Ethan. It made her feel more and more depressed.

She glanced at the clock and saw Poppy wouldn't be there for two more hours. She decided to shut off the movie and picked up a book to calm her mind, but she found herself daydreaming about what their relationship could have been instead of reading. Nora slowly started to doze off until her phone began ringing and woke her up. It was Poppy saying she was on her way over. Nora went downstairs in the same sweats she had worn for three days to let her in. She gave her the biggest hug and felt slightly eased that she wouldn't be alone for the night.

Nora burst into tears. "I don't get it. I thought everything was great."

Poppy hugged her. "What did he say when he ended things?"

Nora tried to calm herself down and catch her breath. "He said I depended on him for everything, and he needs more personal time to pursue his own goals."

Poppy quizzically looked over at Nora. "Do you think that is true?"

Nora wiped away her tears. "I mean, sometimes I call him to vent. But not every day. My life is very stressful."

"I get it. Sounds like he wants to be alone. I'm sorry he did this to you. I know how much you love him."

Nora threw her hair up in a ponytail as she was overheated from crying. "Thank you for being here. Can you stay over?"

"Of course. I know break-ups aren't easy."

"You're such a great friend. Thank you."

After their dinner, Nora and Poppy started watching some reality television. As the show played, Nora finally felt like she was able to take her mind off Ethan. It had been days since she had genuinely laughed or even smiled, and it felt good to be comforted. Poppy was happy to see Nora back to feeling like her usual self, even if it was only for a few hours.

Nora slept through the night for the first time in a few days. The next morning over coffee, Poppy told Nora to call her if she needed to talk while she was at work. Poppy reassured Nora she would take breaks to check-in.

After a few hours of being alone, Nora called Poppy. Poppy quickly went to the break room and called her back. Nora was in tears again telling Poppy how much she missed Ethan and kept going on about how her life was over. Poppy tried to convince her otherwise, with no success. She told Nora to try taking a warm bath or going for a walk to get some fresh air, and she promised to give her a call later.

Nora agreed to Poppy's advice. She began filling the tub with bath salts and lavender oil while listening to her favorite music. She laid in the tub for about thirty minutes before her hands started to turn prune-like. After her bath, she tried to nap but was restless and just tossed and turned. So, she called Poppy again.

Poppy answered, "Hey, what's going on?"

Nora's voice trembled, "Nothing. I can't sleep."

Poppy said, "What have you eaten today?"

Nora sighed and took a deep breath. "Nothing. Everything makes me nauseous."

Poppy leaned her head on her hand while sitting at her desk. "I know. But, at least eat some toast with jam or crackers."

"I will. When does this pain stop?"

Poppy showed empathy, "It will take time. But, please eat because it will help you sleep."

Nora replied, "Okay, I'll try."

Poppy looked at the clock. "I have to go back to work now. Chat later."

Nora ordered chicken noodle soup from her favorite noodle shop down the street. Afterward, she slept for an hour before she started dreaming about Ethan. It woke her up in a panic, and she immediately called Poppy.

"I had the worst dream. I thought Ethan came back."

Poppy replied, "Ugh! That is awful."

"I seriously want him to go away forever."

Poppy was beginning to regret telling Nora to call her anytime while at work. "Let me call you after work. I really can't be on the phone right now."

Nora sulked lying on the couch. "Okay, well you told me to call you when I needed to talk."

"Yeah, but my boss is looking at me right now. I have to go."

Emotional regulation is the ability to effectively respond to life challenges without devaluing your worth or projecting onto others.

Insight

Nora was heartbroken by her break-up with Ethan, as it came as unexpected news that he no longer felt the same way about her. While she believed they were on good terms, Ethan felt overwhelmed by her emotional dependency, yet rescued her from her daily distress. This resulted in them parting ways without resolving the relationship disconnect due to his lack of transparency.

In response to Nora, Ethan struggled to communicate assertively and let Nora know that his value of personal space was being violated. Instead, he went into a flight trauma response and remained passive by abruptly leaving the relationship altogether rather than setting a boundary and addressing the disconnect. While each partner is responsible for their emotions, neither practiced emotional regulation; instead, they projected their feelings onto their connection. Displacing emotions onto a relationship will eventually repel the other person and lead to a disconnect.

Once Ethan was out of the picture, Nora started emotionally flooding Poppy with excessive phone calls. Nora was so overly consumed by her emotional state that she neglected to realize she was repeating the same pattern with Poppy that she had with Ethan. Nora's poor emotional regulation and lack of boundaries kept her feeling emotionally powerless. Operating solely on emotion can make life challenging and lead to feeling chaotic inside. When someone looks to others to rescue them, it can often be a sign they have an unresolved emotional wound or an insecure attachment style. Over time, they develop a deep fear of being alone, but in the process of trying to seek security from others, they can end up pushing them away.

Definition of Emotional Boundaries

Emotional boundaries are the ability to recognize and regulate one's emotional needs and limits without imposing them onto others. These boundaries allow individuals to offer support without assuming responsibility or the weight of others' emotions. Additionally, they serve to protect individuals from emotional harm and manipulation.

Emotional Regulation

Emotional regulation is the ability to effectively manage emotions and respond to provoking environments or experiences that may elicit an emotional reaction. Sometimes these responses may be healthy, and other times they may be unhealthy if emotionally dysregulated. Having strategies to self-soothe your nervous system when challenges arise allows you to adapt to stress or to your environment with a regulated response that supports what you need.

Being emotionally dependent or unable to regulate one's emotions can be detrimental to any type of relationship, as it creates dysfunction in the connection. An individual who finds themselves emotionally dependent on external sources for comfort, or suppresses their emotions altogether, most likely grew up in a home with family dysfunction during early developmental years. These types of situations can lead to unhealthy emotional responses. Unhealthy responses may look like expecting others to save you from painful experiences, emotional flooding, stonewalling and avoiding emotions, using aggression and uncontrollable outbursts, raising your tone of voice, or seeking reassurance. These behaviors indicate the person is unwilling to take responsibility for their emotions.

On the contrary, healthy coping strategies enable individuals to effectively manage and process their emotions within the present environment. Coping strategies can help diffuse unhealthy emotional responses, allowing for greater self-awareness and self-management of emotional discomfort. When you feel emotionally regulated, you are more likely to experience personal freedom and protect yourself from manipulation. Effective emotional responses include pausing before responding, removing oneself from unsafe environments, asking if a person is available before speaking, and honoring self-care and self-love through deep breathing, meditation, and journaling.

Emotional Enmeshment

Emotional enmeshment occurs when there are poor or unclear boundaries between two or more people in a relationship. Individuals may displace their emotions onto a partner, family member, colleague, or friend, expecting the other person in the connection to feel or believe their viewpoints as the collective truth. It can feel suffocating or agonizing to the person whose voice is being silenced.

Enmeshment often begins in the family home where trauma has occurred or when there is a generational or cultural family dynamic of blurred lines. The repercussion of trauma or poor boundaries may cause a parent or child to suffer from bouts of anxiety or depression throughout their life. As this occurs, an individual seeks constant reassurance and emotional support from their child or spouse for emotional security. The spiraling effect makes it challenging for the child to become independent of the parent because they feel pressured to be responsible for their parent's emotions. When children are forced to meet their parent's emotional needs or to live according to their parent's belief system, this hinders their personal development and psychological well-being. Spouses may also thrive off of being enmeshed due to insecurities or fears, which can be projected onto the connection as a way of survival or control.

When a child experiences enmeshment with an unhealthy parent, it can result in the child's inability to form a healthy identity, which may lead to codependency tendencies. The enmeshed relationship can induce fear in the child when setting boundaries, or they may feel guilty when they do because it conflicts with their parent's belief system or the family's collective truth. The loss of self becomes present in their adult relationships later on, often attaching to unhealthy people who give them a false sense of security. Depending on others to heal an emotional wound creates a cycle of codependency or emotional obsession, known as emotional trauma bonding.

Codependency leads to an unhealthy relationship dynamic where neither person's needs are being met, yet they feel unable to leave due to needing or depending on a person to coexist. One or both people tend to display destructive relationship behaviors where the relationship is often one-sided, emotionally abusive, or exploitative. Trauma bonding is quite similar to codependency; however, one person typically forms an obsession or an emotional addiction to the other person who is abusive or high-stress. The person with the obsession will go to great lengths to maintain the relationship at the expense of suffering or negative consequences. The highs and lows of the connection become an emotional cycle that makes a person crave the excitement, fear, or shame they may have felt within their familial patterns. This ongoing pattern creates an emotional dependency within the connection, the same way a person can form a chemical dependency on a drug.

While emotional enmeshment is more common in families and romantic relationships, emotional enmeshment can also occur in the workplace. For example, a boss may look to their employee for emotional support because their spouse is emotionally unavailable at home, or colleagues may assume they can emotionally flood co-workers without asking if they have the mental space to listen. A workplace that falters on professional boundaries can lead to a toxic work culture. This can make it uncomfortable for the employees to do their jobs and creates an unnecessary obligation to a boss or colleagues.

Signs of Codependency:

- Needing approval from others
- Avoiding conflict at all costs
- Taking on more responsibilities than manageable to maintain peace
- Ignoring or minimizing your desires and needs
- Feeling guilty or anxious when doing something for yourself

- Feeling sorry for others even when they hurt you
- Having overwhelming feelings of rejection or abandonment
- Remaining in an emotionally reactive state
- Struggling to set clear boundaries
- Refraining from articulating uncomfortable emotions
- Apologizing even when you have done nothing wrong

Enmeshed Family Dynamic Roles

Enmeshed family dynamics can involve intricate patterns of unhealthy roles that family members unconsciously adopt to maintain a reputation and safeguard internal struggles, but these roles can become detrimental to one's emotional well-being and the family unit due to poor or nonexistent boundaries.

Common Roles of Enmeshed Families:

- **Hero**: The hero is typically the responsible and high-achieving family member. They often excel academically, in their career to achieve success, or in other areas to maintain the family's reputation and compensate for internal family issues. They may suppress their own emotions and needs to uphold the appearance of a perfect family.

- **Scapegoat:** The scapegoat is the family member who is consistently blamed for the family's problems and shortcomings. They may be criticized, shamed, and made to feel responsible for the family's dysfunction or be seen as the identified patient. This role serves as a distraction from the family's deeper issues and allows others to avoid addressing their problems.

- **Golden Child:** The golden child is the family member who is put on a pedestal and receives an excessive amount of praise, attention, and validation. They are often pressured to excel and meet the family's high expectations, sometimes at the expense of their own needs and desires. They are the source of pride and a representation of the family's success.

- **Lost Child:** The lost child is often quiet, withdrawn, and overshadowed by other family members. They may try to avoid conflicts, remain invisible, and seek solitary hobbies or activities. This role can provide relief from the chaos within the family, but it can also lead to feelings of isolation and low self-esteem.

- **Martyr:** The martyr often sacrifices their own needs and desires to cater to the needs of other family members. They may seek approval and validation through self-sacrifice, constantly putting family members' needs first. While they may appear selfless, this role can lead to resentment and exhaustion.

- **Peacemaker:** The peacemaker attempts to mediate conflicts and keep the family together. They often try to maintain harmony at all costs. This role can lead to stress and a sense of responsibility for the family's emotional well-being.

- **Caregiver/Parentified Child:** The caregiver or parentified child takes on adult responsibilities at a young age, often caring for younger siblings or even their own parents. This role reversal can lead to a lack of a normal childhood and difficulties in forming healthy relationships.

- **Black Sheep:** The black sheep is the family member who doesn't conform to the family's values. They may have a lifestyle, beliefs, or choices that are significantly different from the rest of the family. The family may even shun them for going against the family's collective truth or reputation. The black sheep may even move away from the immediate family in adulthood to create space between them and the family dysfunction

Empathy and Mutual Understanding

Empathy is the ability to understand and be attuned to the emotional expressions of others. It provides increased compassion and deeper comprehension of a person's feelings or experiences. When comprehending another person's feelings or thoughts, this doesn't necessarily imply sharing the same feelings or viewpoints. It signifies the ability to connect or grasp their feelings from their unique perspective.

Empathy is essential for healthy relationships, as it provides a safe space for vulnerability and cultivates greater connectedness. Being understanding allows others to feel heard and understood and can be beneficial to helping others process their emotions. A lack of empathy for perspectives outside your own can make it challenging to bridge the gap between differences and establish healthy boundaries.

Conversely, an excess of empathy can make you susceptible to exploitation and prevent you from making healthy decisions. For instance, if you are inclined is to rescue someone who is facing challenges, you may overextend yourself by helping them while neglecting your personal values and worth. As much as you want this person to experience a better life, knowing your limits prevents you from losing yourself in the relationship. Imbalanced interpersonal relationships can become unfulfilling territory for those who possess a profound empathy for others.

Establishing a healthy support system requires mutual respect and acknowledgment of everyone's personal space, emotional capacity for listening, and experiences. Healthy relationships are a balance of individuals who are interdependently supportive of one another while maintaining independence within the relationship. It creates a harmonious emotional bond where each person can be vulnerable without compromising who they are or their values.

Emotional Coercion

There are times when an individual may use emotions to control the relationship dynamic. This type of individual will operate from an inferiority complex because they deeply fear getting hurt based on past experiences. Due to this person's unresolved emotional wounds, they tend to project their issues onto the connection. While they may or may not have self-awareness of their defense mechanisms, they are most likely aware of how they are treating you. A person may use emotional manipulation tactics like stonewalling – shutting you out altogether. Or they may use gaslighting – avoiding responsibility for their actions and making you think it is your fault by distorting the reality of what has occurred. Additionally, a coercive individual may use manipulation tactics, such as denying, blame-shifting, criticizing, or deflecting, to exert power over the other person by creating discomfort and tension to silence or weaken the other person. This is the result of a coercive person being emotionally underdeveloped and having limiting beliefs.

The coercive individual gains control by attempting to break down another person's self-worth, so they can feel more powerful than the person they view to be more superior, admirable, or valuable than themselves. The coercive individual experiences an internal struggle as they yearn for love or success, yet they often feel unworthy. This leads to a destructive pattern of self-sabotage in their relationships, driven by fears of abandonment, rejection, or betrayal. Unfortunately, this behavior often results in a self-fulfilling prophecy, where the person who is being coerced may leave due to the psychological or emotional abuse experienced by the coercive individual. If you find yourself in this situation, it is best to disengage from the destructive behaviors and set personal boundaries for your emotional or physical well-being.

Triangulation is another manipulation tactic individuals with an inferiority complex will use to elicit fear within another person to gain power or control through the use of a third party. For example, a romantic partner may bring an outsider into the conversation to create jealousy or superiority in the relationship, making themselves the center of attention to boost their ego. Or a parent may use the success of something your sibling did to hold over you so that you will follow through on a similar achievement. Likewise, a professional colleague may leverage a business associate to force you into a decision or agreement you do not wish to engage in but feel obligated to avoid losing the deal or your job. Triangulation can also serve as a tactic to undermine or disregard a boundary established by one party. The coercive person seeks a third party who is familiar with both individuals in order to sidestep the boundary. With the help of the third party, the coercive person attempts to convince the initial party to forgo the boundary for their own advantage. This tactic is used to create a two-against-one mentality to make the initial party feel powerless with nowhere to turn but to agree to the coercion. These types of situations will require setting a new boundary to create mutual respect within the relationship by removing the third party.

Additionally, emotional flooding can often be used as a source of power for individuals who experience noncompliance from others. The coercive individual will attempt to get others to comply out of guilt or fear rather than respect. Emotionally flooding may look like being overly emotional to gain control, such as a false expression of crying, repetitive demands, excessive talking, or tantrums. However, once their need is met through coercion, the initial non-compliant individual will likely default back to their old habits.

Coercion cannot be used as a resolution tool or to inspire a person to change for the better. An individual who feels manipulated may create emotional distance from the coercive individual because they feel forced into complying with demands or ultimatums. Emotional coercion is often a ploy to elicit an emotional reaction but fails to address the root cause of the disconnect, leaving the relationship to cycle on patterns of control rather than mutual respect.

Types of Emotional Boundaries

- Practicing emotional regulation with self-soothing techniques
- Communicating needs and feelings constructively
- Honoring your emotional needs through relationship values
- Protecting your privacy and only sharing what feels good to you

- Accepting responsibility for your happiness
- Disengaging or shutting down emotional manipulation
- Calling a timeout when feeling overwhelmed
- Requesting or offering emotional support in times of need, hardship, or loss
- Addressing boundary violations promptly
- Protecting personal space from emotional flooding
- Refraining from the use of sarcasm or humor during serious conversations
- Speaking up when feeling uncomfortable or unsafe
- Using emotions for healthy engagement and building connection
- Asking others for availability to talk
- Allowing time to process emotions before responding
- Refraining from feeling responsible for others' emotions

Example of the Boundary Badass Method for Emotional Boundaries

ASAP: Assess with discovery questions, Set a boundary, Agree to a mutual plan, and Proceed with accountability

*Step 1: **Assess** with Discovery Questions*
> Boundary Setter: How come you keep calling?
> Boundary Receiver: You told me I could call you.

*Step 2: **Set** a Boundary*
> Boundary Setter: I think there is a miscommunication when calls become frequent during work hours. I value work-life balance. Can we find a time to talk after work?

*Step 3: **Agree** to a Mutual Plan Using "I" Statements and Discovery Questions*
> Boundary Receiver: I didn't realize I was bothering you. I

thought you said to call if I needed you. Can you share what changed?

Boundary Setter: I can't take unlimited breaks at work to talk on the phone. I know your break-up is painful, and I want to be there for you. What time can I call you after work?

Boundary Receiver: I am free whenever. Sorry, I can't stop crying. If I can't call, can I text you while at work?

Boundary Setter: Yes, texting is fine.

Boundary Receiver: Okay, thank you again for being there for me.

Step 4: **Proceed** *with Accountability*

Boundary Receiver: (Texting the next day) I can't eat. I can't sleep. What do I do to make the pain go away?

Boundary Setter: I'm sorry. I know break-ups are so hard. It will take time but I'm here to support you in any way I can. What can I do to support you?

Boundary Receiver: It's beyond hard! How come I couldn't see the signs?

Boundary Setter: None of us saw it coming. Sometimes people don't know how to work through things and give up before trying. It's not your fault he didn't communicate with you.

Boundary Receiver: Thank you for listening. Maybe you are right. I do need a partner who can communicate.

Examples of Discovery Questions and Emotional Boundaries

Discovery Questions:

- Who did you hang out with last night?
- How come you are involving family in our relationship problems?

- How come you're upset?

Emotional Boundaries:

- I feel frustrated when I am constantly questioned about my friends. I value trust. What steps can we take to strengthen our trust?

- I feel betrayed when the opinions of external family members are regarded as superior. I value privacy. Can we keep our relationship issues between us?

- I feel anxious when conversations become emotionally overwhelming. I value personal space. Can we revisit this topic tonight after dinner when we've had more time to process our thoughts?

TWELVE

PHYSICAL BOUNDARIES

Tanner would talk to anyone about his passion for playing the guitar, but most of his friends knew him as being a bit of a wallflower. He enjoyed spending time at home writing new songs, often declining social invitations to avoid a crowded room. Each time Tanner received a new invite, he found himself trapped in memories of the night he attended a concert and got trampled on by the crowd. The mere thought of experiencing it all over again left him socially paralyzed.

Remi, one of his closest friends, messaged Tanner inviting him to grab dinner on Friday night at the newest French restaurant in East Village. While Tanner was excited to see Remi, he immediately contemplated how crowded the restaurant would be. Tanner asked Remi who was going and if the restaurant had a photo gallery online, as he wanted to get a feel for the environment. Remi assured Tanner he specifically requested a table off to the side.

As Tanner skimmed the website for photos, he didn't find much on the layout of the restaurant. He admired how appetizing the food looked and was enthusiastic to try the steak frites.

On Friday afternoon, Remi sent a group text reminding everyone to arrive at eight because the restaurant would only wait a few minutes before giving up the reservation. While Tanner got dressed for dinner, he felt a pit in his stomach. His mind began racing, dreading how jam-packed the restaurant would be. All he could think about was a hundred people being stuffed in the place like sardines. He tried listening to some chill music to drown out his thoughts, but nothing could take his mind off being crammed shoulder-to-shoulder with other patrons.

On the way to the restaurant, Tanner began to fidget and started tapping his fingertips repeatedly on his temples. He asked the car service driver if he could turn up the music. As he looked out the window before exiting the car, he took a big sigh. The palms of his hands were beginning to sweat. The place was overflowing with people waiting outside on the sidewalk to get in.

Tanner found Remi and followed him into the restaurant. Remi told him it would be about thirty-five minutes before they would be seated, as the kitchen was running behind. He asked Tanner if he wanted to grab drinks at the bar while they waited for their table. Tanner had zero interest in being at a packed bar, but he also didn't want to make a big deal out of it. Tanner and Remi ordered drinks and talked about Tanner's upcoming concert he had at a local venue next month.

As they waited on their drinks, Tanner and Remi were unintentionally being shoved left and right. Then, a woman accidentally spilled her drink all over Tanner's left shoe. Tanner was trying to keep his cool, but he was extremely uncomfortable. He started to get light-headed and felt panicky.

He yelled at the woman, "Watch out."

The woman glared and shouted, "Chill dude, it was an accident, and it's only water."

Tanner frantically stepped outside for some fresh air. He texted Remi, letting him know he needed a break and would return in a few. He walked around the block to decompress and stopped to listen to a man playing the saxophone on the street. He was unsure if he was going to go back to the restaurant or if he was going to bail and head home. The thought of being bumped into by random people left him feeling breathless.

After he pondered about what to do, he went back inside and saw the rest of their friends had shown up. They all gave Tanner a hive-five and handed him a beer.

As the hostess walked them to a table in the middle of the restaurant, Remi asked if they had anything next to the wall, but she said, "No."

Remi looked back at Tanner. "Are you good?"

Tanner hesitated. "Yeah, I'm good." But he felt his breath begin to shorten.

The friends talked about Tanner's last performance and how they were looking forward to his next show. One friend brought up his latest song and asked about the story behind it. Tanner explained it was about his journey with anxiety and how music had always been his stress reliever.

As they ordered a round of drinks, another waiter brushed by their table, accidentally nudging Tanner's chair.

Tanner got up from his chair. "What the heck, man?"

The waiter apologized and offered to send over a few appetizers for the table.

Tanner threw down his napkin and took another breather outside.

Setting boundaries is living in alignment with your authentic truth.

Insight

Prior to the dinner, Tanner tried calming his nerves with self-soothing coping mechanisms. From listening to music to an emotional freedom technique in the car, nothing worked to soothe his discomfort. However, despite his uneasiness, Tanner was still looking forward to spending quality time with his friends at the new restaurant.

Once Tanner entered the restaurant, he tried to keep his cool but was easily triggered when a woman spilled water on his shoe. This led to Tanner lashing out and leaving the restaurant for fresh air to meet his need for physical space. As soon as Tanner collected himself, he regrouped with friends, and they were seated for dinner. But he was faced with another incident when the waiter bumped into him. Tanner became emotionally distressed as he found himself in a position where his physical space was jeopardized again. Projecting his emotional discomfort onto others left him feeling powerless and unable to effectively set a physical boundary. This is an indication he had disconnected from his values, allowing his emotions to control his reaction.

Individuals who become emotionally heightened in response to new incidents resembling past catastrophic events, where their sense of safety was lost, often experience emotional reactions rather than logical responses. Over time, if a person neglects to heal from an emotionally charged event, they will continue carrying the emotional trauma and may unintentionally project onto lesser tragic events. For Tanner, the flashback from the concert incident reappeared each time his physical space was invaded at the restaurant.

Definition of Physical Boundaries

Physical boundaries pertain to personal space, comfort level with physical touch, and the ability to establish what feels safe in a given environment or with others. Prioritizing one's physical well-being involves attending to basic needs such as self-care, rest, food, shelter, clothing, and water consumption.

Social Cues for Physical Space

Being aware of your personal space and others' space is essential to demonstrating well-developed social cues and etiquette. The level of social awareness, which can vary across different cultures, can potentially harm a relationship before it even has a chance to develop. Social cues for personal space will depend on the type of relationship.

Types of Proxemics:

- Intimate relationships 0–2 feet
- Personal relationships 2–4 feet
- Social relationships 4–12 feet
- Public relationships 12 feet or more

Developing the ability to interpret social cues is crucial for one's comfort level when interacting with others, whether in a personal or professional setting. Some of these cues, such as hand gestures, may be subtle, while others could be more apparent like leaning forward or moving closer to someone. These social cues offer valuable insights into the emotions and thoughts of others, serving as a guide in conversations. For instance, if someone stands closer than usual during a discussion, it might signify heightened interest in a particular subject. Additionally, it might demonstrate a greater sense of comfort, if they have an open stance and position their feet towards the other person. When a person feels they can trust another individual, they will innately mirror their body language for mutual alignment.

On the contrary, if someone wants to keep their distance, they will appear reluctant to engage. This can be a sign of discomfort or hesitation to build a deeper connection. They may give physical cues like crossing their arms, blocking their body with a physical object, turning their feet away, or taking a step back to create space and establish a conservative distance within the relationship. These actions collectively serve as indications that the person is seeking a balance between the interaction and maintaining their personal comfort zone. A good rule of thumb to cultivate healthy physical space is to keep an arm's length distance between you and another individual. This establishes an appropriate and safe space for trust.

Besides physical cues, eye contact is another strong indicator to consider when engaging or meeting new people. Looking people in the eye can help you understand whether or not this person feels pleasure or discomfort based on their gaze. When a person disengages from eye contact while discussing a particular subject, it may be an indication the person is feeling uneasy. As a result, it's important to pause and assess for better understanding before continuing the conversation. This is your cue to ask discovery questions, gain insight into their thought process, or suggest regrouping later when each person is available to engage effectively. The more we can pick up and interpret these social cues, the better we can understand and strengthen our relationships.

Self-Care

Having physical needs and boundaries is essential for living a healthy, balanced lifestyle. Physical needs are vital for ensuring that our bodies are well-nourished and supported. Self-care essentials, such as rest, exercise, hygiene, or healthy nutrition, play a huge role in determining how we feel every day. Additionally, it can impact how we interact and show up in our interpersonal relationships, affecting the overall health of the connection. Whether it's through mindful eating or self-care breaks, tending to our physical needs will help us build a strong foundation for overall wellness.

At the same time, it is important to recognize and respect our personal limits. Being aware of our physical bodies and knowing when something doesn't feel good allows for greater self-awareness around our physiological responses. These responses help us set boundaries to support what we need to remain balanced amongst the pressures of modern life. With a daily self-care routine, we can begin to cultivate the physical boundaries we need to thrive and remain resilient through the ups and downs of life.

Physical Touch

Every individual has the right to body autonomy, allowing them to make decisions that honor and protect their physical well-being. It is important to recognize and communicate your physical boundaries when interacting with others, whether in public or private settings, to ensure comfort and to promote healthy engagement. Before engaging in physical contact, such as a hug or a casual pat on the shoulder, you will want to obtain consent. However, not all individuals will ask for consent before engaging in physical touch. If someone makes an unwelcome physical advance, you can protect yourself by setting boundaries or removing yourself from the situation altogether.

While declining physical advances from a friend, family member, colleague, or stranger can be straightforward, the lines for romantic relationships can become occasionally blurred. Although the relationship is intimate, it doesn't give one partner the freedom to engage in physical affection or sexual activities without the consent of each partner. Each partner is responsible for their body and for communicating limits, regardless of the relationship status. When in an intimate relationship, if one partner denies physical touch, it is important to avoid internalizing this as rejection and instead explore where they are coming from. A partner may have had a stressful day or not be in the mood, leading them to decline the affectionate gesture. During these times of uncertainty, it's important to use discovery questions to gain clarity for the lack of physical intimacy. Understanding why your partner doesn't want to be affectionate can help identify ways to build emotional intimacy and maintain healthy boundaries. *See Chapter 16 for more on sexual boundaries.*

Types of Physical Boundaries

- Respecting your and others' physical space
- Communicating when you need personal space to recharge
- Disengaging from uncomfortable or threatening social cues
- Addressing unwarranted physical advances or contact
- Acknowledging appropriate distance in the gym or workout classes

- Maintaining a suitable space when standing in line
- Establishing an appropriate distance when driving on the road to prevent accidents
- Being aware of a partner's comfort level for public displays of affection
- Prioritizing physical health and basic needs
- Seeking privacy to prevent eavesdropping
- Honoring physiological cues
- Keeping doors closed when needing personal space
- Prioritizing a secure and safe home environment
- Disengaging from unsafe environments or individuals
- Being aware of your surroundings for physical safety
- Seeking consent for physical affection and sexual activity

Example of the Boundary Badass Method for Physical Boundaries

ASAP: Assess with discovery questions, Set a boundary, Agree to a mutual plan, and Proceed with accountability

Step 1: **Assess** *with Discovery Questions*

Boundary Setter: What tables do they have available in the corner?

Boundary Receiver: The hostess said they don't have any corner tables.

Step 2: **Set** *a Boundary*

Boundary Setter: I feel anxious when cramped between tables. I value personal space. How about we wait for a table in the corner?

Step 3: **Agree** *to a Mutual Plan Using "I" Statements and Discovery Questions*

Boundary Receiver: I'm starving. Can we see how much longer the wait will be?

Boundary Setter: Sure. Let me check on the time.

Boundary Receiver: Okay.

Boundary Setter: They said an extra twenty minutes. What do you want to do?

Boundary Receiver: I don't want to wait an extra twenty minutes, but I understand you don't want to be uncomfortable.

Boundary Setter: Okay. So, should we wait?

Boundary Receiver: I guess we can wait. But can we agree if it is past thirty minutes, we will take the first available table?

Boundary Setter: Yes, that works.

Step 4: **Proceed** *with Accountability*

Boundary Receiver: (Thirty minutes later) Hey, they still don't have a table in the corner, but they have one outside on the patio. Can we take it?

Boundary Setter: Sounds good to me.

Examples of Discovery Questions and Physical Boundaries

Discovery Questions:

- Can I please have some space?
- How come you are reading over my shoulder?
- Can you please not put your seat back all the way?

Physical Boundaries:

- I feel smothered when I can't sprawl out on the couch after work. I value physical space. How about we cuddle after I have had time to decompress?
- I feel uneasy when someone reads over my shoulder. I value personal space. Can we agree not to read over each other's shoulders?

- I feel restricted when I can't stretch out my legs during long car rides. I value physical space. How can we adjust the seat position to create more room?

THIRTEEN

FRIEND BOUNDARIES

Two weeks before the Super Bowl, Brady called Justin to convince him to throw a party at his new house for the game. Justin was hesitant since he didn't want his new custom white couch to get stained. His home was exquisitely designed like it was out of an interior magazine. He had worked hard and had been saving for a long time for his dream home. The beach house had floor-to-ceiling glass windows and a spectacular view of the ocean, making it great for hosting social get-togethers.

After some persuading, Justin agreed to throw a party and asked Brady to only invite ten guests. Justin even offered to hang a television and set up heaters on the deck in hopes of keeping most of the guests outside for the game.

Brady immediately began messaging people but found it challenging to keep it under ten people. Both being social, they knew a lot of people from work and the surf club.

The day before the party, Brady met up with their surf buddies Tyler, Zack, and Maxime. When Maxime asked the guys what they were doing for the Super Bowl, Brady kept quiet because Tyler was invited over to Justin's place, but Zack and Maxime didn't receive an invite. Zack mentioned he had no plans, and Tyler said he was going to Justin's party.

Maxime felt confused. "Justin is having a party? Why was I not invited?"

Zack flipped his hair behind his ear. "Neither was I. Are we not cool enough for the party?"

Brady stated, "Yes, Justin is having a party, but he is trying to keep it small. You guys should just come. It won't be a big deal to have a few more."

When Brady dropped off Zack and Tyler, he told them to be at Justin's tomorrow by noon.

On Sunday morning, as Brady was preparing to leave for Justin's house, he received a call. Justin asked Brady to pick up some extra ice. Without hesitation, Brady jumped into his jeep and made a quick stop at the nearby grocery store on his way to Justin's place.

When Brady arrived, Ryan and Oliver from work were there, and Landon and Lucas, the neighbors, were there as well. Tyler showed up with Theo and both of their partners. It was starting to be a full house, and there were still more guests arriving. None of the guys had mentioned they were bringing their significant others, even though Brady didn't think it was a big deal. He thought the more the merrier, although he knew Justin would not to be happy. Maxime and Zack showed up as well as a few more guys from the surf club.

Justin immediately pulled Brady to the side. "How come there are more than ten people here?"

Brady nonchalantly replied, "I invited Maxime and Zack yesterday because we were all surfing together. I did not know anyone was bringing their significant other."

Justin looked at Brady sternly with anger in his eyes. "Well, you know we only agreed to ten. Are there still more people coming?"

Brady shrugged his shoulders. "I'm not sure. Maybe one or two?"

The party grew larger and larger as Justin moved everyone outside on the roof deck. He was nervous someone was going to ruin his new couch and rug. The house was scheduled to be featured in an editorial article by a local architectural design magazine the following week. As an interior designer, Justin aspired to be recognized for his passion, and the last thing he wanted to do was cancel the shoot.

When Justin came inside and saw two women drinking red wine on his white couch, his heart started beating rapidly. He graciously asked the ladies if they could drink their wine outside or in the kitchen.

By this time, Brady had extended the invite to a few more friends. Five more buddies showed up and everyone gathered in the kitchen during halftime. Justin was polite and greeted them, but he was livid with Brady for not respecting the guest count.

Justin clenched his jaw and whispered to Brady. "I asked you to stop inviting people. What are you doing?"

Brady smirked. "I know. Chill. I'm just having a good time."

Justin pulled Brady closer. "Please do not invite anyone else. Or, you can personally leave yourself."

Brady took a step back. "Geez. I got it."

Boundaries honor the relationship with yourself while simultaneously strengthening the connection for mutual respect.

Insight

Justin and Brady had been part of the same social circle for years. Their friendship shared many interests, including a love for sports, which is what brought them together for the Super Bowl party. However, despite having mutual friends, they held distinct values and views on party hosting. Justin vouched for an intimate and low-key gathering, given his upcoming editorial feature, whereas Brady went all out, inviting as many guests as possible and turning it into a grand event.

Even though Brady agreed to Justin's preference for a small party, he disregarded the guest count. While Brady didn't think it was a big deal, Justin felt angry and disrespected. This led to a boundary breach where the value of trust was broken, creating a rift in their friendship. Brady's carefree attitude violated Justin's value of physical space and mutual respect. However, Justin emotionally reacted by giving an ultimatum to Brady out of defensiveness, demanding Brady leave the party if more guests showed up. Instead, Justin should have respectfully asked Brady to excuse himself if he was no longer able to honor their mutual agreement. By giving an ultimatum, Justin disconnected from his values by allowing Brady to influence his behavior versus staying aligned with his inner truth and power. In the future, Justin may need to consider whether he wants to co-host parties with Brady or redefine their relationship where mutual respect is honored.

In scenarios like these, it's crucial to acknowledge that trust can be fractured in a split second when a friend disregards boundaries. Breached boundaries can reveal that the friend might have poor boundaries in their own life or hold vastly different values from their friend. When friends hold conflicting value systems, maintaining the friendship can become challenging because neither side feels that their needs are being met. As a result, Justin and Brady's clash over the Super Bowl party guest count highlighted the significance of effective communication, mutual respect, and trust in their friendship.

Definition of Friend Boundaries

Friend boundaries maintain the integrity of the relationship by respecting the well-being and values of each friend involved. They involve a harmonious balance between showing mutual respect and support for individual differences while enhancing each other's lives.

New Friendships

New friendships often stand out from long-lasting ones because they tend to be more exciting and adventurous in the initial connection stage. However, certain qualities can help you identify whether or not someone is truly a good friend for the long haul. True friends are those who offer unwavering support in both your successes and struggles. They are known to be supportive listeners who genuinely value your opinions and perspectives. Whether you're facing problems in your life or just need someone to talk to after a long day, they are receptive to being there for you.

When creating new friendships, it's important to consider how this person will fit into your life. While it can take time to get to know them, it's much easier to form new friendships when there's value alignment. For instance, if you have plans to attend a workout class with a new friend and they don't show up, but you value integrity, then you may want to reconsider if this person can meet your friendship needs. Or, if you call a friend and they don't call you back for over a week, then they may not be the best resource for support if you value communication.

In new friendships, individuals can hesitate to speak up about their values because they do not want to rock the boat, have a fear of being disliked, or worry they will be judged for their life choices. Sacrificing your values for the sake of acceptance in new friendships can lead to an unhealthy connection, leaving you feeling disrespected and under-valued. Honoring your values and setting boundaries is the healthiest way to create common ground when building long-lasting friendships.

Unhealthy versus Healthy Friendships

From childhood to adulthood, you may acquire new friendships and acquaintances along the way. As you evolve, friendships can shift due to personal or professional growth. Some friendships can become less fulfilling or even one-sided as priorities alter. One-sided friendships begin to form when there is an imbalance in the connection due to finances, seeking external validation, competitiveness, personal commitments, mental or emotional distress, life transitions, etc. Keeping one-sided or unhealthy friendships can take a toll on your mental health, life path, and purpose, and it can drain your emotional energy.

Unhealthy Friendships Look Like This:

- Failure to initiate communication
- Inability to repair a friendship after a disagreement
- Neglecting the need for emotional support
- Desire to control the friendship or shared plans
- Showing competitiveness and jealousy
- Incapacity to show support for successes and losses
- Ungrateful for generosity
- Avoiding accountability for hurt feelings
- Disregarding privacy for confidential information
- Engaging in dishonesty to uphold a perceived reputation
- Applying peer pressure to engage in activities that contradict values
- Inconsistency in keeping plans
- Judging each other
- Excessive focus on gossip
- Continual breach of boundaries

On the other hand, healthy friendships add immense value to your life. These healthy friendships are built on mutual respect and understanding of each other's differences and similarities. While two or more friends may share similar interests, a friend cannot assume each friendship will align on every topic of conversation or individualized belief. Each friend will have their own unique upbringing, which will impact how they form and maintain friendships. True friends, who enhance the quality of your life, are present to support you through both challenging times and moments of celebration. They are friends you can count on because the connection is authentic and trustworthy.

Healthy Friendships Look Like This:

- Reciprocal initiation of plans and communication
- Mutually respecting differences
- Honesty between both parties, even if it may lead to hurt feelings
- Listening to each other and offering support
- Both sides acknowledging mistakes and apologizing
- Shared support for each other's successes and challenges
- Maintaining confidentiality of each other's information
- Looking out for each other's best interests
- Collaborative resolution of disagreements
- Respecting each other's boundaries
- Avoiding judgment of each other's life choices
- Contributing value to each other's lives
- Acceptance of one another
- Balancing giving and receiving
- Respecting each other's time

When it comes to friendships, without question, quality is valued over quantity. Having surface-level friends does not define your social status, relationship skills, or personal value. After all, relationships with a few close friends can be much more meaningful and rewarding than with many casual acquaintances. Healthy friendships thrive on reciprocity and positive interactions over time. This requires effort from both parties to maintain and develop the connection for longevity. When growing meaningful friendships, focus less on how many people you know and more on building genuine connections with the people around you. With time and effort, those friendships will become your most valuable confidantes. At the end of the day, your friends can become some of the greatest influences in your life.

If you find yourself emotionally drained or taken for granted, be willing to do some life cleansing of friendships or acquaintances who are not in alignment with your inner truth and values. Friends who aren't supportive of life's ebbs and flows may be hindering your own happiness and success. It may scare you to lose people, but then you have to ask yourself the following questions:

- How supportive are they of my life goals?
- Can they actively listen when I need a friend to talk to?
- Can they respect my life choices?
- How do they add value to my life?
- Can I count on them during a time of need?

Types of Friend Boundaries

- Honoring privacy and personal space
- Valuing time and commitment for shared plans
- Establishing timelines for borrowing and returning items
- Asking for reimbursement on loaned funds
- Refraining from controversial topics to prevent discord
- Communicating in a timely and respectful manner
- Respecting significant others, family, and mutual acquaintances
- Honoring confidential personal matters
- Respecting differences of opinions or feelings
- Engaging in mutually beneficial friendships
- Asking before posting or tagging photos on social media
- Refraining from gossiping or speaking ill of others
- Showing support for losses or achievements
- Addressing judgmental statements
- Choosing quality friendships over quantity

- Apologizing for disrespectful or harmful behaviors
- Being mindful of house guest etiquette

Example of the Boundary Badass Method for Friend Boundaries

ASAP: Assess with discovery questions, Set a boundary, Agree to a mutual plan, and Proceed with accountability

Step 1: **Assess** *with Discovery Questions*

Boundary Setter: Who invited all these people?

Boundary Receiver: I did. What is the problem?

Boundary Setter: What happened to our agreement?

Boundary Receiver: They are all our friends. What is the big deal?

Step 2: **Set** *a Boundary*

Boundary Setter: I feel blindsided when additional guests show up to the party. I value integrity. Can we agree to communicate before inviting more guests than originally planned?

Step 3: **Agree** *to a Mutual Plan Using "I" Statements and Discovery Questions*

Boundary Receiver: I know you said to keep the party small. I didn't know how to say no to the other guys, especially when we always see them. Sorry for not keeping my word.

Boundary Setter: I understand. It normally wouldn't have been an issue, but I'm a little cautious with the upcoming editorial shoot.

Boundary Receiver: I know I should have asked before inviting the other guys.

Boundary Setter: We could have figured out a plan. I can handle two extra guys, but it turned into an extra ten real fast.

Boundary Receiver: I hear you.

Boundary Setter: After the feature in the design magazine, we can have a celebration party. Cool?

Boundary Receiver: Let's do it!

Step 4: **Proceed** *with Accountability*

Boundary Receiver: (Magazine feature celebration) I can't wait for the party tonight! I'm pretty sure all the guests are coming. I know we planned for twenty-five.

Boundary Setter: Great, I've ordered food and drinks. The caterers will be here at four o'clock.

Boundary Receiver: I'll be over early to help prepare.

(An hour after guests arrive)

Boundary Setter: Hey, thanks for sticking to the guest count tonight.

Boundary Receiver: Of course! I value our friendship.

Boundary Setter: Same here.

Examples of Discovery Questions and Friend Boundaries

Discovery Questions:

- How come you told our group of friends about my break-up?
- How come I am being judged for the type of car I drive?
- When can you pay me back?

Friend Boundaries:

- I feel betrayed when my break-up is the gossip amongst our friends. I value privacy. Can we agree not to share sensitive information with everyone?
- I feel judged when I am criticized for driving an economy car. I value open-mindedness. How can we respect each other's personal choices?
- I think it's inconsiderate when I haven't received reimbursement for the concert tickets. I value financial responsibility. Can we establish a specific timeframe for reimbursements?

FOURTEEN

DATING BOUNDARIES

Taylor had gotten home from work and was rummaging through the refrigerator to find a quick snack before heading to tennis. As she pulled out an apple, she turned around and saw that a notification had popped up on her phone. It was from her dating app – she had matched with a guy named Ellison.

Ellison said, *Hey, Taylor. How is your Tuesday going?*

Taylor excitedly texted, *Hi, Ellison! I'm just getting home from work and heading to tennis. What are you up to?*

I'm trying to finish a work project that has been dragging on. How long have you been playing tennis?

For about a year now. It's a great workout! Do you work out or play any sports?

Ellison wrote back. *I'm into running and playing basketball once in a while. Do you run?*

Taylor responded, *Not much, but once in a while. Well, I have to get to tennis. Let's catch up later!*

After tennis, Taylor noticed she had another message from Ellison. How was tennis?

Taylor smiled. *Great! Feel so refreshed!*

Ellison blasted a text back, *Awesome! Maybe we could play together one day. What does the rest of your week look like? Would you like to meet up?*

For sure! Let's do it…I'm pretty busy this week. What about Friday evening or Sunday during the day?

Cool. Friday works.

Taylor replied, *Great, what time?*

Hmmm. How about seven?

Taylor happily confirmed, *That works!*

The next day, Taylor began to feel overwhelmed. She had her hands full at the office trying to ensure the marketing materials for the upcoming product launch would be sent to the new vendor on time. The account details had to be solidified by Friday morning, or else she knew her boss would be in her ear pressing for answers. She felt like no matter how efficient she was with her time, there were still never enough hours in the day. Taylor was so distraught she had completely forgotten about her date Friday night until Ellison messaged her.

Hey, Taylor. Hope you are having a good day. Are we still on for tomorrow?

Taylor quickly replied. *Yes, where are we meeting?*

Ellison typed back. *I can pick you up if that is okay with you, and we can head to this restaurant on 5th Street.*

Taylor rapidly typed as she multitasked. *I'm working late. How about I meet you there? By the way, what is your number?*

Ellison smiled, *Great! Looking forward to it.*

Thanks! I'll text you.

Friday morning rolled around, and Taylor was in a mad dash to get out the door for work. She had less than three hours to launch the online campaigns. She ran into the break room and poured herself another cup of coffee.

As the clock ticked, Taylor finally completed the project with minutes spare. She gathered her materials, went by her boss's office and handed him everything. Her stomach was in knots. Her boss Jaxson slowly began examining her materials, looking over every last detail before he finally approved the marketing campaign. She sighed with a sense of relief and couldn't wait to go out and celebrate the completion of her project.

While she started to get ready for her date at the office, Taylor checked her messages one last time. She saw a text from Ellison. He was running late and asked to push back the time until 7:30 p.m. Since she had an additional thirty minutes, she stopped rushing and took a breather from her long day.

Taylor sat down on the bench in the ladies' room and called her friend to pass the time. She told her how annoyed she was that Ellison was running late. While on the phone, Taylor looked in the mirror one last time before throwing on her black heels and gold necklace. As she left the ladies' room, Ellison texted her again.

Hey sorry, but I'm still at the office. Do you want to just come over to chill and watch a movie at my place around nine?

Taylor froze as she stared down at her phone. *Umm…what happened to going out?*

I apologize. I can't leave yet, and I don't want to cancel.

Taylor decided to go with the flow. *Okay, I guess that works. Where do you live?*

Ellison replied, *Cool. I'm at the corner of Willow St. and Pine Ave.*

Okay. See you soon!

Taylor went home after work to change clothes and threw on jeans to head over to Ellison's house. While putting on her shoes, she ordered a car service to pick her up. When she got to his house, Taylor felt nervous but tried to play it off like she wasn't. Ellison offered a few beverage options and made a charcuterie board while Taylor chilled in the living room. Once Ellison was done, he joined her on the couch. Chatting away, he asked her what type of movies she enjoyed watching. They agreed on a drama film.

After the movie, Ellison said she could stay over at his place, but Taylor insisted on going home. Ellison grabbed his car keys, and they walked to his car so he could drive her home. As they arrived at her house, Ellison leaned over to kiss her cheek and said he had a good time. He suggested they should do it again. Taylor agreed and said she would enjoy that.

The rest of the weekend went by and Taylor didn't hear from Ellison. Sunday, she had lunch with an old friend and told her all about him. She expressed how much she liked Ellison but was disappointed she hadn't heard from him since their movie night. Her girlfriend said to give it some time and he would probably reach out.

On Monday, while working, she received a text message from Ellison.

Hey! Hope you had a great weekend. How's your Monday going?

Taylor immediately blushed. *Weekend was great. Hung out with a friend and my Monday is moving along. How's yours?*

Mine was great too. Watched baseball with the guys. What does your week look like? Want to grab lunch since we work so close to each other?

Taylor typed back. *Sure, I can meet on Tuesday or Thursday. How about you?*

Perfect, let's do Thursday.

Taylor was so excited about her new date with Ellison that she immediately shared the news with her co-worker. She began to feel giddy over Ellison, but she couldn't figure out what it was about him that she liked so much.

It was Thursday morning around ten o'clock when Ellison messaged Taylor.

Any particular place you want to grab lunch? And, does twelve o'clock work?

Taylor replied, *Noon works. What about the pizza place on the corner of Adams St. and Bennett Ave.?*

Ah yes, I know the place. See you there!

Taylor stood up swiftly as she walked over to print her client's materials. While they were printing, she responded, *Perfect. Just a heads up, I only have an hour lunch break.*

Ellison messaged, *No problem.*

She waited in the lobby area of the restaurant for Ellison. It was 12:10 and he still hadn't shown up. Taylor messaged him to see if he was on his way. He replied that he would be there in five minutes because he got caught up in a meeting. She waited another five minutes and still no Ellison. She asked the hostess to seat her because she only had forty-five minutes left on her break. She messaged Ellison to see what kind of pizza he liked, but there was no answer. When the waitress returned to the table, Taylor ordered a medium pizza with pepperoni and green peppers on one half and sausage and onions on the other since she didn't know what Ellison liked.

Another ten minutes went by and Ellison finally showed up at 12:30 p.m. He apologized for being late, but Taylor was already frustrated with him.

Taylor said, "Happy you made it. I already ordered since I'm short on time. And, I don't know what you like so I guessed."

Ellison smiled and looked at her apologetically. "Thank you for ordering. Sorry, today is extremely busy."

Taylor joked, "I'm starting to think you need a watch."

Ellison smirked. "Ha ha, yeah maybe."

The pizza arrived at the table and they both began eating. Before they knew it, Taylor had to get back to work. She hugged Ellison goodbye, and he stayed to finish eating his pizza.

Your values set the tone for the connection, regardless of the opinions or behaviors of others.

Insight

Due to conflicting values, Taylor and Ellison's first date did not start well. Ellison demonstrated a lack of consideration for Taylor's time, believing that his personal schedule took precedence over their date. Furthermore, Ellison failed to properly plan for the occasion, and this turned their date into a casual hangout at his home, which disappointed

Taylor. Ellison's absence of time management and personal integrity showed his *me mindset*.

Despite Ellison's lack of accountability, Taylor compromised her values by remaining silent, as Ellison continuously pushed back the time of their date. When Taylor accepted Ellison's invitation to watch a movie at his home without any prior dates or quality time together, Taylor unintentionally conveyed that she didn't know her personal boundaries and that she trusted everyone. This can give off the impression she doesn't have standards, and it can potentially put her physical safety at risk.

After the first date hiccup, Taylor was immersed in her emotions and decided to go on another date with Ellison. Unfortunately, Ellison repeated his previous behavior and arrived late again due to his professional obligations. Even though Taylor had informed Ellison of her time constraints beforehand, Ellison once again showed disrespect for her value of time. During the date, Taylor made a sarcastic remark about Ellison needing a watch since he couldn't manage to be on time. Although Taylor felt undervalued at that moment, she used sarcasm to address the disconnect instead of setting a dating boundary. With poor dating boundaries, the other person will not understand their behavior is an issue and can continue to take advantage of the other individual.

When it comes to actively dating, each individual is responsible for setting the tone of the connection based on their personal values and standards of how they want to be treated. If someone is incapable of aligning with one's values, it can clarify that this individual is unlikely to fulfill their emotional needs long-term, leading to an imbalanced connection.

Definition of Dating Boundaries

Dating boundaries define an individual's standards concerning time, health, needs, personal space, individuality, and physical safety. These preferences may address standards for dates, comfort level for physical intimacy, individual and relationship goals, and communication style. It is important to respect personal limits and values at the onset of a connection to create alignment and growth.

Setting the Tone for the Connection

When dating someone new, it can be easy to get caught up in the excitement of the honeymoon phase. Setting dating boundaries in the initial stage is essential to building a healthy connection with mutual respect. This highlights the importance of effectively expressing one's values and limits all while being open to understanding the limits of the other individual. While being flexible or overly accommodating can be seen as easygoing, this can potentially lead to unfavorable behavior patterns down the road. The sooner you set boundaries, the easier and more fulfilling the relationship will be in the long run.

Dating can come with thrills or instantaneously bliss; however, letting intense emotions or physical chemistry override your values of compatibility can cost you the relationship later on. For first dates, meeting someone in a public location versus a private residence is the initial step to establishing respectful standards, especially if you have no previous connection to this individual. Knowing your boundaries of what feels safe or unsafe when getting to know someone is important for honoring self-respect.

The way you treat yourself sets the standard for how you desire a romantic partner to treat you in return. At times, individuals may try to test the waters or push your limits to see what they can or can't get away with. Your instincts will naturally react when something feels off, potentially leading you to feel uneasy, emotionally distant, or defensive. If you have high self-awareness and live by your values, you will be better equipped to recognize unhealthy behaviors as soon as they arise in a relationship.

When the nervous system gets activated, the body sends a physiological response that something doesn't feel good, creating a sense of discomfort. Many times, people will ignore this gut instinct because they are more fixated on their feelings or seeking validation than on building a valuable connection. However, the more an individual focuses on long-term growth and how this person aligns with their values, the greater clarity they will have of who can truly meet their emotional needs. If a person seeks short-term admiration and instant gratification, then it is a clear indication there is a disconnect with regard to one's values. These experiences and connections generally fizzle out as quickly as they start.

At the end of the day, we can't convince someone to see our worth. If the person you are dating isn't valuing you or respecting your boundaries, it may be best to cut ties and move on so you can build a healthy connection with someone who has similar values, interests, and goals. Instead of viewing this as a loss, see it as an opportunity to attract a person who aligns with your values. Attempting to convince yourself that you can change a person's interest only creates an internal war within yourself. This is because you are trying to prove your worth instead of believing you are worthy of love. Over time, an individual who settles for less than what they deserve lowers their self-esteem and devalues their self-worth because they are accepting behaviors that are deemed disrespectful. The longer you accept or stay in these types of connections, the more challenging your dating life will become because you cannot trust who has your best interest at heart. When you believe you are valuable, you will attract a high-value partner who is emotionally available for love.

On a final note, if you're an individual who consumes alcoholic beverages on dates, it is best to keep your consumption to a two-drink maximum. Finding yourself under the influence on the first few dates can distort your perception of whether or not this person is a great fit. It can also lead to poor decision-making that may not align with your relationship values. Your relationship values are your roadmap to relationship success, and they are the key to meeting your relationship goals.

Ghosting

You may come across variations of ghosting behavior during your dating journey. Ghosting, disappearing without warning, may come in the form of a person not showing up on a date. Or, an individual who dates you for a few months, leading you to believe they desire a relationship before ghosting altogether. Often, a ghoster will passive-aggressively vanish and abruptly cut off all contact without an explanation because it is easier than having a heart-centered conversation that may make them feel uncomfortable.

Ghosting is not about you or the relationship itself but rather a reflection of the ghoster's lack of integrity with themselves. Such individuals are often disconnected from their values and view relationships as one-sided, transactional interactions intended solely to meet their own needs. Ghosters tend to be emotionally underdeveloped and lack the assertive communication skills needed to express their true desires or the need to move on. They may have self-limiting beliefs of being rejected and, as a result, prematurely leave the person they are dating before they can experience rejection themselves. These individuals may have a self-fulfilling prophecy that they continuously reinforce through their ghosting behavior.

Love Bombing

Love bombing is when a person tells you everything you want to hear to get you hooked on them within the first couple of months. They entice you with grand romantic gestures or extravagant gifts, charm you with nonstop compliments and excessive communication, quickly move the relationship to the next level by saying "I love you," and offer you a better world together before they get to know you on a deeper level. A love bomber tends to have low self-worth and believes a romantic companion wouldn't be attracted to them if they didn't offer all their surface-level promises. This type of person will lead with a false persona and try to sell the dream life, whether they can offer it or not. They attempt to create a euphoric feeling, like an addiction, so when you think about them, you crave their admiration. The reason they shower you with excessive attention and affection in the first ninety days is because psychologically, that is the maximum threshold of how long a love bomber can keep up with their facade.

When being loved bombed, it can often cloud your mental ability to assess whether or not this person has your best interest because of the illusion the love bomber has created. They will base the connection on feelings of intensity or a grandiose vision of what the relationship could look like. If an individual lacks personal boundaries, they may find themselves attaching their relationship goals to a person's words without assessing if they have the integrity to follow through on these grand visionary plans. When determining if someone has integrity, taking things slow can help you assess whether the connection is worth pursuing and will provide fulfillment or not. Ultimately, words are meaningless in the absence of integrity.

Values versus Checklist

When it comes to choosing a compatible partner, some people will use a selection process of ideal traits, also known as a checklist, to determine their match. Characteristic traits are seen as one-sided ideals or surface-level expectations that an individual may desire in a potential partner. Displacing expectations onto a partner stems from the ego and a *me* mindset, and it has no bearing on relationship success and how someone will treat you. Having a checklist of superficial attributes, a vision of how you want the connection to play out, or what you expect a potential partner to possess is operating out of fear and control rather than building a loving connection. Checklists may include preferred height, physique, financial status, the color of eyes or hair, location of residence, similar sex drive, social status, the vehicle they drive, date expectations, or the need to be married by a certain timeline, etc. And, the list can go on and on. This mentality can lead to a never-ending cycle of relationship sabotage if the ideals, or self-limiting beliefs, are unmet.

While you may find specific characteristic traits attractive, they will not meet your emotional needs for a healthy relationship or sustain it long-term. Focusing solely on physical appearances or conditional terms can often lead to unhealthy relationships, as these are superficial qualities that prevent a deeper connection for growth. Over time, physical attributes may fade, financial assets may be lost, and social status may change, leaving the relationship without a foundation to stand on. Additionally, expecting the connection to evolve according to futuristic outcomes indicates a lack of presence in the connection. This can hinder deeper vulnerability, growth, and mutual fulfillment.

Having standards and values will guide you in choosing a healthy partner who can meet your emotional needs. Values such as loyalty, honesty, and trust are fundamental in respecting and upholding your self-worth within a relationship. If you find yourself searching for overly idealistic qualities, this may indicate that you are selling yourself short in meeting your needs for longevity, respect, and happiness. For relationship fulfillment, authentically living according to your values is imperative.

Transitioning from Dating to a Relationship

Dating can be mysterious and exhilarating; however, determining if a person is a great match for a meaningful relationship can take time. It is important not to commit until you feel comfortable and confident that this partner aligns with your relationship values. If an individual tries to evolve the relationship to the next level too soon and forgoes their values, it creates an open invitation for disrespectful behavior. On average, it takes a few months of spending quality time together to determine if a person can meet your relationship values. If they lead with a false persona, this is also the time by which you'd see their true colors and destructive patterns begin to emerge.

What happens when you meet someone and discover, after dating for a couple of months, that their values align with your values? Transitioning the connection from dating to an exclusive relationship can be a hurdle in modern times. Using boundaries is one of the simplest communication techniques to take the relationship to the next level without feeling nervous or uneasy. When approaching it from a *we* mindset, this takes the pressure off both individuals, clarifying whether either person is ready to move the relationship forward or if they still need more time. Before you ask for a commitment, here are some questions to clarify if this person is worthy of a commitment with you.

Ask Yourself These Questions Before Committing:

- Do they align with at least three of my relationship values?
- Do I feel respected by them?
- Do we share similar long-term relationship goals?
- Do I feel calm in their presence?
- Do they fully incorporate me into their life with friends and family?
- Do we have common interests?
- Do they listen during times of need?
- Do they communicate openly and honestly?
- Do I trust they have my best interest at heart?
- Do I feel like a priority in their life?
- Do we spend quality time with each other to deepen our connection?

Types of Dating Boundaries

- Respecting personal and physical space
- Valuing each other's time
- Establishing integrity for commitments
- Withholding private information until trust is built
- Honoring relationship values
- Communicating when ready for physical intimacy
- Sharing and understanding each other's viewpoints
- Choosing mutually fulfilling connections
- Expressing the need for quality time
- Refraining from internalizing others' emotions
- Asking for exclusivity for growth in the relationship
- Being transparent about children or pets that may come with you in the relationship
- Respecting each other's privacy
- Knowing your limits for alcohol consumption on dates
- Presenting an authentic persona online
- Disengaging from connections that feel one-sided or manipulative
- Maintaining a harmonious balance between personal and relationship goals
- Being transparent about the type of relationship you're looking for

Example of the Boundary Badass Method for Dating Boundaries

ASAP: A*ssess with discovery questions,* **S***et a boundary,* **A***gree to a mutual plan, and* **P***roceed with accountability*

Step 1: **Assess** *with Discovery Questions*

Boundary Setter: How about we meet at the restaurant?

Boundary Receiver: I have plenty of food and drinks at my place.

Step 2: **Set** *a Boundary*

Boundary Setter: I think a public place would be great when meeting for the first time. I value integrity. Can we stick to our original plan and meet at the restaurant?

Step 3: **Agree** *to a Mutual Plan Using "I" Statements and Discovery Questions*

Boundary Receiver: Sure. Can I ask if everything is okay?

Boundary Setter: Of course. I prefer meeting in a public place when getting to know someone.

(Three hours later)

Boundary Receiver: I've had a long day. How about we chill and watch a movie?

(Boundary receiver disregards initial boundary and tests the setter)

Boundary Setter: Can we do that another time? Let's check out the restaurant.

(Boundary setter redirects the conversation back to the boundary)

Boundary Receiver: Okay, sounds good.

Step 4: **Proceed** *with Accountability*

Boundary Receiver: (Date two) Hey, want to grab dinner Thursday night?

Boundary Setter: I would love to. What time do you want to go?

Boundary Receiver: I can make a reservation for seven or eight. What do you prefer?

Boundary Setter: Seven works. I'm looking forward to it!

Boundary Receiver: Ditto. I'll send you the reservation.

Examples of Discovery Questions and Dating Boundaries

Discovery Questions:

- Help me understand, how come we agreed to be exclusive if you aren't?
- What are your thoughts about us?
- How come I haven't received a call back?

Dating Boundaries:

- It appears we are on different pages when it comes to exclusivity. I value transparency. Can we talk about what exclusivity means to each of us?
- It feels good when we spend time together, and I am looking forward to going on more dates. I value growth. Can we talk about where we see our connection growing from here?
- I feel ignored when I don't receive a call back. I value communication. How can we find a balance between our communication styles?

FIFTEEN

COUPLE BOUNDARIES

Addison asked Jules what his schedule looked like for work this upcoming week.

Jules looked at his calendar. "I have a huge conference Wednesday through Friday, remember?"

Addison gazed out the kitchen window. "Ah yes, I forgot. So, I'm on my own those days for dinner?"

"Yes, I will be attending dinners with colleagues after the presentations. I'll try not to be home too late. On Saturday, we should definitely go out for date night. What do you want to do?"

Addison propped her hands on her hips. "Well, in case you forgot, it is our tenth anniversary this weekend…"

Jules replied, "I didn't forget!"

Addison mumbled under her breath, "Sure you didn't…"

"I swear. Why do you think I brought it up? I can make a reservation and get tickets to a show."

Addison glanced back at Jules. "Sounds perfect. Hmmm, what should I wear?"

Jules walked over and kissed Addison. "Something red would be lovely."

It was the start of a new week, Addison and Jules were out the door with a quick kiss goodbye. Addison, a chiropractor, had appointments throughout the week, but her schedule was pretty flexible. She booked a private yoga class on Wednesday night for her and her friends.

That night around ten o'clock, Addison pulled into the driveway, but Jules still wasn't home. She sent a quick text to see when he would be home. Jules said he was still at dinner but would be home in an hour or so. Feeling tired, Addison climbed into bed and began reading the news. She lathered her hands in moisturizer before realizing it was past her bedtime. With a flick of the switch, she turned off the light and sent Jules a text saying goodnight.

Jules arrived home at midnight and began making a lot of noise as he fumbled around in the kitchen for a snack. He walked upstairs and flipped on all the lights in the master bedroom.

Addison woke up. "What are you doing, Jules? I'm freaking sleeping."

Jules stumbled over the clothes on the floor. "Uh sorry, I can't see where I'm going. Just go back to sleep."

Addison angrily yelled, "Shut off the lights. I swear you only think about yourself."

"Sorry, I'll shut off the lights in a minute."

Addison snapped back. "Stay on your side of the bed. I'm so annoyed right now! You know I need at least seven hours of sleep. Geez, how many times do I have to tell you."

Jules apologetically softened his voice. "Yes, I know. It won't happen again."

Jules finished brushing his teeth in the bathroom and shut off the rest of the lights before climbing into bed. He knew Addison was not happy with him. Normally, he would kiss her goodnight, but he knew to keep his distance until tomorrow when he could try and smooth things over.

When Jules woke up, he had the worst headache ever. He went to the kitchen to make himself an espresso to ease his throbbing pain. Addison had left a note for him on the counter.

Jul-

If you are going to be late again this evening, please sleep in the guest bed-room. I have an early appointment tomorrow morning.

Addy

She had never told him to sleep in the guest bedroom before, nor did she ever forget to leave out *I love you* in her little notes. He didn't know what he had done for her to be this upset, but he thought he was better off giving her space than pushing the issue. Jules knew he had their anniversary night to make it up to her.

Later that day, he ran to the jewelry store to get Addison some-thing special. He picked out an emerald stone necklace that he knew would complement her bright green eyes. He also ran to her favorite flower shop and ordered a bouquet to be sent to the house on Satur-day morning. He ordered her a large arrangement of white florals. He picked hydrangeas, garden roses, and orchids – her favorites.

After work, Jules went to dinner again with his co-workers and cli-ents. He loved entertaining but also knew he shouldn't stay out late two nights in a row. Jules called it an early night and was home by eleven. He didn't want to wake Addison, so he slept in the guest bedroom. He thought it was better to be safe than to start another argument. Plus, they didn't speak much yesterday, as Addison had given him the silent treatment.

The next morning, Jules and Addison woke up at the same time and had coffee together. The tension in the air was thick. Neither of them said much to each other, except to have a good day at work. Nor was there a kiss goodbye. It wasn't like Addison to hold grudges, but Jules didn't want to poke the bear, so he avoided asking Addison what was still bothering her. All Jules knew was he could not mess up Satur-day.

When Jules went to work on Friday, he decided he would skip the client dinner that evening, and instead, he would play an early morning round of golf with the guys on Saturday. Jules sent Addison a message letting her know.

Hey, change in plans. I'll be home tonight. We decided to golf tomorrow instead.

Addison wrote back. *Okay. See you tonight.*

Jules hesitantly asked, *Should we go out or watch a movie?*

Movie is fine.

Jules knew she was being short and couldn't take the tension much longer. But he was also hopeful because she had agreed to watch a movie together.

Addison sent another text. *Also, what time are the reservations tomorrow?*

Jules smiled at his phone with relief. *At six. I should be home from golf by four o'clock.*

Addison responded, *Thanks.*

The next day after golf, the guys grabbed a bite to eat at three o'clock. As Jules was about to get the tab for lunch, one of his prospects he golfed with mentioned he was ready to sign on as a client. Shortly after, Jules received a text from Addison thanking him for the flowers. But Jules was too distracted by his client and didn't respond. He asked the new client when he wanted to get started.

The client mentioned, "I was hoping we could sign everything today, as I fly out tomorrow."

Jules replied, "Let me message my assistant to have the contract drawn up."

While waiting on the contract, Jules started to get antsy and kept glancing down at his watch. It was pushing five o'clock. He still needed to get home and shower to make their six o'clock anniversary dinner. He messaged his assistant again for an update. He then sent Addison a message. *Darling, I see you got the flowers…I'm running late. I got a last-minute client, and I need to get the contract signed.*

Addison was fuming mad. *You're doing this on our anniversary. Are you serious?*

Jules felt torn but proceeded. *He literally just dropped this on me as we finished lunch. I will make it, don't worry!*

Addison continued to get ready. *I'm not holding my breath on this one. You only care about your work.*

Not true. I sent you flowers and got you a surprise for later. Please let me close this deal, and I will be there. Do you want me to meet you at the restaurant?

Addison slammed down her hairbrush on the counter. *Seriously, Jules? No, I don't. But, whatever, I will just meet you there. This anniversary is going downhill really fast.*

Jules quickly replied so he could get back to his client. *Thank you for understanding. Love you.*

Jules's client signed the paperwork at exactly 5:45 p.m. He rushed home and showered, grabbed the necklace, and ran out the door. He arrived at the restaurant thirty minutes late. Addison was in a chic red dress sitting in the lounge looking stunning. Jules couldn't believe how beautiful she was, and he was starting to feel guilty for being late. He walked up to her from behind and put the necklace on her. He whispered in her ear, "I'm sorry for being late. Happy Anniversary."

Addison turned around and kissed him.

Achieving relationship goals requires prioritizing long-term commitment over short-term emotions.

Insight

Addison and Jules had a healthy connection, except when Jules's career took precedence over their relationship. While Jules desired to be a devoted husband, his actions conveyed a lack of mutual respect. Jules valuing his work as his top priority led to an imbalance in their marriage by not maintaining a work-life-love balance. This led to Addison feeling taken for granted and undervalued. Rather than seeking understanding behind Addison's silent treatment, Jules became passive by shoving the issue under the rug and hoping it would dissipate on its own.

In response to Jules disturbing Addison's sleep, she became emotionally reactive by demanding Jules sleep in the guest bedroom. Shutting Jules out may have made Addison feel powerful in the moment, but it failed to get her needs met with her husband long-term. Silent treatment is often used when a person has stepped away from their values and is consumed by their feelings. This tactic can be used to punish the other person, yet in this case, Jules didn't understand Addison's intentions. Addison's inability to communicate and set a boundary kept unresolved discord between her and Jules. This behavior shows they are stuck in a problem state versus being solution-focused and resolving their differences amicably as a couple. Remaining in an emotional state can lead to each partner holding onto resentment and walking around on eggshells instead of repairing the relationship.

Overall, Jules had room for improvement in managing his time effectively, prioritizing his relationship with his wife, and establishing clear boundaries between his professional commitments and personal life. On the other hand, Addison needed to focus on developing emotional regulation skills and asserting couple boundaries within the dynamic, especially when she felt undervalued, to foster a stronger foundation of mutual respect. Often, couples unintentionally trigger each other but fail to address these issues openly, resulting in unhealthy patterns within the relationship.

Definition of Couple Boundaries

Couple boundaries support the foundation of an intimate connection by maintaining a balance of independence and interdependence. Each partner will have standards and values that meet their personal needs while still honoring and mutually respecting what the relationship needs to thrive and evolve.

Attachment Styles

Attachment styles refer to patterns of emotional and behavioral responses that individuals develop in close relationships, particularly during childhood. These attachment styles are shaped by an individual's early experiences with their primary caregivers or parents. These interactions create one's interpersonal relationship patterns and beliefs about relationships in general. With that being said, attachment styles are crucial as they influence how individuals perceive and respond to emotional intimacy, trust, and connection in their adult relationships.

There are four different attachment styles. Secure attachment develops when caregivers consistently respond and are emotionally available to a child's needs, providing a safe and nurturing environment. In contrast, the three insecure attachment styles emerge when caregivers are inconsistent, neglectful, or abusive in their responses to the child's needs. For instance, anxious attachment can result from caregivers who are sometimes responsive but unreliable and inconsistent, leading the child to seek constant validation due to a fear of abandonment. Avoidant attachment may develop when caregivers are emotionally distant and consistently reject, dismiss, or neglect the child's emotional needs, prompting the child to develop self-reliance as a coping mechanism. Lastly, disorganized attachment often arises from caregivers who are erratic, abusive, or traumatizing, leading to a lack of consistent coping strategies to emotionally regulate and ongoing trust issues.

When couples are unaware of each other's attachment styles, it can lead to misunderstandings, false assumptions, and increased relationship discord. For instance, a person with an avoidant attachment style may feel uncomfortable discussing emotional issues and shut down, while someone with an anxious attachment style may want to address the discord because unresolved conflict causes them distress. In this situation, their contrasting approaches to managing relationship discord can result in a greater disconnect, possibly even pushing the other person away. Aligning their attachment styles will require patience, setting boundaries, and effectively communicating each person's needs to achieve harmony. It's important to note that attachment styles are not fixed; they can be influenced and modified by later experiences and relationships, as well as through self-awareness and personal growth.

Four Types of Attachment Styles: Secure, Anxious, Avoidant, and Disorganized

- **Secure Attachment** refers to the ability to form healthy, loving relationships with a partner. A secure individual feels they are able to love, trust, and interact with ease throughout their connection due to their positive view of themselves and others. Emotional and physical intimacy of closeness feels good, as does personal time away from a partner. An individual will communicate what they need if something becomes unfulfilling, or they will request adjustment for better alignment. Secure people tend to be naturally cooperative and flexible and engage in healthy interactions for relationship success. Their daily habits define what works best to support themselves and the foundation of the relationship for longevity.
  - Common Core Beliefs:
    - "When I'm upset, I let others know how it makes me feel."
    - "Mistakes are difficult, but I learn and evolve from them."
    - "I want to feel close in my relationships and build foundations with time."
- **Anxious Attachment** forms when an individual has a deep fear of abandonment. Having an insecure attachment style, an

individual can find it challenging to trust and love a partner freely as they fear their partner could leave them at any given time. An anxious individual can have self-doubts and need a partner's constant reassurance or approval to feel worthy of love. An anxious attachment can cause an individual to be reactive or act out when they feel emotionally triggered, as they struggle to ask for what they need from their partner. Being unable to articulate their needs or limits can keep their emotions bottled up out of fear. Eventually, this can lead to verbally unleashing on their partner because they have a dysregulated nervous system and feel challenged to regulate their emotions.

- ○ Common Core Beliefs:
  - • "I'm not good enough; otherwise, they wouldn't treat me that way."
  - • "I know I'm not going to hear back from them."
  - • "I need an answer right now."

- **Avoidant Attachment** forms when an individual experiences emotional discomfort with vulnerability and intimacy. An avoidant attachment style leads to distrusting a partner, even if the partner has their best interest at heart because of their own insecurities. They stay emotionally detached and unavailable as getting too close creates too much fear. They prefer to be self-reliant to protect themselves from being vulnerable and expressing what they need in the relationship. Most often, they show vulnerability only when they are about to lose someone they love or a crisis happens.
  - ○ Common Core Beliefs:
    - • "I don't trust anyone with my feelings."
    - • "I can't deal with people's emotions."
    - • "I refuse to be controlled and rather be on my own."

- **Disorganized Attachment** is a combination of anxious and avoidant attachment styles. This individual feels fearful they will not be loved enough by a partner and may experience rejection. They often have a wide range of fears and worries due to their low self-esteem and limited self-worth. At the same time, they will keep a partner at arm's length due to the intense anxiety they experience when a partner wants to form a deeper connection. Due to the complexities, there can be extremes of sexual behavior, increased violence, and difficulty regulating emotions. They are typically in a constant state of confusion about love and tend to live in survival mode.
  - Common Core Beliefs:
    - "Everyone is untrustworthy, so I'll end up alone."
    - "No one could possibly love me for who I am."
    - "I am completely worthless and empty."

Destructive Communication

Conflict is inevitable and can arise with a partner at any given moment when facing differences. Couples can view conflict as "something is wrong," yet conflict can be an opportunity for partners to have a constructive conversation and strengthen their connection through establishing healthy boundaries. This allows them to work through each perspective for growth and mutual alignment. However, couples may find themselves stuck in problematic communication patterns when addressing everyday life stressors or relationship issues. This is a direct result of poor boundaries and insufficient conflict resolution skills present in their interactions. Couples may resort to emotional reactions of frustration, anger, sadness, or shame to name a few. When couples resort to taking out their emotions on their partner, they often will engage in one of the four horsemen. The four horsemen – criticism, contempt, defensiveness, and stonewalling – are destructive to relationships, especially romantic relationships because they break down the communication channels leading to an impasse or a relationship disso-lution.

The first horseman, criticism, occurs when one or both partners verbally attack their partner for some type of hurtful or disrespect-ful behavior. They tend to react by criticizing their partner's character out of frustration or anger. A partner who passes negative judgment onto their partner's character is shifting blame to them for how they feel, rather than accepting responsibility for their behavior or emo-tions. When one partner refuses to take responsibility for their part of a disagreement, this becomes a violation of mutual respect. This com-munication pattern is emotionally and psychologically harmful to the relationship and each partner. One partner may feel disrespected and undervalued while the other who is being critical is abandoning their authenticity and needs.

When criticism intensifies, it will lead to the second of the four horsemen – contempt. Contempt is considered one of the most de-structive communication patterns. A partner who engages in contempt will tend to be impulsive and reactive with condescending language that is disrespectful, scornful, and arrogant. The contemptuous partner will likely use this tactic as a means to seek superiority in the relationship due to their loss of internal control. They may deflect from their be-haviors by twisting and turning the facts of an incident by gaslighting their partner to feel guilty or mentally unstable for even questioning their behavior. This can cause the receiving partner to doubt their own reality or memory of how the event or situation occurred. Over time, this emotionally toxic cycle can weigh heavily on a partner's self-esteem and confidence, making them feel unworthy or fearful of leaving the relationship.

Gaslighting Phrases:

- "That never happened"
- "You're too sensitive"

- "You're imagining things"
- "You're crazy and need help"
- "I'm sorry you think I hurt you"
- "You should have known how I would react"
- "You're too controlling"
- "You're defensive all the time"
- "Maybe that is what you heard in your head, but it's not what I said"
- "It's your fault"
- "I was only joking"
- "Don't get upset over nothing"
- "Stop being so insecure"
- "You're the only one who thinks there's an issue"

A partner who avoids accountability will make it challenging to build a healthy relationship. It can often indicate there are personality complexities present, they are disconnected from their value system, or they refuse to self-reflect. An emotionally underdeveloped partner often finds it easier to hide behind a false narrative in an attempt to cover up their inadequacies within the relationship. They believe they are entitled to make or break the "rules" in the connection; however, their partner cannot. Most of the time, a psychologically or emotionally unhealthy partner believes their opinions are facts when, in reality, they can be limiting beliefs from unresolved wounds that are being projected onto the connection.

The third horseman, defensiveness, occurs as a response to criticism. A partner who resorts to this style usually is trying to recover from the criticism and may try to reverse blame onto their partner out of self-protection. Defensiveness involves denying responsibility, giving poor excuses, or counterattacking, which only fuels greater discord and a power struggle, rather than shutting it down altogether. When a partner is critical or contemptuous, the worst thing for the other partner to do is to defend themselves against false accusations or projections of control. Instead, it is vital for the partner being verbally attacked to hold their value and follow the *Boundary Badass Method* or call a timeout.

The final horseman, stonewalling, is a response to contempt where a partner shuts down or withdraws from the conflict. The stonewalling partner may refuse to engage in conversation or act as though they are not affected by the relationship issue. This behavior can leave the other partner feeling punished for speaking up, frustrated, unheard, and disconnected.

Stonewalling Can Be Interpreted As:

- I'm not going to give you what you want
- I'm going to punish you until you comply
- I'm scared you will see the real me
- I don't have to tell you how I feel
- I don't have time for this
- I don't care what you have to say

It's important to note that the four horsemen are often a response to overwhelming emotions or a perceived threat that results in an overreaction and exertion of power. Most likely the individual who is contemptuous or stonewalls grew up in a home where they were not heard or understood; they learned these modeled behaviors through family dynamics. However, these approaches are a counterproductive way of working through relationship disconnects. Addressing these maladaptive behaviors requires open communication, active listening, taking responsibility, and a willingness from both partners to work on healthier ways of resolving conflicts. If the four horsemen remain present in the relationship dialogue long enough, it will likely lead to relationship dissatisfaction and poor psychological health.

Relationship Privacy

Relationships aren't community projects. The airing of relationship tension on social media or sharing with family and friends can create more problems than the initial relationship issue. While seeking an outside perspective can be helpful in understanding each partner's role in the relationship problem, family and friends can be biased. They tend to support the partner they share a close relationship with, which can lead to a greater divide between the couple. In fact, most people value their family or friends' opinions, yet it may not be conducive to an amicable resolution that honors both partners' needs. Sharing your concerns with others also can cause humiliation, embarrassment, betrayal, or the undermining of your partner with those you or your partner share close relationships with. When seeking to resolve relationship differences, it's best to seek an unbiased neutral party if the discord cannot be resolved on its own.

Authors' note: In the case, where emotional, psychological, physical, sexual, or substance abuse is present, please seek professional help for guidance and safety.

Keeping the Spark Alive

Whether your relationship is in the beginning phases or you have been together for many years, all relationships will go through their ebbs and flows. People often wonder what it takes to keep a relationship healthy, functioning, and thriving. Relationships don't have to be complicated to be healthy or require rigorous amounts of undivided time. However, they do take commitment, consistency, and communication to truly reap the benefits. While a couple doesn't need to spend eight hours a day to deepen their connection, daily touches can create emotional intimacy for longevity.

When a relationship begins to fizzle out, it can be due to different value systems, a partner's needs no longer being met, relationship goals shifting over time, misaligned attachment styles, loss of physical and emotional intimacy, or disagreements over finances. Nonetheless, there are ways to increase connection opportunities with a partner and to make the relationship a priority.

How to Keep a Romantic Relationship Healthy and Thriving:

- Respect each other's relationship values
- Establish a weekly date without distractions
- Spend quality time together
- Show daily appreciation for each other
- Enjoy a shared hobby or common interest
- Engage in an active sex life
- Establish monthly check-ins about finances, emotional needs, etc.
- Create couple goals for the relationship
- Set healthy boundaries for mutual respect
- Resolve differences and emotional wounds in a timely manner
- Calmly communicate even when it's uncomfortable

Types of Couple Boundaries

- Respecting each partner's personal or professional commitments
- Knowing your personal limits or emotional triggers
- Communicating constructively and consistently for emotional intimacy
- Honoring your relationship values
- Creating guidelines for entertaining guests
- Implementing a daily self-care and self-love regimen
- Refraining from rehashing past and resolved topics
- Agreeing to mutual consent for physical intimacy

- Finding the balance between love, work, and social lives
- Establishing financial agreements for spending, saving, and investing
- Respecting each other's differences of opinions, beliefs, and feelings
- Requesting personal space or privacy
- Spending quality time together
- Respecting your partner's appearance and body image
- Supporting each partner through challenges and achievements
- Talking in person about significant concerns
- Balancing household tasks and responsibilities
- Keeping couple discord private unless there are critical safety concerns
- Supporting each other's friendships and family relationships
- Asking for a timeout if things become heated during an argument

Example of the Boundary Badass Method for Couple Boundaries

ASAP: Assess with discovery questions, Set a boundary, Agree to a mutual plan, and Proceed with accountability

Step 1: **Assess** *with Discovery Questions*

Boundary Setter: When can we go on a date?

Boundary Receiver: I'm not sure. I'll look at my schedule. Maybe we can go next week.

Step 2: **Set** *a Boundary*

Boundary Setter: I feel undervalued when work takes precedence over our relationship. I value work-life-love balance. How can we make time for our relationship?

Step 3: **Agree** *to a Mutual Plan Using "I" Statements and Discovery Questions*

Boundary Receiver: I know I've been busy, but this week was an exception with clients in town. I do value you and want to spend time together. What do you have in mind?

Boundary Setter: I was thinking about a weekly date night for just the two of us. What do you think?

Boundary Receiver: It's a great idea. What day do you prefer?

Boundary Setter: I prefer Saturday, but if something comes up that day then we can reschedule for Sunday. How do you feel about this?

Boundary Receiver: Works for me.

Step 4: **Proceed** *with Accountability*

Boundary Receiver: (Monday morning at the office) I am looking at the calendar and I can't do Saturday the 21st of this month. Can we do Sunday that week?

Boundary Setter: Let me check!

Boundary Receiver: Okay.

Boundary Setter: I can't do Sunday because I have brunch that day. Can we do Friday instead?

Boundary Receiver: Sure, that works.

Boundary Setter: Thank you for making sure we keep our weekly date night. It means a lot to me.

Examples of Discovery Questions and Couple Boundaries

Discovery Questions:

- Can you please stop yelling at me?
- How come I am the only one who unloads the dishwasher?
- How come you're not listening?

Couple Boundaries:

- I feel uneasy when there is yelling and screaming. I value constructive communication. How can we respectfully work together to find a resolution?

- I feel stressed when all the chores fall on my shoulders. I value teamwork. Can we collaborate on creating a chore list to split the responsibilities?

- I feel disconnected when I share my thoughts and they are dismissed. I value empathy. How can we be more understanding of each other's feelings and thoughts?

SIXTEEN
SEXUAL BOUNDARIES

Whitney and Levi met in their junior year of college at the city's art gala fundraiser. Whitney, a featured artist, was showcasing her avant-garde paintings in hopes of raising money for children's developmental research. As Whitney wandered around the gala, she saw a man admiring her work. She casually walked over to her displayed painting and asked him what he thought about the piece.

Levi replied, "It's brilliant. It's simple yet catches my imagination."

Whitney beamed with curiosity. "What strikes your imagination?"

Levi whispered, "The way the colors merge together reminds me of the sunsets in Bali."

Whitney was amused. "Bali? Hmm. Have you been?"

"No, I haven't, but it's on my bucket list. Maybe we should go one day?" he said with a flirtatious smile.

"Perhaps! If someone buys my painting, then we shall go. Half the proceeds go to research and the other half I get to keep. I can buy my plane ticket with the proceeds."

Levi replied, "Then we can experience it together."

Whitney gave him a subtle smile and walked away. At that moment, Levi was mesmerized. He had never seen her before and began to wonder who she was. Her long wavy hair and poised essence made his heart flutter in a way he had not felt before. He knew he had to talk to her again, but he forgot to ask for her number. He began brainstorming how he would get in touch with her. He called his father, telling him he just met the woman of his dreams at the gala and needed to buy her painting. He sent his father a photo of the painting and begged him to help him out. His father agreed to purchase the painting since it was for a good cause.

Levi began making his rounds at the fundraiser searching for Whitney, but she was nowhere to be found. Levi told the host of the fundraiser he wanted to purchase her painting. As he was finalizing the purchase, he asked if he could get in touch with the artist. The host said they don't give out personal information about the artists but would be happy to give him information on where she features her work regularly.

The next day, Levi found her studio in the art district. His legs were trembling with nerves as he entered the front door. He knew this was his only chance to get her number. As Whitney heard the door open, she immediately turned around and saw him. Their eyes met, and they both grinned at each other.

Whitney walked toward the door. "Hello, mister."

Levi replied, "Hi, I wanted to come see the rest of your work. I hope you don't mind."

"Of course, I don't. I heard you purchased my painting last night."

Levi charmingly said, "Well, actually my father did. I wanted to support a great cause and a talented artist."

Whitney modestly looked away. "Well, thank you. You're too kind."

"And, you're amazing. These paintings are spectacular! How long have you been painting?"

Whitney thought about it for a moment. "Since I was about twelve."

"I'm so impressed. It looks like we can go to Bali now," Levi said with a wink.

"When is the best time to go and see the sunsets?"

Levi replied, "How about we talk about it over dinner tomorrow night?"

Whitney walked over to her desk to check her schedule. "I would like that. I will be finished around six."

Levi reached his hand into his front pocket to grab his phone. "Perfect. Can I have your number? I'll find a place for us to go and message you the time."

"Sure"

Fast forward fifteen years later, Levi had just finished telling his business partner the story of how he and Whitney fell in love. Levi and Whitney hadn't skipped a beat and celebrated their fifth trip to Bali last month. Even though they were deeply in love, they were also complete opposites, which caused them to clash from time to time. Whitney, an art professor at a local university, was a free-spirited go-with-flow type of person. Whereas, Levi, a fine art agent, was much more method-ological in his day-to-day life.

One night, Levi came home late after reviewing artists' contracts for an upcoming exhibition. He was drained, but he had no choice but to keep treading ahead. Over dinner, Whitney and Levi talked about the new artist he was looking forward to seeing featured. Whitney could tell he was tired by the look in his eyes, but she asked if he wanted to watch a television show after dinner. Levi agreed. He went and sprawled out on the couch. Whitney sat down and cuddled up beside him.

Levi flipped through the channels. "What show do you want to watch?"

Whitney looked up at Levi. "Can you look to see what's trending?"

Levi began to throw out suggestions. "We can watch a crime show, a real-life story about a family living on a haunted ranch, or a documen-tary about the ocean."

Whitney got up from the couch and headed for the stairs, saying over her shoulder, "Okay, let's do a crime show. But I'll be right back. I need to go upstairs."

Whitney quickly rummaged through her dresser drawers looking for her black lace lingerie. She had been waiting all day for Levi to come home so they could have sex. She finally found what she was looking for when Levi yelled at her to hurry up. Whitney threw on her lingerie and slowly walked down the stairs. As she came to the landing on the staircase, she dimmed the lights. Levi was already asleep on the couch. She kissed him to wake him up but he wasn't opening his eyes.

"Levi, wake up! Look what I have on."

Levi muttered, "You look hot, babe, but I'm too tired. I had a fourteen-hour day of talent calls, press, and contract signings."

Whitney demanded, "But, Levi, I want sex now!"

"How about tomorrow?"

Whitney got more aggressive. "No, now! We haven't had sex in like two weeks. What is your deal?"

"I'm worn out, what do you expect? I can barely stay awake."

"So, you don't want to have sex with me anymore? This marriage is awful, and you have become so boring and self-centered."

Levi replied, "I didn't say that. Can you let me sleep? Geez. All you ever care about is sex."

Whitney felt rejected and shouted, "That's not true. But I didn't marry you to be sexually frustrated my whole life. Clearly, we aren't on the same page. I need sex regularly, and you need it like once a month. I don't get it. Maybe you should see a doctor and check your hormones!"

Whitney stormed upstairs with tears streaming down her face. She had always known she desired more physical intimacy than Levi, but not having consistent sex made her think they were growing in different directions. She didn't understand how a man who used to be so mesmerized by her all of a sudden didn't want to have sex with her. It was killing her internally, and she felt like their marriage was falling apart.

The following morning, Whitney was in the kitchen prepping for breakfast when Levi came in and sat at the kitchen table. Whitney angrily chopped up some fresh fruit and made yogurt bowls. She was still visibly upset, but Levi said nothing. He began scrolling through his emails as he would any other day.

Whitney decided to break the ice. "Do you want to talk about last night?'

Levi sulked in his chair. "Not really."

Whitney found herself becoming more annoyed. "So, we are going to ignore that we have a sexless marriage."

Levi got agitated. "Why do you have to be so dramatic? We don't have a sexless marriage. You just want sex more than I do."

Whitney started to raise her voice as her eyes began to well up with tears. "I married my best friend who I love having sex with, but if you don't want to talk about it, I don't know how we can find a resolution."

Levi slapped his hand on the table. "Whitney, enough. We will have sex when I'm not tired. I need to land this deal for one of my artists."

Whitney stood up. "All you care about is your talent. It's like I don't exist. Nothing turns you on anymore. Is there someone else?"

Levi started to collect himself. "Babe, don't be ridiculous right now. How about tomorrow? I don't have any events and will be home early."

Whitney glared back. "We will see if you keep your word. Just so you know, I'm done cooking dinner until you give me sex. You can starve for all I care."

She stormed out of the kitchen with her coffee in hand.

Boundaries speak volumes when differences arise and emotions are high.

Insight

Levi made a bold move by buying one of Whitney's paintings and discussing future travels to Bali together in an attempt to sweep her off her feet. His self-doubt led him to believe that Whitney might reject him unless he went to great lengths to impress her. However, in his pursuit, he unintentionally undermined his own value and lacked the confidence to be his authentic self. Trying to captivate someone with grand gestures before fully understanding their values can potentially lead to later disconnects in the relationship.

Many years later, Whitney became frustrated with the shift in their marriage, feeling undesirable due to Levi's lower sex drive. She valued physical intimacy as an essential part of their marriage, while Levi found this to be less of a priority. When emotional and physical intimacy deteriorates, it can be challenging for couples, like Whitney and Levi, to reconnect without healthy boundaries and conflict resolution skills. When a consistent pattern is present in a romantic relationship, where one partner experiences sexual rejection repeatedly, it can turn into an ongoing power struggle, creating further discord.

Levi's avoidance of their relationship issues, an avoidant attachment style, only pushed Whitney further away, highlighting how their communication channels had become closed off. This left Whitney questioning whether she felt loved by Levi. As a result, Whitney showed poor emotional regulation when her value for physical intimacy was not met. To further exacerbate the situation, she made personal insults toward her husband and went into a fight trauma response, instead of setting a sexual boundary to create alignment. Using reactive language hurt Whitney's chances of receiving what she needed because she didn't create a safe space for open dialogue.

When Whitney approached her husband again the next morning, he deflected from the sexual intimacy issue. This led to her reacting from a place of emotion, giving him an ultimatum rather than responding to their relationship disconnect. Being vengeful keeps the relationship in an ongoing toxic cycle without ever getting to the root cause of the disconnect and moving forward in a healthy way.

Definition of Sexual Boundaries

Sexual boundaries are guidelines for sexual pleasures in a relationship that honors each partner's emotional and physical well-being. It defines limits that include the frequency of sex, types of sexual engagement or positions, sexually explicit comments or content, sexual consent, sexual health testing, and contraceptive choices.

Using Sex for Power

In relationships where sexual intimacy plays a role, some individuals may resort to using sex as a tool for coercion to assert dominance over their partner. This unhealthy dynamic often leads to emotional power struggles, toxicity, and a buildup of emotional resentment, ultimately sabotaging the connection between individuals. While one person is in a position of power or control, the other can be left feeling powerless or voiceless. Whether it involves making sexual promises or gestures to manipulate someone into doing things they are uncomfortable with, withholding sex for leverage, or engaging in transactional exchanges of sexual favors, all of these behaviors fundamentally exploit sex as a means of power. When individuals feel coerced or pressured, this can have detrimental effects on their mental and emotional well-being. Such transactions can lead to feelings of objectification and dehumanization, as individuals can be seen as a resource in the eyes of those seeking to exploit them.

These actions are rooted in ego-based thinking, making it challenging for either person to develop a genuinely healthy and fulfilling relationship. The individual using coercive tactics may be driven by fears of not being loved or accepted for who they truly are, concerns of their partner leaving them for someone else, or a lack of understanding about how to form a genuine and authentic connection. It is important to recognize and address these harmful patterns to foster an environment of respect, consent, and emotional well-being within the relationship.

There are consequences for surrendering our sexual boundaries and allowing ourselves to be used for someone else's gain. In the long run, allowing yourself to be exploited will likely leave you feeling devalued and disempowered, and it can have lasting effects on your physical and mental health. When faced with sexual coercion, it is much healthier to maintain sexual autonomy rather than to agree to a short-term gain with a person who uses sex as a form of control. Knowing your limits and having sexual boundaries can prevent these types of occurrences.

Sexual Trauma Bonding

Sexual trauma bonding is when a relationship revolves around the gratification of sex and control. Both individuals thrive on being desired sexually and seek the intense high of excitement through sexual engagement, which prevents forming a strong foundation for a healthy connection. Constantly looking for an intoxicating experience can become a sexual addiction to the point neither individual knows how to physically or emotionally disengage from the connection. The euphoric high can temporarily eliminate an individual's fear of abandonment or rejection, but this often highlights deeper unresolved wounds and the inability to create emotional intimacy. These individuals can find a healthy relationship often boring or mundane due to the lack of intensity.

Relationships that are primarily centered around sexual intimacy often follow a pattern characterized by a cycle of makeup-and-breakup sex, with minimal consideration for needs or values. In these types of partnerships, sex can become a quick fix or a band-aid solution to temporarily cover up conflicts and disagreements, while the deeper disconnect is frequently overlooked. Failing to address underlying issues can contribute to an unsustainable and emotionally unfulfilling relationship.

When a relationship exhibits signs of sexual trauma bonding, these patterns often originate from past experiences where each partner might have faced rejection or abandonment by a parent or caregiver. Consequently, this unresolved emotional wound can manifest in adult relationships, leading to seeking external validation through sexual pleasure with others.

To build healthier and long-lasting partnerships, individuals will need to consider addressing the root cause of their unresolved emotions and need for sexual gratification. Open and honest communication, trust, and shared values can form the foundation of a meaningful relationship, allowing for a deeper and more authentic connection that goes beyond the superficiality of sex.

Sexual Preferences

Sex is much more enjoyable when an individual feels safe and comfortable exploring their sexual preferences and desires in the bedroom with another. Having a conversation prior to any sexual experience can help create a positive outcome and build trust within the relationship where both individuals know their limits or intentions. Knowing what turns each individual on or off allows for vulnerability and exploration without hindering the connection.

During intimate conversations, if an individual brings up something that feels uncomfortable or doesn't turn them on, it is important not to shame them for their sexual desires or limits. Instead, you will want to use this moment to gain clarification about intimate pleasures they are willing to engage in. If you judge a romantic interest or partner by immediately shutting down their ideas without further inquiry as to why it may be fulfilling to them, then you are denying yourself of potentially deepening your emotional intimacy with them. An open conversation will allow each person to further understand their desires, bridge the gap between the differences, and find common pleasures.

While sex is a healthy aspect of bonding with an intimate person, some people may find themselves prioritizing other aspects of their relationship over sex, like raising kids, friendships, careers, etc. It can be natural for intimate relationships to experience phases where partners may have different sex drives throughout their life cycles. The differences allow the partnership to grow by establishing sexual boundaries and how it will be prioritized within their overall lifestyle.

Responsibilities and Risks of Sex

Engaging in sex involves personal responsibility as well as risks one may encounter during a sexual experience. Giving verbal consent is a personal choice when deciding whom you wish to engage in sexual relations with. While a person may give consent for sex, they can revoke their consent at any time if they do not feel like having sex or feel like their mental or physical health is threatened in any such way.

When deciding whom you want to have sex with, it begins with understanding your limits concerning your body and values. Honoring your self-worth and physical body protects you from unwarranted emotional harm and unhealthy attachments with individuals who may not be good for your overall health. If you prematurely engage in a sexual experience when you aren't emotionally ready, feel pressured, hormones are heightened, are under the influence, or were love-bombed in the relationship, you can violate your own sexual boundaries. To prevent experiencing negative emotions around sexual pleasure, it is wise to date someone for a good amount of time to ensure they align with your values or provide transparency of intentions upfront.

Similarly, emotional health needs to be considered when it comes to sexual relations. Some may view sex as a solely physical pleasure, while others may find it creates an emotional connection with another individual. It is well-known that women have higher levels of oxytocin than men. This feel-good hormone can sometimes play a role in transforming a physical act into an emotional connection. Unfortunately, this can cloud one's perception of the connection if both individuals aren't on the same page. Both men and women benefit from increased levels of oxytocin, as this hormone is known for playing a role in sexual satisfaction, reducing stress, and increasing trust and warmth within a committed relationship.

While everyone is responsible for voicing sexual consent to support their emotional health, physical risks are involved in every choice. Some of these risks may entail sexually transmitted diseases and pregnancy. Safety measures to ensure your physical health and prevention of pregnancy may look like discussing contraceptive methods, protection, and taking sexual health tests prior to engaging in sex. At the same time, if you are in a healthy committed relationship, these risks may not be as much of a concern for your relationship and family goals.

Lust versus Love

Using sex to create a connection in the initial stages of meeting someone can leave the relationship ending up with poor boundaries. Lusting after an individual or chasing the intensity of physical chemistry prevents the formation of a solid foundation for growth and stability within the relationship. When the connection hyperfocuses on physical features and sexual desires for fulfillment, this can cause the relationship to fizzle out just as quickly as it started due to the lack of deeper intimacy. Lust can be seen as fun, exciting, and adventurous, but it is often short-lived because one or both people stay on the surface instead of learning about each other.

Lust can show up in various forms, where it can lead to being emotionally blindsided if you are unaware of someone's intentions. Lust may look like flirty messaging to seek sexual admiration and gratification, buying affection with lavish gifts, disappearing and reappearing, feeling pressured to spend time together, calling excessively, trying to control the connection, spending time together only in privacy, and much more. When this occurs, it can create a distorted perception of the connection and lack meaningful value. The easiest way to know if someone only wants lust is if they avoid talking about life goals, desires, or values for long-term fulfillment.

On the contrary, when someone is seeking a long-term commitment with a partner, they will not rush the process to become sexually involved, as they have yet to uncover compatibility of similarities or differences. They will gradually explore the connection to see if and how they can add value to each other's lives one date at a time. Each individual is willing to show respect and be open to emotional intimacy while simultaneously using their values to maintain healthy boundaries. While sex is part of a loving relationship, it does not sustain it. Quality time, emotional connectedness, friendship, respect for each other's values, acceptance of differences, relationship boundaries, and aligned long-term goals are essential to a remarkable relationship.

Types of Sexual Boundaries

- Communicating sexual desires, preferences, needs, and limits
- Agreeing or disagreeing to sexual consent
- Discussing differences in sexual frequency
- Using a code word for when you want to stop a sexual act
- Exploring when a person shares their sexual desires, fantasies, or preferences
- Respecting body autonomy until sexually ready
- Sharing current methods of contraception
- Requesting sexual health testing
- Healing from traumas that may hinder your sexual relations
- Refraining from the use of sex for power or control
- Knowing your limits when sharing sexually explicit content
- Shutting down sexually degrading language
- Practicing celibacy
- Being open and honest about sexual intentions
- Establishing sexual exclusivity

Examples of Following the Boundary Badass Method for Sexual Boundaries

ASAP: Assess with discovery questions, Set a boundary, Agree to a mutual plan, and Proceed with accountability

Step 1: **Assess** *with Discovery Questions*

Boundary Setter: How come you don't want to have sex?

Boundary Receiver: I'm tired and not in the mood.

Boundary Setter: It's been over a month. What's going on?

Boundary Receiver: I have a lot on my plate right now.

Step 2: **Set** *a Boundary*

Boundary Setter: I feel hurt when my sexual advances are rejected. I value physical intimacy. Can we talk about our individual sexual desires and frequency?

Step 3: **Agree** *to a Mutual Plan Using "I" Statements and Discovery Questions*

Boundary Receiver: I know you prefer sex more than me. I will try to make an effort.

Boundary Setter: I don't want you to make an effort if you don't want it. I want us to figure out a plan that works for us so it doesn't become an issue. How often do you need sex a week?

Boundary Receiver: Probably once a week. What do you prefer?

Boundary Setter: I prefer three times a week. How can we find a balance?

Boundary Receiver: Let's strive for twice a week.

Boundary Setter: Okay, but I don't want to be the only one initiating.

Boundary Receiver: I will try to initiate too.

Step 4: **Proceed** *with Accountability*

Boundary Setter: (End of the week on Saturday) Hey, babe, I know we committed to twice a week, but we have only had sex once. When can we have sex?

Boundary Receiver: Sorry, it was a long week. We can tonight.

Boundary Setter: Can't wait!

Examples of Discovery Questions and Sexual Boundaries

Discovery Questions:

- Can we take our connection one step at a time?
- How come I'm the only one who initiates sex?
- What contraceptive method do you prefer?

Sexual Boundaries:

- I believe it would be best for us to wait to have sex until we've had more time to get to know each other better. I value quality time. How can we spend more time together?
- I feel undesirable when I have to initiate sex every time. I value mutual partnership. What can we do to create more physical intimacy?
- I feel uneasy when engaging in sex without contraception. I value safety. What method can we agree to use?

SEVENTEEN

FAMILY BOUNDARIES

Everyone sat in the living room and began planning the annual snow-boarding trip. Johnny, twenty years old, the oldest, requested to stay in a rustic cabin. The triplets, Molly, Michelle, and Monica, sixteen years old, begged to stay at an all-inclusive resort. And, of course, Tommy, the youngest at fourteen years old, wanted to stay at a vacation home up in the mountains so he could bring two friends along. They were all talking over one another at the table arguing about who had the best lodging idea for their family vacation. By the end of the discussion, Monica claimed she was no longer going, and Tommy threatened to go on vacation with his friend Matt if none of his friends were invited. And Tim, their dad, wasn't even home from work yet to throw in his two cents. What was supposed to be a fun family trip was turning into a complete whirlwind of chaos.

Jackie, a stay-at-home mom, was more focused on shopping for the trip rather than where they would be staying. She loved spoiling the kids, as they were her pride and joy, and she liked being known as the cool mom. She wasn't one for household rules and generally let things slide under the rug when the kids were being mischievous. She left most of the disciplining up to Tim, even though he was generally at the office working long hours.

When Tim got home from work, he was greeted by everyone shouting over one another. Each kid started to list all the reasons why their choice of lodging was the best option. He could hardly even hear what each kid was saying to him and began to tune it out. The kids knew their father would make the final decision since he had business meetings to attend while they were on holiday.

Overwhelmed by the chatter, Tim looked at Jackie and asked, "Why are you letting them decide?"

Jackie replied, "I thought we could try something different, but you can decide."

Jackie went upstairs and began ordering the kids their new snowboarding gear. While she added items to her online shopping cart, Tim came into their bedroom and glanced over at the computer to see everything she was buying for the trip.

"How come the kids can't wear the gear they already own?"

Jackie kept scrolling. "I didn't ask. They told me they needed these things, so I'm ordering them."

Tim gave a perplexed look. "Do you know the word no? Every year we go on this trip, and it ends up costing us double what it should because the kids need new snowboards or outfits. Yet, you and I continue to use the same gear we've had for the last several years."

"You're right. I'll tell them you said no."

Tim could feel his face getting flushed with anger. "How about you tell them instead of making me the bad cop?"

"You know I can't do that. I'll feel guilty if I tell them no. You tell them I'm going to go make dinner now."

Jackie was baking salmon and vegetables for her and Tim and stuffed chicken for the kids since they refused to eat fish. As Jackie got the vegetables prepped for dinner, Johnny told her about how he and his girlfriend were fighting about him leaving on the family vacation. Jackie offered to call Johnny's girlfriend to talk to her about it and smooth things over. While on the phone, Jackie extended the invitation for her to join the family trip in hopes of keeping the peace with everyone.

When they all sat down for dinner, Tim let the kids know they would have to use their snowboarding equipment and gear from last year. Immediately, Monica started pouting, saying it wasn't fair. Tim told her to stop with the nonsense or they would not be going on vacation at all. As they continued to eat and talk over each other, Tim interrupted and shared that he had decided to stay at a rental home in the mountains. Then, Jackie announced that she had invited Johnny's girlfriend on the trip.

At that moment, Tommy slammed down his fork because his friends had yet to be invited on the trip. He got up and left the dinner table and stormed off to his room.

Jackie tilted her head slightly and gave Tim a pleasing look. "Can his friends come?"

Tim finished chewing his bite. "I guess. Also, just a heads up, I invited my parents to join us on vacation too."

"Since when? Now I have to listen to your mother tell me all weekend how I'm too nice to the kids and I don't know how to parent."

"I will talk to her beforehand," Tim said. "Or…better yet, why don't you just ignore her?"

Jackie started to feel overwhelmed. "It's kind of hard when she is your mother. What am I supposed to tell her – to mind her own business?"

"No, just leave the room or let it go."

Michelle yelled over everyone, "Seriously, you both are giving me a headache. Can't everyone come and just get along for once? Why is it so hard for our family to be normal?"

When they arrived at the mountain, the house had four bedrooms and a loft for sleeping. Immediately, the kids argued over which room was theirs, as no one wanted to stay in the loft. Eventually, Tim stepped in and told Tommy he and his friends could sleep in the loft, giving the other bedrooms to the adults and older siblings. Tommy got angry and stomped up the stairs yelling that he never gets what he wants because he is the youngest and still gets treated like a child.

Once everyone unloaded their gear and luggage, Tim started a fire in the living room. Jackie made tea for everyone, then hung out by the fire to catch up with Tim's mom, Nancy.

Jackie wrapped herself up in a blanket and sipped on her tea. "How have you been?"

Nancy put down her magazine and looked over at Jackie. "Great! We just got back from sailing in Florida."

"Sounds like retirement life is treating you well."

"It is. How have you and the kids been?"

Jackie paused for a minute. "The usual teenager mood swings and fighting with each other. It's a full house most days."

Nancy crossed her arms. "Teens can be challenging. They need household rules."

Jackie glared at her. "We have rules."

Nancy huffed, "You're just a bit more laid back than I ever was."

"I think we can agree that we are opposites when it comes to parenting. I'm going to check on Tim. Let's catch up later." Jackie calmly exited the room.

Healthy families set clear boundaries. Dysfunctional families are unsure where to draw the line.

Insight

When it came to raising their family, Jackie and Tim had different perspectives on parenting. Jackie believed in pampering her children, and she deflected from setting boundaries so she could be seen as the cool mom, whereas Tim desired to set limits with the children. When children are pampered, this often robs them of developing healthy self-esteem and can create a long-term effect of entitlement and an inferiority complex. Neglecting to remain a united team in front of the children can make it challenging for children to develop trust within the family home due to conflictual messages. Despite Tim and Jackie having good intentions, they felt criticized by each other for their parenting choices. Their parenting styles were likely influenced by their own childhood experiences, as many parents learn how to raise children by observing their own parents.

As for Jackie and Tim's marital dynamic, they were misaligned financially as a couple. Jackie and Tim had opposing spending styles when it came to maintaining their family budget. While Jackie enjoyed spending without much concern for limits, Tim believed in being financially savvy. This discrepancy in their approach to money is a common cause of marital discord, making it crucial to have a family budget in place.

Additionally, Tim and Jackie lacked transparency when inviting extra guests on the family vacation. They each made their own decisions without consulting with one another, which resulted in heightened tension among the entire family. Executing unilateral decisions can cause ongoing power struggles, as neither partner is prioritizing the relationship. While it's not necessary for either spouse to seek their partner's approval, it's mutually respectful since the decision impacts all family members.

When Jackie took it upon herself to invite Johnny's girlfriend, she overstepped a boundary with her son. Jackie showed a fawn trauma response by feeling the need to resolve Johnny's relationship issue, which wasn't her responsibility. Also, appeasing one child's needs and not the others is playing favoritism between the children. This can negatively impact their self-worth and take a toll on their personal well-being and psychological development, questioning their role within the family. Additionally, it creates family discord and causes the child who didn't get their needs met to feel emotionally neglected. When Jackie showed favoritism towards Johnny, Tommy felt slighted that he was not given the opportunity to invite his friends. Tommy became emotionally dysregulated with aggressive behavior rather than asking a discovery question. By asking a discovery question, it would have highlighted the parental issue and prevented sibling rivalry from being created.

Not creating healthy boundaries within a family causes long-term emotional effects on each family member and their relationships. Children learn relational skills by mirroring their parental figures during their prime developmental years. Jackie and Tim's interpersonal relationship challenges influence their children's chances of becoming prone to similar interpersonal relationship issues as they reach adulthood.

Definition of Family Boundaries

Family boundaries outline each family member's responsibilities and roles within the family dynamic while honoring each individualized connection. Parents will establish boundaries both individually and collectively with their children, while children may set boundaries amongst their siblings without parental involvement. Family boundaries will be unique to each family, depending on how they relate to extended family members and the outside world.

Prioritizing a Partner

When a couple neglects the initial relationship that started the family unit, the relationship will likely begin to experience fundamental issues that create family discord. Once children are born into the family, the couple will need to make a shift by setting quality time aside for each other outside of maintaining the family and their careers. The time they will spend together as a couple will need to focus on emotional and physical intimacy, instead of how they are raising children, daily life stressors, or financial decisions. While the latter three are necessary to discuss for maintaining a healthy home, it's important to set up family meetings outside of romantic dates to address household matters.

Going on romantic dates promotes positive growth between partners and decreases the chances of either partner experiencing emotional neglect outside their personal ambitions, obligations, or children. The focus should be on what brings pleasure to you and your partner while minimizing external distractions. Scheduling weekly dates can be as simple as playing a board game, learning a new hobby together, attending a show or concert, or going on an adventure. Prioritizing time to listen to your partner, openly communicate, and continuously grow together will help you stay connected so you can weather any storm as a team.

Aligning Parenting Styles

When parenting, each parent has a responsibility to help their children thrive and grow up to become self-sufficient individuals. It is essential to teach them how to be emotionally, mentally, spiritually, and physically fit during their prime developmental years. However, if you and your partner have different parenting styles, it can cause great confusion and impact how well your children perform academically, manage adversity, and feel emotionally secure with who they are.

Children learn how to manage conflict as they mature based on their parent's conflict resolution skills within the home. If the safety of open dialogue is not established between the parent-to-parent or parent-to-child relationship, a child can feel highly conflicted as to whether they should be forthcoming about their mistakes and personal needs. Additionally, children may stay silent or hide the truth if they have a great fear of being punished or judged to avoid feeling embarrassed, shameful, or unlovable. The misunderstood child will continue to struggle with self-esteem and confidence issues into adulthood versus learning to love and trust themselves.

When children experience an insufficient family structure within the home, it can lead to life-long emotional hardships. Children who are shunned from expressing their feelings, thoughts, or beliefs can display emotional outbursts of anger, use manipulative language, give ultimatums, become withdrawn, or have people-pleasing tendencies. A child without boundaries will often have an underdeveloped identity and emotional immaturity, making it challenging to cultivate healthy relationships. They tend to struggle with communicating their personal needs, which can complicate their adult connections, personally and professionally.

In best practices, both parents will need to be on similar pages about fostering healthy independence and coping strategies to support their children's psychological and emotional well-being. This encourages children to honor their authentic selves by utilizing healthy boundaries, so they feel worthy in every facet of their life. When parents or caregivers are consistently present and mentally healthy, children are more likely to adapt and thrive with the ups and downs of life.

Four Types of Parenting Styles: Authoritative, Authoritarian, Permissive, Uninvolved

- **Authoritative** refers to a healthy parent-child relationship by setting clear guidelines and boundaries while taking the child's needs and emotions into consideration. The parents encourage thoughtful and respectful communication while implementing discipline when necessary. They invest time and energy into their children's development to prevent behavioral issues, and they nurture the connection to create respect between the parent and child. This parenting style raises developmentally healthy, happy children who are socially aware and tend to do well in life as they display independence, express self-discipline, and use creative and critical thinking skills for decision-making.

- Authoritative Parental Behaviors:
  - Maintains a healthy, consistent relationship with a child through interactive engagement
  - Explains reasons behind healthy boundaries or guidelines within and outside the home
  - Encourages respectful and open communication while considering a child's needs

- **Authoritarian** refers to when a parent engages with a child under their rigid rules without exception. The parent is often demanding and strict, controlling every interaction or relationship the child engages in. They often prioritize discipline over a nurturing relationship, leaving the child without a voice in the connection. If a child disobeys, the parent will use punishment over discipline to exert their power. They often make a child feel guilty for their mistakes instead of seeing them as an opportunity to learn and grow. This parenting style raises a child who displays low self-esteem, suffers from poor decision-making, becomes deceitful to avoid punishment, expresses aggression, and shows difficulty in social interactions.
  - Authoritarian Parental Behaviors:
    - Has total control and prevents a child from having a voice within the home; there is limited room for negotiation
    - Punishes the child without giving reasons or discussing misbehavior
    - Refuses to consider a child's needs, emotions, or thoughts when making decisions

- **Permissive** parents tend to be lenient and take on more of a friend role while encouraging children to come to them with their problems. They are quite responsive to their child's needs, and they fail to have boundaries, guidelines, or consequences.

Parents keep communication channels open without addressing misbehavior, which can impact a child without knowing their limits of healthy or unhealthy choices. This parenting style raises a child who exhibits low self-esteem, lacks healthy boundaries, struggles with self-control, suffers academically, and shows resistance to authoritative figures.

○ Permissive Parental Behaviors:

- Refuses to enforce discipline, boundaries, or consequences even after establishing them with a child
- Keeps lines of communication open and friendly
- Allows the child to voice their needs, desires, or problems without discouraging unfavorable behavior or setting limits

- **Uninvolved** refers to parents who are disengaged or uninvolved in their child's life and often provide minimal support, attention, or guidance. They have little knowledge of what goes on in their child's life and lack an emotional connection to the child. Parents rarely enforce consequences for misbehavior and lack boundaries altogether. A child is often expected to raise themselves, as the parent tends to suffer from mental health issues, substance abuse, or is absent altogether by neglecting the child. This parenting style raises a child who experiences low self-esteem, lacks self-trust, struggles to form healthy relationships, and displays sadness or dissatisfaction in life through behavioral issues.

○ Uninvolved Parental Behaviors:

- Shows disinterest in a child's life and doesn't ask about the child's hobbies or educational experiences
- Forgoes communication and neglects a child's needs, desires, or boundaries
- Lacks quality time or engagement with a child

Treating Children Fairly

Children need to be loved, accepted, and encouraged by their parents or caregivers, but this doesn't mean they won't test their parents' patience. At times, children will be unruly or cross familial boundaries within the home because they are developing their own belief systems, identity, and personality. When a child's behavior defies the parental guidelines, this can lead to a power struggle dynamic between the child and parent. The power struggle can continue to grow over time, creating further discord within the relationship if the parent doesn't remain outside of the conflict. When this conflictual dynamic remains present for a period of time, the parent can begin to resent or treat this child differently due to their own struggles they are displacing onto the parent-child relationship.

While each child may have a unique relationship with their parents or caregivers, it is important for children to be treated fairly while maintaining respect for the family boundaries. When there are multiple children within the home who are treated differently, it can create self-doubt, insecurity, or a sense of estrangement within the child who is seen as "less than" or as the "scapegoat" amongst their siblings. Shattering a child's confidence and self-worth is detrimental to how they approach life, whether or not they choose to love themselves, and to the types of relationships they will form throughout their lifetime. A child who believes they are "not good enough," due to not meeting their parent's projected expectations, can find themselves in unhealthy adult relationships where their partner reflects a similar dynamic as their caregivers. Favoring children, or choosing a golden child, can lead to long-term effects of entitlement, perfectionism, external gratification, self-abandonment, codependency, and trauma bonds in relationships. If the golden child is ever denied by a romantic partner, this can be a challenging experience for them since they are used to getting their way.

We cannot emphasize enough the impact a parent or caregiver has on a child's developmental years, from infancy to age seven, and how it will play a role in the relationships they create socially, professionally, or romantically throughout their lifespan. If you are a parent, know that you are the most critical person in your child's life. Their joy for life and how they engage with others comes from the love and respect they receive within the home.

Extended Family Outside the Home

Extended family members often play a significant role in our lives. Their presence can provide a sense of connection, familiarity, and support that adds value to our familial relationships. However, like any aspect of life, the involvement of extended family members in our immediate family requires a delicate balance. At times, extended family members can insert themselves into the immediate family household without permission. While you or your partner may deeply care about these family members and value the relationship, there comes a point where extended family members need to be aware of your immediate family boundaries. Whether it's in-laws or a second cousin, biological family roots shouldn't prevent an individual from setting healthy boundaries.

It's important to recognize that these family boundaries are not a rejection of extended family or an indication of a lack of love and respect. Instead, they are a vital component of maintaining the happiness and integrity of the immediate family unit, as well as nurturing the relationships both inside and outside the home. Having the courage to constructively set a boundary when a violation occurs prevents resentment toward family members while respecting the immediate family. Some of these boundaries may involve choosing not to answer invasive questions, eliminating unannounced visits, minimizing excessive texting or phone calls, and keeping relatives out of marital disputes and parenting decisions. This allows family members to resolve conflicts within the confines of the immediate family, fostering a sense of unity within the relationships.

Types of Family Boundaries

- Respecting each family member's opinions, beliefs, and values
- Establishing a family financial budget
- Treating children fairly and respectively
- Providing structure and guidelines for healthy or unhealthy behavior
- Finding alignment in parenting styles
- Contributing to the family housework (age-appropriate for kids)
- Implementing guidelines for hosting guests
- Using proper manners, etiquette, and appropriate language
- Giving children healthy options for decision-making
- Being respectful of each member's personal time or physical space
- Establishing privacy guidelines for information shared with extended relatives
- Sharing only age-appropriate information with children
- Creating a schedule to use the family vehicle
- Partnering with teens on creating behavioral boundary contracts for responsibilities
- Consulting with your significant other prior to making major family decisions
- Finding the balance between parenting, careers, couple's romance, and personal time
- Disengaging from family gossip
- Choosing to break away from detrimental generational patterns
- Respecting each family member's comfort level for physical affection or touch
- Refraining from triangulating children or other relatives into the couple's discord

Example of the Boundary Badass Method for Family Boundaries

ASAP: *Assess with discovery questions,* **Set** *a boundary,* **Agree** *to a mutual plan, and* **Proceed** *with accountability*

Step 1: **Assess** *with Discovery Questions*

> Boundary Setter: How come you invited your parents on our family trip?
>
> Boundary Receiver: They are family too.

Step 2: **Set** *a Boundary*

> Boundary Setter: I feel blindsided when additional guests are invited without my knowledge. I value transparency. Can we consult with each other first before extending the invite to others?

Step 3: **Agree** *to a Mutual Plan Using "I" statements and Discovery Questions*

> Boundary Receiver: I'm sorry, I didn't think it was an issue. I will ask you next time before inviting my parents. How come you don't want them to come?
>
> Boundary Setter: I was looking forward to spending time together as a family without worrying about entertaining others. How about we figure out another trip they can join us on this coming year?
>
> Boundary Receiver: I am fine with that. And I understand my mother can be a lot at times.
>
> Boundary Setter: Thanks for understanding.

Step 4: **Proceed** *with Accountability*

> Boundary Receiver: (Next family trip) I've been looking at flights for our family trip. What are your thoughts about my parents joining us at the beach next month?
>
> Boundary Setter: Thanks for asking. I don't mind if they join us.
>
> Boundary Receiver: Great, I will invite them. Hopefully, they can help with the kids so we can enjoy a few date nights as well.
>
> Boundary Setter: That would be nice!

Examples of Discovery Questions and Family Boundaries

Discovery Questions:

- How come the kids know about our argument?
- Who gave the kids permission to go swimming?
- How come I'm the last one to find out we are hosting a family cookout this weekend?

Family Boundaries:

- I feel betrayed when the kids are caught in the middle and forced to choose sides during our disagreements. I value trust. How can we ensure the children are not involved in adult matters?
- I feel disrespected when the kids are given permission to do activities that we didn't agree upon together. I value mutual respect. Can we discuss the kid's extracurricular activities before giving them an answer?
- I think it's inconsiderate when family gatherings are planned without discussing them in advance. I value open communication. Can we include each other in the planning process for family gatherings?

EIGHTEEN

SIBLING BOUNDARIES

Violet and Hazel, a year apart, were inseparable. For the longest time, they ruled the roost together and were the center of their parents' world. Together, they dedicated countless hours to their studies, striving for straight As to earn their parents' admiration. That was until their parents welcomed their younger brothers, Grayson and Gabe, eight years later.

The arrival of their siblings turned their lives upside down. And, no matter how hard the sisters tried to seek their parents' attention, Violet and Hazel found themselves brushed aside. Even their exceptional achievements in gymnastic competitions and attempts to assist at home with their brothers went unnoticed. This caused their frustration to grow, which led them to stay up late and even skip school. Violet and Hazel were called to the principal's office on a few occasions for ditching, but their parents weren't alarmed by their rebellion.

As time passed, Violet and Hazel became jealous of how much time their parents dedicated to their brothers. It even got worse when Violet and Hazel decided to have a standoff and no longer ate dinner with the family. They insisted on their parents bringing their dinners to their room where they ate together.

Twenty years later, not much had changed between the four siblings as they went on their annual horseback riding retreat.

Prior to leaving for the trip, Violet called Hazel. "Hey, girl! Can't wait for this trip. How are you? Have you packed yet?

"Not yet. What are you taking?"

Violet sat on her bed staring at her closet. "Mostly riding clothes and a few casual outfits for sitting around the fire."

"Ditto! Have you talked to Gabe or Grayson yet?"

Violet shook her head. "Nope. Have you?"

Hazel jokingly said, "I haven't. We should really give it to them this week. Ha ha."

Violet twisted her ponytail as she pondered. "Okay. What did you have in mind?"

"Not sure. But I'll let you know once I have a plan!"

"Let's do this! See you soon." Violet hung up and began packing.

As the siblings arrived at the ranch with their spouses, they were greeted by their host and directed to their lodging accommodations.

The next day, they headed down to the barn to meet their horses. Violet and Hazel, who had grown up horseback riding, were saddled and ready to go before their brothers. Grayson and Gabe looked to the barn hand for assistance to get their horses saddled, even though they knew how to saddle up.

Violet started laughing as she walked out of the barn. "What's new? They still need everything done for them."

Hazel laughed along with Violet. "Right! It is just like when we were kids."

Violet snapped back, "Too bad Mom or Dad isn't here to help. Ha ha."

Grayson was getting annoyed. "Don't you two have anything better to do with your time?"

"Oh what, we can't tease you? You both were so spoiled growing up, and it shows years later. I can't imagine how things get done in your homes," Violet laughed shaking her head.

Grayson replied, "Leave our spouses out of this. And so what if Mom and Dad spoiled us? Are you jealous?"

Hazel chuckled to herself. "Ha, jealous of what? Of being dependent and helpless?"

Gabe decided to put in his two cents. "Geez. Are you guys really fighting about this? Seriously, we aren't kids anymore. Get over yourselves."

Violet continued to tease her brothers. "I guess some quarrels never go away, but at least we can saddle our horses."

Gabe sarcastically replied, "Oh did you want a blue ribbon for that?"

Violet responded sharply, "Nah, just for you and Grayson to acknowledge you never had to do anything growing up."

Hazel started to get antsy. "Anyways, let us know when you're ready to go. We will be out in the field waiting to head up the trails."

Grayson said, "Yep, we will be out in a bit. And this is the first and last fight I'm having on this trip. I'm not ruining my retreat."

After a few hours of riding, they reached the top of the mountain where they decided to break for lunch. They got off their horses and tied them to the posts.

While they began eating, Grayson realized he had forgotten his water bottle back at the cabin. Immediately, Hazel shouted out, "Ha, did you expect your wife or one of us to pack a water bottle for you?"

Grayson was fed up. "No, I didn't. Knock it off already."

Hazel smirked, "I just love giving you a hard time. It's too much fun."

"It's rather annoying and not even funny at this point," Grayson sternly replied.

Hazel belted out a huge laugh. "It is funny. Nothing has changed in twenty years. We used to do everything for you guys."

Grayson replied, "Okay, but we see you three times a year, and it's dumb to keep bickering like we are kids. Do you think we owe you for helping us?"

"I agree. It's getting old," Gabe expressed as he crossed his arms over his chest.

Violet jumped on her horse. "Okay, enough. Let's go ride!"

While we don't get to choose our family, we can choose our boundaries.

Insight

Growing up in the same home can lead to various childhood experiences, especially for siblings who may have encountered different parent-child relations. Over time, the growing sense of favoritism the parents showed Grayson and Gabe led to the sisters' rebellion. This can make it challenging for the siblings to form a healthy bond, often creating dysfunctional family dynamics.

As the sisters began competing for their parents' attention and love, it was continuously denied. This led the sisters to go from being overachievers in school to becoming disobedient – a reaction to their parents' emotional neglect. When children's basic needs are inconsistently met, they resort to ill behavior to seek attention, whether positive or negative. Violet and Hazel felt they no longer had a voice within the family, so they created their own alliance for emotional security.

With lingering childhood wounds that remained unresolved, the sisters carried their sibling rivalry well into adulthood. During their horseback riding retreat, the sisters displaced their feelings of parental betrayal onto Grayson and Gabe. Rather than expressing their concerns directly to their parents, they resorted to passive-aggressive remarks. With the sisters valuing independence, they continued to pass judgment on their brothers, who relied on others for support. Unfortunately, Violet and Hazel took their teasing to an extreme when they publicly undermined their brothers in front of their spouses, displaying a lack of mutual respect. Simultaneously, Grayson and Gabe struggled to comprehend the sisters' perspective, as they perceived the world through entirely different lenses. The lack of mutual understanding among the siblings only fueled their competitiveness and envy further.

The core of the sibling rivalry stemmed from the parents' failure to acknowledge their role in creating an imbalance within the parent-child relationships. As the parents favored the brothers over the sisters, they effectively dethroned the sisters, leaving them powerless within the family dynamic. Building healthy sibling relationships requires the ability to empathize and understand each sibling's perspective while respecting their individual differences and boundaries.

Definition of Sibling Boundaries

Sibling boundaries help establish mutual respect and clarity among siblings by defining acceptable or unacceptable behaviors. The specific types of boundaries may differ depending on the unique bond between each sibling and their personal values.

Sibling Rivalry

Sibling relationships can be unique depending on cultural norms, gender, age gaps, achievements, personal choices, where each child falls in the birth order, and what roles are modeled throughout the family's interactions. Siblings can be very close and have similar interests, whereas some may drift apart and become estranged after leaving the family home. While having a sibling can be the greatest experience, it can also wreak havoc on one's emotional health if siblings are unable to show mutual respect when resolving differences.

When raising children, parents may unintentionally treat their children differently during their prime developmental years. They may use favoritism, double standards, or different sets of guidelines for children, indirectly promoting sibling rivalry. This can lead to jealousy and envy when competing for their parents' attention or approval. Parents who don't encourage children to express their feelings constructively, establish respectful boundaries, or develop secure parent-child attachments can hinder the siblings' relationships.

Additionally, sibling rivalry or competitiveness can build up over the years and become continuous as each sibling tries to find their place within the family structure. One sibling may develop a superiority or inferiority personality type over another as a way of survival. This is often due to an insecure parent-child attachment. If this happens, sibling relationships can become strained leading to greater conflict in their interactions due to lack of self-esteem and trust within the home. Sibling rivalry may look like verbal arguments, name-calling, physical fights, or trying to one-up each other to win over their parents' admiration or to exert control.

When sibling personalities continue to clash throughout adulthood, it is often due to opposing belief systems and choosing to live out their childhood family dynamic. The unhealthy behavior stems from poor emotional regulation skills, past emotional wounds, or personality complexities. However, some siblings may decide to strengthen their relationships and become amicable as they evolve into adulthood. They find greater appreciation or acceptance of their differences and develop boundaries for emotional safety.

Signs a Sibling Relationship Needs Boundaries:

- Avoid taking responsibility for actions
- Engage in competition and strive to outdo each other
- Make critical or judgmental remarks about one another
- Resort to coercion to gain an advantage
- Hold on to past grudges or conflicts
- Undermine relationships with others
- Borrow money or belongings without returning them
- Neglect to provide support for successes or losses

- Engage in constant arguments with each other
- Monopolize conversations or activities
- Show a lack of trust or honesty

Sibling Support System

A close relationship with one or more siblings provides a built-in support system that is invaluable throughout life. Siblings can often understand each other, empathize with their shared experiences within the family home, and become trusted confidants. They tend to be more honest than friends, as they often know you better than anyone. Siblings can offer emotional and practical support, whether it's sharing advice, lending a shoulder to cry on, a listening ear, helping out during times of need, or sharing a good laugh when life becomes overwhelming.

Establishing boundaries early on in sibling relationships can reduce conflict or competitiveness by honoring each sibling's needs and values. This allows siblings to keep a close-knit bond with open communication while advocating for their independent values and life choices. Having a go-to person in your life who is reliable and trustworthy gives you peace of mind knowing you don't have to face challenges or stressors without support.

Types of Sibling Boundaries

- Respecting privacy with journals or personal messages
- Valuing each other's time
- Requesting borrowed items to be returned
- Asking for reimbursement of financial loans
- Communicating needs, feelings, or opinions
- Ensuring disagreements remain within the bounds of the sibling dynamic
- Abstaining from excessive texting and calling

- Respecting differences in personalities and viewpoints on life
- Refraining from criticizing or undermining each other in family group text messages
- Addressing favoritism and unfairness with parents
- Shutting down manipulative or abusive language
- Supporting each other during challenging times or achievements
- Knowing when to take a timeout to diffuse heightened emotion or arguments
- Showing empathy and understanding for personal experiences
- Disengaging from competitiveness or comparison
- Respecting each sibling's comfort level for physical affection or touch
- Knocking before entering bedrooms or bathrooms

Example of the Boundary Badass Method for Sibling Boundaries

ASAP: Assess *with discovery questions,* Set *a boundary,* Agree *to a mutual plan, and* Proceed *with accountability*

Step 1: **Assess** *with Discovery Questions*

Boundary Setter: How come we are talking about something that happened years ago?

Boundary Receiver: Oh, I'm just joking with you.

Step 2: **Set** *a Boundary*

Boundary Setter: I feel frustrated when we continue to repeat childhood issues that we had no control over. I value growth. How can we put this behind us and focus on our relationship today?

Step 3: **Agree** *to a Mutual Plan Using "I" statements and Discovery Questions*

Boundary Receiver: I agree. I'm tired of arguing and feeling misunderstood.

Boundary Setter: What are you feeling misunderstood about?

Boundary Receiver: It doesn't feel like you are able to see my perspective. I feel our conversations are one-sided and we can't see eye-to-eye.

Boundary Setter: We have had different perspectives our whole lives, and I doubt it will change now. I'm tired of being harassed about our parents' choices. Can we stop rehashing the past?

Boundary Receiver: Fair enough. I want to work on letting the past go and moving forward.

Step 4: **Proceed** *with Accountability*

Boundary Receiver: (The following month) Something has been on my mind, and I want to know if you have time to talk about it tonight. When are you free?

Boundary Setter: What's going on?

Boundary Receiver: I'm bothered there's favoritism going on again.

Boundary Setter: Can you share more?

Boundary Receiver: I spoke with Mom, and she told me she is helping you out financially. How come you keep the favoritism going?

(A boundary violation occurred – an indication it will need to be restated)

Boundary Setter: I needed help this month. How come you aren't sticking to our agreement?

Boundary Receiver: We did agree not to revisit the past. I shouldn't have overstepped.

Boundary Setter: Thank you for understanding. I will be paying them back.

Examples of Discovery Questions and Sibling Boundaries

Discovery Questions:

- When can I get my shirt back?
- How come I haven't received reimbursement for your flight?
- What was the reason for telling Mom/Dad about our argument?

Sibling Boundaries:

- I feel annoyed when there is little regard for borrowing and returning my shirt. I value integrity. Can we agree on a timeframe for returning borrowed belongings?
- I feel taken advantage of when I haven't been reimbursed for the flight. I value integrity. Can we create a plan for reimbursements?
- I feel betrayed when our parents are asked to take sides during our disagreements. I value trust. How can we keep our disagreements between us?

NINETEEN
CHILDREN BOUNDARIES

Madeline was extremely excited to celebrate her eighth birthday with family and friends. All she could think about was getting her new pink unicorn bike so she could zip around the neighborhood with her older brother Cameron. She was in awe of everything he did and wanted to be just like him. And, while Cameron found Madeline to be a bit annoying at times, he was a good sport and let her tag along with him and his friends.

Bethany, their mother, was busy preparing for Madeline's birthday party Saturday morning when she noticed the backyard still wasn't set up. She had stayed awake until midnight, tirelessly baking and decorating the unicorn cupcakes that Madeline had eagerly requested. Completely drained and struggling to keep her eyes open, Bethany dragged herself toward the backyard. One by one, she began placing the chairs, determined to ensure that Madeline's day would be nothing short of special.

Bethany had sent out invitations to thirty guests, which included extended family members and Madeline's close friends from the neighborhood. Madeline, naturally reserved and uneasy in large social settings, presented a challenge for Bethany, who was determined to make everyone feel included. Deliberately, Bethany decided not to share the guest list with Madeline in the hopes of preventing any potential emotional distress. While Madeline felt completely at ease around her immediate family and grandparents, she had concerns about interacting with extended relatives and neighbors, especially when it came to receiving hugs.

It was 3:45 p.m. when the kids from the neighborhood started to show up for the party. They all carried in their birthday gifts and began grabbing snacks and party favors from the kitchen island. Bethany made sure she included all of Madeline's favorites in the goody bags.

As the kids filled up on snacks, they ran to the backyard to play hide-and-seek. They divided up into two teams of five and began to hide. After an hour went by, the kids sprinted back into the house to get cold drinks. When they got back inside, Madeline began sipping her juice box. Standing in the middle of the room frozen in panic, her eyes swelled up and she burst into tears. She stared around the room looking at everyone who was there. Embarrassed in front of her friends, she ran upstairs to her room and slammed the door shut.

Bethany ran upstairs to Madeline's room and asked her to open the door. Madeline refused. So, Bethany picked the lock with a bobby pin and sat on Madeline's bed so she could talk to her. Madeline was crying hysterically.

Madeline screamed, "Leave me alone."

Bethany leaned over and tried to hug her. "How come you are crying?"

Madeline wiped her tears. "There are too many people, and I don't like it."

"I'm sorry, Madeline. I thought it was okay since it was your birthday," Bethany expressed with guilt.

Madeline anxiously said, "Please leave. I want to be alone and play in my room."

A couple of hours passed, and Madeline had yet to come out of her room. The guests continued to mingle and carry on at the party as if everything was normal. Bethany was not sure if any of the adults even realized Madeline was in her room, but the kids from the neighborhood did since she no longer wanted to play.

It was finally time to sing "Happy Birthday" to Madeline. Her father, Steve, headed up to Madeline's room to see if he could talk her into coming downstairs. "Madeline, can I come in?"

Madeline mumbled softly, "Yes."

"It's time to sing 'Happy Birthday' and blow out your candles. Do you want to come down?"

Madeline resentfully looked up at her dad. "Who invited all these people?"

Steve said, "I don't know why Mommy and Daddy didn't tell you. We are sorry and should have asked you before inviting this many people."

Madeline focused on the game she was playing, "Well, I don't like it."

Steve compassionately asked, "I know, but will you come down so we can sing to you at least?"

Madeline paused and thought for a second. "Yes, as long as no one hugs or kisses me on the cheek afterward. It's so gross. I just want to play."

"Okay, deal. I'll make sure no one kisses or hugs you after we sing, and you can go play with your friends."

Ultimatums create defiance; healthy boundaries create alliance.

Insight

Madeline felt extremely uncomfortable and anxious around large family gatherings due to sensory overload. Despite Madeline's sensitivities, her parents kept to their agenda without considering Madeline's limits. Hosting a big birthday bash breached Madeline's physical boundaries, causing her to feel unsafe and unheard.

Upon realizing that the entire house was filled with guests, Madeline became emotionally triggered and ran to hide in her room. As Madeline sought safety, Bethany created another boundary violation by entering her room without permission, forgoing Madeline's need for personal space. While this can be a challenging situation for any parent, having awareness of a child's limits and respecting their comfort level helps prevent unwarranted situations.

When a child's boundaries are ignored, it not only hinders the parent-child relationship, but also silences the child's inner voice. If a child's voice is repeatedly silenced, they may develop emotional wounds and limiting beliefs that don't support their best self. Children are highly impressionable and will learn coping mechanisms to protect themselves from the pain of being ignored, humiliated, or disrespected. In Madeline's case, she could develop a flight trauma response to escape uncomfortable situations if her parents continued to dismiss her boundaries.

Disregarding a child's boundaries, like Madeline's, can create a profound sense of emotional distress, not only within the home but also in other environments. This can trigger a range of adverse behaviors as the child tries to cope with these overwhelming emotions. These behaviors may include seeking isolation in their room for safety, resorting to lies as a form of emotional security, experiencing physical symptoms like stomachaches, suffering from recurring nightmares, having emotional outbursts, or even expressing a desire to run away. While children may not be able to make all their life decisions or articulate their feelings at a young age, they do deserve to have boundaries. A child may be perceived as naive or ill-equipped to regulate emotions, but it does not give anyone permission to disregard their comfort zone, perspective, or boundaries.

Definition of Children Boundaries

Children boundaries establish personal safety and security while learning to trust choices that benefit their psychological, emotional, and physical well-being. By defining limits, children attain a clear understanding of their own comfort zones, supporting their growth and nurturing their self-identity.

A Child's Individuality

Recognizing a child's individuality and curiosity is essential to their development. It's important to understand that a parent's aspirations might not correspond with the child's interests or beliefs. At times, a child might resist taking part in extracurricular activities or wearing a specific outfit, while you hold the belief that it's in their best interest. Do you enforce your decision upon them, going against their wishes to fulfill your expectations, or do you honor their unique preferences? Overlooking a child's need for self-expression infringes upon their boundaries and individuality.

Children are not meant to live out their parent's wishes or unfulfilled life goals. Every child deserves to have a voice when it comes to deciding what types of activities and hobbies best suit them, how they want to wear their hair, what style of clothing makes them feel good, and who they want to have relationships with, as long as their choices do not cause mental or physical harm to themselves or others. Respecting your child's personal preferences honors the connection with your child while creating trust and mutual understanding. Accepting your child for who they are can establish a healthy relationship with them.

When it comes to forcing a child to do something against their desires, outside of beneficial fundamentals like school work, eating healthy, cleaning their room, respectful manners, personal hygiene, etc., it can be emotionally unhealthy and traumatizing for them. When a child is expected to do something that violates their limits, they are bound to establish new worries or fears. They may feel the need to tell lies or stories as to why they don't want to participate in something because saying no isn't good enough. A child may even fake illness, like an upset stomach or headache, to avoid a situation that causes more discomfort to their nervous system. Over time, their fears can build up, causing a child to resent a parent, feel unworthy about who they are, or fear they will be punished for not meeting their parent's expectations. As a result, it can set a child up for failure in their adult relationships due to the absence of emotional support and the kind of secure attachment children need from their parents.

If a parent or caregiver continuously oversteps a child's boundaries, then the child can develop a false sense of self. When one's self-worth and personal identity are underdeveloped, it can potentially lead to suffering from deeply rooted insecurities, unhealthy coping mechanisms, experiencing shame, struggling with vulnerability, and feeling voiceless in relationships. As an individual transitions from childhood to adulthood, they may unknowingly seek out unhealthy adult relationships that mirror the unhealthy parent-child dynamic, thereby blurring boundaries. Additionally, they may crave external validation and indulge in vices that temporarily fulfill an internal void stemming from unaddressed childhood issues.

Child's Physical Limits

When it comes to physical touch, it's crucial to recognize it as a personal choice. Expecting a child to engage in physical interactions that make them uncomfortable can convey a message that their boundaries are not valuable. From a parental perspective, it may seem like the child is being uncooperative or disrespectful. However, it's important to understand that children begin to learn about boundaries in their first few years of life. If a child is pressured to hug, kiss, or shake hands when they're uncomfortable, it can undermine their sense of respect and limits for personal space and body autonomy. This can result in children feeling unsafe or voiceless, particularly in environments where they should feel protected by their parents. When children aren't taught the importance of their physical boundaries within the home, it can lead to poor boundaries outside the home.

Encouraging children to make healthy choices regarding their physical limits without the fear of judgment or potential consequences establishes self-trust and self-advocacy. This promotes the development of healthy relationships and diminishes the likelihood of unwarranted physical or sexual abuse, both in childhood and adulthood. Teaching children about the significance of physical boundaries is vital to ensuring their well-being, nurturing their self-esteem, and fostering a foundation of respect that will continue to influence their relationships throughout their lives.

Child's Emotional Limits

Children reveal their personal boundaries and values through the narratives they share during everyday moments, whether it's around the dinner table, after school, or during interactive play. Often a child will be open about their feelings when describing a character in a movie or book, the pictures they draw, or when talking about their best friend. By gaining insight into their inner world, you can better understand their level of comfortability, emotions, and thoughts. Every child is unique and will have a different emotional capacity for their needs and limits. Being attuned to their emotional needs creates a safe space for open communication to establish a secure attachment and trust. If a child does not feel they can trust their parent or caregiver, they will withdraw or withhold their thoughts and feelings. Trust is established in the first two years of life between parent-child, yet it can be broken in a split second when their emotional needs are not met.

If a child is unable to verbally express themselves and their boundaries, they may tell you through nonverbal behaviors about what makes them feel safe and secure, or adversely unsafe. An innocent child is less likely to reject someone unless they have reasonable cause. Children are very perceptive and pick up on the slightest behaviors or interactions that are modeled in their homes or environments. The majority of the time, children don't learn from what their parents say but by watching what they do. When you notice a child experiencing discomfort, it is important to assess their emotional expression through discovery questions, provide words of encouragement and safety, and validate their feelings. When safety or security is absent, a child may feel unsafe and begin to develop defensive coping mechanisms. These coping strategies, also known as trauma responses, are implemented to protect oneself from future distress.

Phrases That Support a Child's Safety and Security:

- "I love you, no matter what"
- "You are safe and I'm here to protect you"
- "I believe in you and in your abilities"
- "You are important and your feelings matter"
- "I'm here to listen, even when things feel tough"

Children Boundaries versus Household Rules

Children boundaries uphold the mentality that all family members are treated respectfully regardless of age. When establishing family boundaries for healthy functioning, it's best to establish a value system that collectively honors each family member's values. Developing family values creates a roadmap to setting boundaries and promoting flexibility within the home, implementing an *authoritative parenting style*. Establishing healthy routines and boundaries for children gives them a sense of clarity and the ability to manage themselves with freedom within those limits.

On the contrary, strict household rules are generally fear-based, controlling, and often demanding, which can lead to ongoing problematic situations within and outside of the home, creating parent-child power struggles. The parent usually has an *authoritarian parenting style* with the mentality of "You will do as I say without question." In this case, the rules are very black and white, and the child has no voice if the parent demands something that causes them distress. This results in a parent-child disconnection because the parent has little respect for the child's limits or needs and has failed to understand the child from their perspective. Instead, the parent is projecting their beliefs onto the child.

Parentification of Child

A role reversal can occur when a parent is personally struggling in their life and is unable to care for themselves or their children. Parentification may be present in homes where there is a single-parent family, an uninvolved parent, generational trauma, or a form of abuse (substance, psychological, or emotional). The reversal occurs when a child is forced to grow up too quickly due to carrying the emotional or physical burden of adult issues and life responsibilities. The child will comply to minimize conflict or disappointment and seek parental approval. Parentification looks like a child being responsible for paying bills, managing household duties, playing referee between parental arguments, watching inappropriate television, exposing them to unhealthy environments, and serving as a parent's confidante.

When a child is overly responsible at a young age or exposed to circumstances that are not age-appropriate, the child suppresses their needs and feelings. The child feels an obligation to care for and prioritize their parents or siblings over their own needs by being their emotional support system or physical caregiver. A parentified child can have a long-term effect on their development, leading to emotional regression later in life, severe anxiety or depression, a sense of entitlement, inability to trust, self-isolation, the inability to experience joy or pleasure, trauma-bonded relationships, confusion regarding their sense of self, ultra-independence, people-pleasing habits, and poor boundaries.

Teenager Boundaries

During adolescence, it can be hard for teens to manage their hormonal fluctuations, resist social peer pressure, and understand their independence as they mature. When teenagers become distressed due to a lack of acceptance or respect, they can take extreme measures compared to younger children. Teenagers may escape the emotional burden by threatening to run away, using substances to numb emotional agony, or engaging in activities without understanding the consequences and how they can negatively impact their lives.

Helping teenagers navigate their decision-making processes is a great way to develop their critical-thinking skills and boundaries while also respecting their need for independence and exploration of life experiences. If a parent or caregiver is resistant to understanding a teenager's personal boundaries, they are more likely to rebel or seek external support outside the home that may not align with their personal values. By striking a balance between firmness and flexibility, parents can help their teenagers navigate this transitional stage of life.

For teenagers, it is important to involve them in the process of establishing boundaries and negotiating consequences for any adverse behavior. This may look like signing boundary contracts for responsibilities, such as curfew times or vehicle usage, to hold them accountable for behavior. By including teens in these open discussions, they have the opportunity to learn vital lessons in regard to accountability and integrity of their actions without judgment. When both the parent and the adolescent reach a mutual understanding and agreement on these boundaries, there is a higher likelihood that these limits will be respected and upheld through cooperation.

Furthermore, this collaborative approach teaches essential life skills to teenagers and encourages them to utilize their inner voice, gain self-awareness, and make healthy choices. It also helps them develop the ability to advocate for their freedoms while simultaneously demonstrating respect for their parents and themselves. As teenagers continue to evolve and the family dynamic shifts based on new responsibilities, these boundaries may naturally evolve over time. Ultimately, by actively engaging in the process of setting boundaries with teenagers, parents can guide them through this period of self-discovery, encouraging their growth and development into responsible, self-aware individuals.

Types of Children Boundaries

- Respecting a child's privacy and personal alone time
- Listening to a child's feelings and perspectives without judgment
- Allowing a child to enter social situations at their own pace
- Honoring a child's body autonomy
- Refraining from displacing adult problems onto children
- Allowing children to share input on family activities
- Avoiding overly rigid rules
- Respecting a child's comfort level for physical affection or touch
- Honoring a child's voice and input on age-appropriate consequences
- Refraining from sharing sensitive matters with extended family
- Treating all children fairly within the home
- Avoiding the use of children as weapons or exploitation
- Accepting a child's uniqueness and individuality
- Respecting age-appropriate bathing with siblings or parents
- Providing a child with their own sleeping quarters separate from parents
- Establishing time limits for electronic usage, curfew, bedtime, etc.
- Respecting a child's choice for extracurricular activities and interests
- Balancing family values and each child's values
- Refraining from using children as an emotional support system

- Abstaining from exposure to endangering environments or unsafe individuals
- Reducing the risk of parentification

Example of the Boundary Badass Method for Children Boundaries

ASAP: Assess with discovery questions, Set a boundary, Agree to a mutual plan, and Proceed with accountability

Step 1: **Assess** *with Discovery Questions*

Boundary Setter: How come there are so many people here?

Boundary Receiver: It's your birthday party and we invited everyone.

Step 2: **Set** *a Boundary (The method is modified for age-appropriate language)*

Boundary Setter: I feel anxious when too many people are at the house. I am going to my room. I need space.

Step 3: **Agree** *to a Mutual Plan Using "I" statements and Discovery Questions*

Boundary Receiver: How come you want to go to your room?

Boundary Setter: (Child begins to cry)

Boundary Receiver: What would you like me to do?

Boundary Setter: I want to be alone. Don't invite this many people ever again!

Boundary Receiver: I understand this many people can be overwhelming. Next time we will talk about what you're comfortable with before sending out invitations. How about I let you know when it's time to open gifts?

Boundary Setter: Fine.

Boundary Receiver: I'm sorry. I'll come to check on you in a bit.

Step 4: **Proceed** *with Accountability*

Boundary Receiver: (Next home gathering) We are having friends over for a dinner party next weekend. What are your thoughts about going to your grandparents or staying here?

Boundary Setter: I don't care. I guess I can go to my grandparents.

Boundary Receiver: Are you sure?

Boundary Setter: I'm sure. I feel safe there.

Boundary Receiver: Okay, I'll let them know. I love you!

Boundary Setter: I love you too!

Examples of Discovery Questions and Children Boundaries

Discovery Questions:

- Can you please not touch me?
- Can I stay home today?
- How come I can't have my phone?

Children Boundaries:

- I don't like to be touched. Please stop.
- I don't feel like going to school when everyone is mean to me. Can I switch classes?
- I feel left out when I can't talk to my friends. Can I have more phone time?

TWENTY

DIVORCE, CO-PARENTING, AND BLENDED FAMILY BOUNDARIES

Following Noah and Grace's divorce, Grace met Charles on a business trip, and the two immediately hit it off. They dated long-distance for some time, but it started to become a strain on their connection. A year later, Grace made the huge decision to pick up her life and move from the West Coast to out East to be with Charles. At the time, Grace and Noah had equal shared parenting time; however, moving cross country created a dilemma in their parenting agreement. Neither parent wanted to give up time with their son, but they were willing to work with each other to make the best of it. Ryder was only four at the time, and Noah felt living with Grace was Ryder's best option for giving him a stable home environment since Noah traveled weekly for work. Noah, left without other options, agreed to have Ryder solely for the summers and one weekend a month.

A few months after Grace and Ryder moved away, Noah unexpectedly eloped with Celine. She had a daughter from a previous relationship and the three of them started their new family. Having a child in the home all the time made Noah start to miss Ryder more and more. Noah immediately regretted modifying the parenting agreement with Grace, but he didn't want to think about it with his summer visitation approaching. He knew it was his time to bond with Ryder, and he couldn't wait to introduce him to his new sister, Serena.

Upon arriving at his dad's home for the summer, Ryder felt a sense of unease as he discovered he would now have to share his father's attention with his new sister full-time. He wasn't used to having a sibling and enjoyed having his dad all to himself. To ease the blending of their family, Noah figured it would be best for everyone to head to their lake cabin for quality family time. He planned their entire summer with fun activities to keep Ryder and Serena entertained while adjusting to their new sibling relationship. The kids couldn't have been more excited about fishing on the dock and riding their bikes around town.

About four weeks into the summer, Noah noticed Ryder was getting comfortable with his new sister, and they were spending a lot of time together. The kids would race to eat breakfast and see who would finish first so they could go fishing. Noah and Celine were thrilled to see their bond was growing stronger by the day. It was almost as if they had grown up together in the same house.

The end of summer had arrived before they knew it. It was the night before Ryder's flight back to the East Coast, and Noah and Celine decided to have a cookout with their neighborhood friends. Ryder and Serena were having a blast with the other kids and started a water balloon fight. While Noah was filling up water balloons, Celine could tell something was on his mind by his somber expression. He said he was sad about Ryder leaving the next day, and he wished he had never agreed to Grace relocating him. Celine consoled Noah and told him he should consider talking to Grace about Ryder living with them full-time during the school year instead of the summer months.

A week after Ryder returned to the East Coast, Noah sent an email to Grace to discuss Ryder's education and to ask about updating their parenting agreement to adjust their parenting time. Grace was completely shocked by Noah's email. She immediately told him the idea was off the table without any consideration. This left Noah angry because he wanted more time with his son. Celine was also upset by Grace's response and felt Noah's agony. She decided she would send an email to Grace on Noah's behalf without telling him. Celine suggested that she and Grace get to know each other, hoping it would change her mind about Ryder living with his dad.

Grace blatantly ignored Celine's email at first and was appalled Noah would even let her be a part of their co-parenting relationship. The thought of Celine being Ryder's motherly figure most of the year left her feeling betrayed.

Another week went by, and Grace was still silent. Noah and Celine became frustrated because they wanted an answer. Finally, Grace responded to Noah again saying she could not wrap her head around the idea of updating their parenting plan. They had already agreed on Ryder's home life during the school year and summer months.

Noah felt heartbroken about not being able to raise his only son. He did not want things to get out of hand between him and Grace, but he could not let go of the pain he was feeling. He was struggling to find a solution on how he could make Grace see this was to benefit Ryder's well-being.

As Noah sat in his living room chair, he sent a text to Grace asking her to hop on a call, but she declined. Celine couldn't take how heavy-hearted Noah was and secretly decided to send Grace another email. This pushed Grace to become more resistant, as she felt they were both trying to monopolize the situation.

Eventually, another month went by before Grace decided to respond to Noah's request and set up a time to talk. He called Grace immediately, as she suggested in her email, but she did not pick up. He was annoyed with Grace. Noah was beginning to think she was taking him on a wild goose chase. Noah sent Grace another email.

Grace,

I'm trying to work with you on this issue and you continue to ignore my call after you set the time. Call me back so we can get this resolved. Thanks.

Grace walked in the door after work and threw down her bags with complete exhaustion. Charles could tell something was wrong because it was written all over her face. She explained to Charles what was happening via text message since Ryder was in the room and she didn't want him to be stuck in the middle of their co-parenting matters. Grace asked Charles what he thought about the whole situation. Charles said it was not his decision and told Grace it was up to her to decide and he would support her either way.

Grace sat in her home office and began anxiously flipping through their parenting plan. The thought of losing her son for most of the year terrified her. She got up to close the door and dialed Noah back, hoping to get his voicemail, but he picked up.

Noah angrily spoke, "I do not appreciate you ignoring my calls, especially regarding Ryder. How can you be a mother and work all the time?"

Grace aggressively put in her two cents. "Do not worry about how I manage it all; that isn't your concern. I really think Ryder should continue to live with me during the school year. You travel non-stop for work. So, Celine would have him versus one of his biological parents. It doesn't make sense to me."

"I am trying to travel less for work. This is something I have been trying to change for a while now so I can spend more time at home," Noah responded.

Grace grew more frustrated. "Of course, you want to stay home more now. If only you did that while we were married. Anyway, I am not here to fight with you. I do not see the point of making such a drastic change to Ryder's life. He is happy here with me and Charles. And please tell Celine to stop emailing me."

"And, he will be happy here too. I wasn't aware she had emailed you. But, I do know she would like to get to know you since she will be a part of his life."

Noah realized things were not going to end well on the call and asked Grace to think about it. Even if they could try it for a year or two, it would be worth it to Noah. He knew Ryder would have a stable home life with him, his stepmom, and his sister. He told Grace she could come and visit anytime and he would accommodate her expenses while visiting. However, no matter how hard he tried to work with Grace, he was left without answers.

Setting boundaries works best when using facts and refraining from personal attacks.

Insight

Noah and Grace wanted to do what was best for Ryder, but their heightened emotions hindered their ability to effectively communicate co-parenting decisions. Upon Noah's request to update their parenting schedule, Grace became emotionally avoidant and ignored him. As Noah and Celine pressed for answers, this pushed Grace further into a freeze response. Grace felt voiceless when pressured for answers, which led to her abandoning the scheduled phone call. When an individual forgoes their integrity, they allow their emotions to overpower their decision-making process and potentially hinder their value. This is a sign of poor emotional regulation and a lack of personal boundaries.

Regarding Grace and Noah's communication, both presented inadequate conflict resolution skills, which eventually led to an impasse. Grace opted for silence and neglected to express her need for more time to contemplate Noah's request. Conversely, Noah repeatedly invaded her personal space by sending numerous messages. He lacked self-awareness regarding how his request might have caught Grace by surprise and how he unintentionally pressured her with such a significant decision. This situation threw them into an emotional whirlwind, as neither knew how to assertively communicate in Ryder's best interest. Once on the call, they both resorted to attacking each other's personal lifestyle choices and cycling back into old marital discord. This fueled a power struggle rather than establishing co-parenting communication boundaries to reduce triggering each other.

In an attempt to get Grace to respond, Celine, Noah's wife, overstepped her role as Ryder's stepmother when she reached out to Grace about Ryder living with them. While Celine may have good intentions, when one household tries to exert power over the other household, this can cause tension or feel like manipulation. Additionally, the communication mishap could have dampened Celine's trust with Noah since she emailed Grace without consulting Noah first. Sometimes this can leave stepparents, like Celine, without a voice regarding the co-parenting relationship and often wreak havoc on a new marital relationship. This is why blended family boundaries are a necessity so everyone feels respected.

As for new sibling relationships, they can take time to evolve. While Ryder felt apprehensive about sharing his father with his stepsister, this is common in blended families as every child is trying to find their role within the new family structure. When children become part of a blended family, it is vital the parents give the children time to adjust and accept each other while also encouraging positive bonding time as a family. Furthermore, it will be essential for each child to have time with their biological parent and not feel rejected or abandoned in the new family structure.

Definition of Divorce, Co-Parenting, & Blended Family Boundaries

Divorce, co-parenting, & blended family boundaries are child-centered agreements that focus on the development and well-being of children. These agreements prioritize safety, consistency, and stability across multiple households while defining each family member's role, responsibilities, and values within the family dynamics.

Transitioning from Divorce to Co-Parenting

Divorce boundaries are beneficial for both parents and children when establishing a respectful co-parenting relationship. After a couple dissolves their marriage, their co-parenting relationship is no longer about past emotional wounds or a competitive game of trying to outdo the other parent. The relationship becomes more business-like with each co-parent solely investing in the raising of their children. Placing the children's needs first can streamline communication and reduce emotion, allowing the co-parents to heal and move forward. If each co-parent continues to share personal details about their new lifestyle choices or attack each other's parenting style, the emotional attachment will stay intact, creating tension that can become displaced onto the children.

While communication styles can greatly differ, especially in cases involving high-conflict co-parenting, it's advisable to maintain minimal communication and focus on keeping the discussions child-centered. Limiting communication serves to reduce the chances of unnecessary conflicts and helps prevent manipulation from taking place. If both parents fail to establish and uphold boundaries and instead operate out of fear, power struggles are likely to persist throughout the co-parenting relationship. Unfortunately, when poor boundaries are present, it's the children who end up shouldering the emotional burden. Children aren't fully equipped with the coping skills to handle adult problems; rather than verbally expressing their feelings, they often show distress through unfavorable behaviors.

If you and your co-parent are unable to keep communication child-centered, then text messaging or in-person co-parenting interactions may not be in your best interest. Other communication resources, such as co-parenting apps or sending weekly emails, can keep you and your co-parent up-to-date on education, extracurricular activities, medical decisions, and child development. This can offer a smooth transition for communication while redefining your relationship from a romantic to a platonic one.

Keeping Children out of the Middle

When going through a divorce or separation, establishing a parenting plan to meet the needs of the children is necessary to keep both parents on the same page and accountable for their parental responsibilities. A parenting plan, a legally binding agreement, will establish provisions and stipulations for medical and mental health, education, communication channels, travel itineraries, holiday schedules, parenting time, extracurricular activities, relocation, and much more. A well-executed parenting plan should be accustomed to your family and have firm boundaries between you and your co-parent to protect the mental, physical, psychological, and emotional safety of the children. As the children develop with evolving needs, or there is a significant change in one parent's life, the parenting plan may require adjustments.

To protect children's innocence, it is crucial not to share adult information with children and expect them to relay it to their other parent. Asking children to become the messenger for the co-parenting relationship can make them feel like they have to choose sides or be the peacekeeper. It can be emotionally draining and damaging to a child's mental health, potentially leading to behavioral concerns and trauma responses. Even the simplest actions like, "Let your Dad/Mom know I'll be at your parent-teacher conference" can leave a lasting imprint on the child. While a child may not show signs of emotional distress, children are wise beyond their years and are perceptive when there is tension in their environment. However, it's unlikely you will see resistance from your child, as they will deliver the message out of fear of punishment or letting you down. A child in this predicament will often stay voiceless to appease each parent while forgoing their own needs and boundaries.

When children are forced to appease their parent's emotional state, this is known as parentification. Parentification develops when a child is neglected and forced to take on an adult role. They unwillingly take on the role of caretaker for younger siblings or become the referee between their parent's arguments. When parents aren't able to fully show up for themselves, children get placed into developmentally inappropriate situations. It can result in self-abandonment, difficulty setting boundaries, anxiety, depression, need for control, and choosing romantic partners or friends they have to care for in their adolescent or adult relationships.

A co-parent who puts their children in the middle is often emotionally dysregulated or has personality complexities. They may weaponize the children against their co-parent by projecting their own inferiority complex and struggles onto the child out of fear of abandonment or rejection. This behavior stems from their inability to let go of the power struggles that existed during their marriage or their own unresolved traumas. This makes the child feel powerless in that they must oblige with their parent, developing a fear mindset within the child.

When tension is heightened, children may experience extreme fears or worries, as they feel torn about whether they can talk about their other biological parent while residing in the opposite home. Forcing a child to feel like they have to choose one parent over the other creates internal conflict for the child. A child may be afraid to speak up about their beliefs or feelings about their other biological parent out of fear of disappointing the parent they are spending time with.

Children who feel stuck as peacemakers can learn unfavorable habits like lying, suppressing their emotions, the inability to trust either parent, perfectionism, self-isolation, and people-pleasing. They live in a constant state of fear, seeking each parent's approval while experiencing a toxic cycle of emotional and psychological abuse. Children who don't feel safe voicing their honest feelings or thoughts can struggle with developing healthy self-esteem, self-worth, and identity.

New Partners and Stepparents

It can feel like a balancing act as everyone tries to find their place in the family household. However, establishing healthy boundaries for each individual's role within the family can help ensure a harmonious environment. Introducing new parental figures can often bring about new family dynamics, which can be rewarding and stressful all at once.

Before introducing new partners, ensuring safety and security within the parent-child relationship is imperative for children. It lets them know they can trust you and that you have their best interests at heart. Introducing a significant other too soon into the children's lives can impact the fundamentals of trust and love, resulting in lifelong complications for the children's understanding of healthy love and attachment style.

Once the children have met the new partner, it will be vital to assess your children's feelings and reactions. At times, a child can feel rejected or replaced by their biological parent who is introducing a new partner into their life. They may express difficulties with sharing their parent or coming to terms with a new parental figure. It can lead to instability in the home and create trust issues with your children if not done in a gradual manner. Ideally, a minimum of six months to a year of committed dating is advised prior to introducing them to the children.

New partners may evolve into stepparents, which can be a great addition to raising children and managing the household. However, it's important to identify their role in their stepchildren's lives to lessen the uncertainty. It will look different from one household to the next, including the level of involvement a stepparent will have based on the children's needs. While a stepparent may be greatly involved in the children's lives, major parental decisions or disciplining the children is best left up to the biological parents.

When a stepparent attempts to take on a disciplinary role in a child's life, this can create tension between the stepparent and the child, or in the co-parenting relationship. With the children having to adjust to the transition between two homes, experiencing the grief of their parent's divorce, accepting new siblings, or potentially switching schools, it can be exceptionally hard to have another parent also telling them how to behave. Being a stepparent requires a fine line of positive emotional support and guidance for the children while also remaining an adult figure in the children's lives for security and safety.

Accepting Each Child for Who They Are

Building a new family structure is not an easy feat when collectively respecting everyone's belief systems. While it can be difficult to balance what works for everyone, it's important to remember each child is an individual with their own needs, emotions, experiences, and values. One of the best things you can do for your new family is to accept each child for who they are and not force them to become like their step-siblings and half-siblings. This means respecting their boundaries, listening to their concerns, and being flexible in your parenting approach. Creating an atmosphere of acceptance and trust makes each family member feel supported and allows for healthy engagement.

When children don't feel respected, valued, or accepted, they may act out in ways that seem oppositional or atypical to their standard behavior. This can be a sign of emotional distress or looking to find their place within the family dynamic because they are struggling to adapt to the new family structure. Spending quality time with each child can help parents gain insight into their child's internal world and build deeper connections. The more a parent or stepparent understands a child's beliefs and values, the easier it will be to meet their needs.

Additionally, it can be tough for a child to share a parent with new siblings. The child may feel rejected or have a sense of entitlement to their parent, creating sibling rivalry. Understanding each child and how they prefer to receive love can help each child feel secure within the family. This creates a personalized approach for each child, helping everyone adjust more effectively to the new family unit.

Keeping Siblings Together

Separating children when going through a divorce or separation can have long-term negative effects and goes against the best interests of the children. Divorce is already a significant change in children's lives, and separating siblings can intensify their emotional distress by creating a second division. Keeping siblings together allows them to maintain a sense of familiarity and consistency when going back and forth between two homes. When siblings share a strong bond, separating them from each other can disrupt their security and their ability to cope with the changes brought about by the dissolution of the marriage.

Siblings can provide each other with emotional support while transitioning from home to home during the divorce process since they share similar feelings. Separating siblings can be traumatic, especially for younger children because they may carry the weight of self-blame for the divorce. Children who are separated from their siblings may experience grief, anger, and confusion, which can lead to behavioral and emotional problems. When they lose this crucial support system, they can experience bouts of loneliness or isolation. This can have a detrimental impact on their mental health, physical well-being, school performance, and social engagement.

Additionally, separating siblings can lead to a breakdown in their relationships, making it harder for them to reconnect later in life. When they are separated for parenting time, they are unable to create new memories and may feel a sense of loss for their shared experiences, holidays, and quality bonding time. This can also create a greater divide and lead to long-lasting sibling rivalry due to favoritism.

Not only is the sibling relationship impacted, but so are the parent-child relationships. Separating children may further distance them from one or both parents because they feel forced to take sides or feel abandoned by one parent. By keeping children together, it's easier for both parents to maintain ongoing relationships and actively participate in their children's lives. Keeping children together simplifies these logistical aspects of visitation schedules and promotes more efficient co-parenting.

Types of Divorce, Co-Parenting, & Blended Family Boundaries

- Communicating with a children-centered approach
- Leaving disciplinary decisions up to legal guardians or parents
- Respecting each family member's need for personal space
- Reserving the titles "Mom" and "Dad" for biological parents
- Allowing children to develop new relationships with family members at their own pace
- Abiding by a mutually agreed parenting plan
- Treating all children fairly and uniquely for who they are
- Redefining relationships with extended family and friends associated with the ex-partner
- Establishing a co-parenting communication plan and platform
- Refraining from undermining, devaluing, or slandering parental figures
- Establishing communication guidelines for parent-child calls
- Respecting the children's belongings transferred between two homes
- Setting a timeline prior to introducing new partners

- Protecting the privacy of your new lifestyle and relationships
- Avoiding the discussion of adult problems in front of the children
- Discussing financial decisions in advance prior to purchases
- Refraining from using children as an emotional support system
- Abstaining from withholding or weaponizing the children
- Arriving promptly for pick-up and drop-off on transition days
- Sharing child's travel itinerary, flight, and hotel accommodations with co-parent
- Respecting each parent's attendance at extracurricular activities
- Notifying co-parent of medical, dental, and mental health appointments
- Giving advance notice for changes to the parenting time schedule
- Refraining from making children messengers with the co-parent
- Balancing the blended and co-parent boundaries simultaneously

Example of the Boundary Badass Method for Divorce, Co-Parenting, and Blended Family Boundaries

ASAP: Assess with discovery questions, Set a boundary, Agree to a mutual plan, and Proceed with accountability

Step 1: **Assess** *with Discovery Questions*

Boundary Setter: How come I received an email from your significant other?

Boundary Receiver: I wasn't aware she emailed you.

Step 2: **Set** *a Boundary (Professional boundary method for co-parenting and blended families)*

Boundary Setter: It seems intrusive when significant others intervene in our co-parenting decisions. I value trust. Can we keep the decision-making between us?

Step 3: **Agree** *to a Mutual Plan Using "I" statements and Discovery Questions*

Boundary Receiver: How did I break your trust?

Boundary Setter: By allowing Celine to email me about our son. When did we decide significant others could be a part of our co-parenting?

Boundary Receiver: We haven't discussed this. I believe she was trying to be helpful because you hadn't replied to my email. However, I understand where you are coming from and agree all parenting decisions for our son should remain between us.

Boundary Setter: I'm glad we are on the same page now. I needed time to collect my thoughts, but I will try to respond sooner next time.

Boundary Receiver: Thank you. I appreciate keeping the lines of communication open.

Step 4: **Proceed** *with Accountability*

Boundary Setter: (The following month) I think it would be great for your wife and I to talk to ensure we are all on the same page about her role in our son's life.

Boundary Receiver: I thought you didn't want her involved in our decision-making. Can you help me understand what you mean?

Boundary Setter: I don't want her making decisions. However, I think if our son is spending time with her, we should have a mutual understanding of her role.

Boundary Receiver: Thanks for clarifying. I will see if she is open to a joint call with both of us. Can I get back to you later this week?

Boundary Setter: Yes, that works.

Boundary Receiver: Thank you.

Examples of Discovery Questions and Divorce, Co-Parenting, and Blended Family Boundaries

Discovery Questions:

- How come the kids aren't using their safety seats?

- When can I receive an update on (child's name) doctor's appointment?

- How come the children are tired when they come to my house?

Divorce, Co-Parenting, & Blended Family Boundaries:

- It appears we have different parenting styles when it comes to safety seats. I value physical safety. How can we ensure the safety seats are used until they reach the required age or weight?

- It seems we are on different pages when sharing our children's medical records. I value transparency. Can we establish a timeframe for exchanging medical information?

- It seems the children are having difficulty falling asleep when they have two different bedtimes. I value collaboration. How can we create consistency for the children's bedtime?

TWENTY ONE
NEIGHBOR BOUNDARIES

Iris and Gabriel purchased their first home after years of renting apartments. They were so excited for a fresh start to have a big backyard, a private pool, and fresh vegetables from the garden. Having their private oasis felt like a dream come true since they had been saving for the past five years. Iris kept telling Gabriel how she couldn't wait to meet all the neighbors and make new friends.

As they pulled into the driveway of their new home, Iris saw an envelope sticking out of the front door. She thought it was odd it wasn't in the mailbox but continued to pull into the garage. She grabbed her shopping bags and walked to the front door to see what was in the envelope. While sitting on the couch relaxing, she opened the letter and noticed it was from the neighbor across the street. She was beyond thrilled as it was the first time she had any communication with the neighbors since settling into their new home. As Iris began to read the note, her heart sank as it wasn't what she had expected at all. The Russo's welcomed Iris and Gabriel to the neighborhood but gave them a long list of guidelines about how to maintain their yard, what was acceptable for holiday decorations, types of security cameras they needed to install, noise limits and hours, the height of a privacy fence, and so on. Iris was shocked and motioned for Gabriel to come read the note.

Iris handed Gabriel the letter. "Can you believe this? We finally moved into our dream home and are expected to follow some neighbor's ludicrous guidelines. I thought that when you bought a house, you had privacy and property rights."

Gabriel skimmed through the long list. "I'm going to go over there and find out what the deal is. Surely, we can clear things up."

"I hope so! I don't want to deal with bossy neighbors living here. I can't imagine them controlling everything we do on our property."

Gabriel kept pacing in the kitchen. "We will work this out. I'm sure it's all a misunderstanding."

The next day, Gabriel and Iris left the house to go to work. Iris was still feeling perturbed, but she knew she could trust Gabriel to fix things. He was great at resolving problems and putting out fires. However, this was definitely a new problem he hadn't experienced before.

After work, Gabriel ran across the street to see if the Russo's were home to talk. But they didn't come to the door. He figured he would try to rectify the situation in person before things got out of control.

As he walked into the house, Iris was busy pulling out their holiday decor for the Fourth of July. She planned to hang star-shaped lights on the front porch, vintage flags, and huge white lanterns that lined the walking pathway from their front door to the main sidewalk. As Iris was untangling the lights, she mentioned to Gabriel she wanted to host a celebration to get to know their next-door neighbors. She asked him to invite the neighbors on both sides of the house and even a few neighbors down the street whom they had recently met on their nightly walk.

As Iris was going through the RSVPs for their party, she realized she had not received a reply from the Russo's. Gabriel told Iris not to worry about it and to continue planning their neighborly party. He said, "If they choose not to come, then that's on them. I have tried to get in touch with them about the list but still haven't heard back. I even left a note for them to call me."

The next morning, Iris saw all her white lanterns had been shoved into a box and moved to the front porch. She couldn't believe it, but her gut instinct told her exactly who it was – the Russo's. At that point, she was livid. And she wasn't about to stay quiet just to keep the peace. Iris began furiously writing them a note while on her lunch break at work. She had reached her limit with the Russo's trying to meddle in their life.

Iris dropped off her note when she got home from work and stuck the envelope inside the front door. She figured she would mimic their actions so they would be sure to find the note.

Iris felt a weight lifted off her shoulders now that she had spoken her mind. She knew she had bigger things to focus on, like planning their party later that weekend.

As Iris placed the lanterns down the driveway for the second time, she looked up and saw Mrs. Russo looking out the window at her. When she bent down to turn on the lanterns, she could feel someone breathing over her shoulder behind her back. It was no other than Mrs. Russo.

Mrs. Russo said, "Hey, not sure if you got my letter, but those are not allowed in our neighborhood. It's kitschy, and we don't allow those types of decorations. Haven't you noticed?"

Iris contained her anger, "I'm sorry, who are you? And I believe this is my property you are standing on."

Mrs. Russo fired back, "I'm Mrs. Russo. I've lived across the street for fifteen years. And we have guidelines in this neighborhood to keep up with our classy presence. We don't want to lower the value of our neighborhood, and we hope you can understand why we all follow the rules."

"Well, I'm Iris and I make my own rules for my property. I hope you can understand. Now, if you don't mind, I'm going back to prepping the decorations for the festivities. I hope you have a good evening and will join the rest of us for the celebration."

Mrs. Russo got snippy. "Celebration? I don't think so. You clearly don't sound like my cup of tea. We will be attending festivities elsewhere. I'm going to have to warn the neighborhood about you."

Iris smiled, "Oh, please do!"

"You can bet I will. We will make sure you don't last long here."

While you cannot control what others say or do, you can control how you respond.

Insight

Iris and Gabriel had high hopes for their new home, but their excitement quickly turned into frustration as they encountered the intrusive guidelines set by their neighbor, Mrs. Russo. The couple was taken aback by the level of interference that Mrs. Russo displayed regarding their property. They felt their neighbor had overstepped their boundaries and violated their values of personal and physical space.

Despite their attempts to be friendly and open with Mrs. Russo, the situation only worsened. Mrs. Russo refused to engage in a neighborly conversation and continued to retaliate against Gabriel and Iris. She crossed a major line of respect when she trespassed on Iris and Gabriel's property and threw their lanterns into a box. Mrs. Russo escalated the conflict by giving an ultimatum and creating a power struggle over their differing decor preferences. Her behavior made it clear that she was unwilling to compromise and was intent on having things her way. This left Iris and Gabriel feeling disrespected in their own home and their neighborly boundaries breached.

To make matters worse, Mrs. Russo resorted to using coercive control. She threatened Iris and Gabriel by making the situation the topic of neighborhood gossip, potentially tarnishing their reputation in their new community. This behavior was not only malicious but also created difficulties for the couple in their attempts to establish a mutually respectful agreement with their neighbor.

Definition of Neighbor Boundaries

Neighbor boundaries refer to the physical property and personal space involved in both individual relationships and communities. By establishing clear boundaries, neighbors can ensure respectful interactions, appropriate borrowing of possessions, consideration for noise levels, and respect for each other's property and privacy.

Intrusive Neighbors

Everyone deserves to have a safe place where they can relax and feel comfortable, especially in the privacy of their own home. Unfortunately, not all neighbors value personal or physical space. Intrusive neighbors can make life difficult and stressful when they engage from a *me* mindset. They may drop by unannounced, enter your property without asking, share gossip, or want to talk your ear off for hours during your free time. While it can be tempting to simply ignore them, this is often not the best solution to resolving conflict and protecting your personal space.

Bypassing a neighbor may give them the impression that their conduct is permissible, only to cause further complications in the long run. When neighbors feel shunned, they may become more aggressive or annoying, complicating matters. This can impact your mental and physical health as you may develop resentment, insomnia, anxiousness, or other ailments that impede your well-being. Failing to voice your value, can perpetuate the power struggle between you and your neighbor as most problems don't disappear on their own. When neighbors are disrespectful, it is important to set healthy boundaries after the violation occurs. Advocating for your beliefs and values respects your boundaries while trying to sustain amicable neighborly relationships.

Borrowing and Returning Items

One of the greatest things about living in a close-knit community is that you can count on your neighbors for a helping hand when you need it. Whether you need to borrow a tool or home equipment, chances are there is someone nearby who is happy to help out. When borrowing items, you'll want to clarify in advance the terms of usage, in case your neighbor plans to use their belongings in the near future. Neighbors won't want to wait weeks to get their possessions back, as they are trusting you in good faith to be an honest neighbor. Having integrity maintains the neighborly relationship while being punctual with time for future borrowing.

When returning borrowed items, you will also want to return the item in the same condition as borrowed. For example, make sure it's clean and there has been no damage to the item. If the borrowed item does become mishandled or damaged, it's proper etiquette to offer financial reimbursement for the repair or replacement. Additionally, you don't want to become the neighbor who continuously borrows the same item on a regular basis, as this can hinder the relationship over time. Eventually, you may need to consider making the investment and purchasing the item yourself. Borrowing your neighbor's snow blower or electrical drill regularly can eventually show you are taking advantage of their good nature. On the other hand, if you are the one who is doing the lending, it will be essential to maintain boundaries on how often you lend or the time allocated for usage. This will reduce resentment or frustration with your neighbors or the feeling of being used.

Additionally, neighbors may lend items, only to expect something in return for the favor. They use their resources to hold leverage over another in case they need something from their neighbor in return at a later date. This forgoes being a good-natured neighbor. Lending under conditional terms, such as "I'll do this for you, but what can you do for me?" is manipulation and creates an imbalance in the relationship.

Noise Ordinance and Privacy

For many people, living in close proximity to neighbors can be a source of tension, anxiety, and frustration if there is an invasion of privacy and peace. Whether it's loud music, construction, or shouting late at night, noise can make it difficult to enjoy your own home. While noisy neighbors are disruptive, it's best to find out if your neighborhood or residential building has a noise ordinance in place before speaking with your neighbor. This can help you best assess the situation and use the ordinance to your advantage if you need to approach your neighbor about a noise disruption. Most noise ordinances have specific hours and a certain decibel of what is acceptable. Generally, neighbors will be open to a friendly conversation to resolve the problem. It is best to attempt this route first and establish boundaries before contacting authorities.

In addition to noisy arguments and sound disturbances, there can be issues regarding privacy. There's nothing worse than having a nosy neighbor who tracks every move you make. These are the types who are caught peeking over the fence to see what you're up to, watching you through the windows, or using binoculars to spy. Nosy neighbors can make you feel like you're constantly under surveillance, and it can be challenging to relax in the privacy of your home. Some people believe that it's their right to know everything that's going on in their neighborhood, deeming themselves the neighborhood watchdog. While there's nothing wrong with being curious about what's happening around you, there's a fine line between curiosity and nosiness. Nosy neighbors often cross that line, making others feel uncomfortable and even unsafe. By taking actionable steps, you can help create a more harmonious relationship with your neighbors and reduce the stress of living in close quarters. A few steps to protecting your privacy from nosy neighbors are installing blinds, curtains, fences, and security cameras.

Types of Neighbor Boundaries

- Borrowing and returning items in a timely manner
- Protecting property from being devalued or vandalized
- Establishing clear yard dividers
- Refraining from offensive signage or decor
- Asking for permission to prevent trespassing
- Respecting noise ordinances
- Practicing pet etiquette
- Maintaining the visual appearance of the property
- Installing privacy fences, blinds, or security cameras
- Respecting physical and personal space
- Refraining from competitiveness or retaliation
- Giving wrongly delivered mail and packages to the recipient
- Shutting down harassment and gossip
- Respecting property management guidelines
- Replacing or reimbursing for damaged borrowed belongings
- Agreeing not to park, block, or restrict each other's driveways or spaces

Example of the Boundary Badass Method for Neighbor Boundaries

ASAP: Assess with discovery questions, Set a boundary, Agree to a mutual plan, and Proceed with accountability

Step 1: **Assess** *with Discovery Questions*

Boundary Setter: How come you took down my decorations?

Boundary Receiver: They don't meet the guidelines.

Step 2: **Set** *a Boundary*

Boundary Setter: I think we are on different pages when it

comes to trespassing and removing items from my property. I value mutual respect. How can we respect each other's property?

Step 3: **Agree** to a Mutual Plan Using "I" statements and Discovery Questions

Boundary Receiver: I gave you the guidelines for property management. It outlines the decorations there. How come you aren't willing to follow the guidelines?

Boundary Setter: Who orchestrated these guidelines?

Boundary Receiver: They are mine. Everyone in the neighborhood follows them. How come you're the only one with a problem?

Boundary Setter: While I understand your preferences for decorations, the guidelines aren't a city ordinance. Can we find a way to respect each other's decor despite our differences in style?

Boundary Receiver: I agree we have very different styles. I will do my best to respect your property.

Step 4: **Proceed** with Accountability

Boundary Setter: (Fall decor) Hey, I love all of your orange pumpkins.

Boundary Receiver: Thanks, fall is my favorite season. I can see you chose white and sage pumpkins and are sticking to your unique style.

Boundary Setter: Of course! I am a big fan of neutral decor.

Boundary Receiver: I can't help but be a traditionalist. However, I can appreciate both styles.

Examples of Discovery Questions and Neighbor Boundaries

Discovery Questions:

- When can you return my ladder?

- How come your security cameras are facing our home?

- Can you please turn the music down?

Neighbor Boundaries:

- It appears we have a misunderstanding when returning loaned items. I value integrity. How about we agree to return borrowed items within forty-eight hours?

- I think we have an issue when it comes to the direction of security cameras. I value privacy. When can we have the cameras redirected away from my property?

- It seems we have different preferences when playing loud music late at night. I value collaboration. Can we agree on a reasonable volume?

TWENTY TWO
HOLIDAY, CELEBRATION, AND EVENT BOUNDARIES

It was a brisk fall day. Heidi looked out the window and saw the leaves blowing across the yard. As she sipped her ginger spiced tea, she thought about how much she needed to get done before next week and realized she had better start prepping for Thanksgiving dinner.

In the midst of writing her shopping list, she began searching through her recipe box for the dishes she would need to prepare. After filtering through them, she considered switching things up this year and adding some new dishes along with traditional side dishes, like mashed potatoes and green bean casserole. She jumped on the internet and began searching for a new twist on the old classic recipes.

Later that afternoon, Heidi headed to the grocery store to get her final shopping done. It was a madhouse, and the store was already starting to run low on items. She started to get a pounding migraine and regretted not going to the store sooner. She kept saying to herself, *Why do I do this to myself? Every year, I turn down help, and then I'm stuck doing it all. I'm getting burnt out. Next year, I'm asking for help.*

Her alarm clock went off at six o'clock on Thursday morning. She got out of bed and fed the cats and dogs before making a stiff pot of coffee to get her through the day of baking and cooking. She had about five hours before guests would begin to arrive. She thought she would bake the sweet potato soufflé and get it out of the way. Next, she began chopping the ingredients for the salad and then threw the pieces of butternut squash and croutons in the oven to bake. She was feeling good about getting things accomplished so quickly.

She poured herself a second cup of coffee and turned on her favorite playlist to keep the momentum strong. The kitchen started to look like a tornado with pots and pans piled up everywhere, which left her in a frenzy. She tried to wash the dishes as she cooked to keep things organized, but it only slowed her down.

It was getting close to eleven and she felt her stress level starting to rise. She had about an hour before guests would arrive. It dawned on her that she forgot to make the green bean casserole. She popped open the cans of green beans, threw them into a glass baking dish with the rest of the ingredients, and placed it in the oven, hoping it would be done on time. Now, she was feeling overwhelmed because she still had to make all the appetizers and there was no way she was going to get it all done in time.

As soon as she set the timer, she heard a knock on the door. It was the first guest arriving way earlier than she anticipated. She started to panic because everything was still in the oven. She told the guests to grab their own beverages, as she would be in the kitchen finishing the final touches. She really needed a break at this point, but she couldn't walk away from the kitchen out of fear she would burn the casserole.

More guests started to arrive, and the intensity of pressure to make everything perfect consumed her mind. Every little detail from the food presentation to the ambiance needed to be done exactly how she envisioned it. It was the only way she could contain her anxiety. One of her nieces came into the kitchen to see if she needed help as she was taking the potatoes off the stove. Heidi was carrying the heavy pot to the sink and didn't see her niece, which led them run into each other. The hot water splashed and drenched the front of their shirts. They both screamed and Heidi dropped the pot on the floor.

The clock was ticking fast and the food wasn't going to be finished on time. Dinner was running thirty minutes behind schedule. Heidi's son started to carve the oven-roasted turkey. At this point, guests were content with their appetizers but the smell of turkey had everyone's mouth watering. Heidi set out the rest of the dishes and serving utensils so everyone could begin to fill their plates. Thanksgiving dinner was officially complete, and she could finally sit down and breathe while everyone began to eat.

As the family members were catching up over the meal, Heidi's second cousin started a political debate with her brother. They had extremely opposing views, which led to him screaming over everyone, throwing his napkin down, and cursing out her brother. She told them to take it outside because they weren't about to ruin the perfectly good meal she had been cooking for hours. But both men were too strong-headed and heated to even hear what Heidi said.

Eventually, Heidi's brother got so fed up, that he grabbed his wife and kids and told everyone they were leaving. His wife begged him to stay and not ruin Thanksgiving for the kids, but it was too late. The kids screamed they weren't leaving either and ran downstairs to hide. However, Heidi's brother was past the point of calming down and needed to get out of there before things got worse.

Heidi, distraught about the meal being a disaster, secluded herself in the kitchen as she washed the dishes in tears. The only thing she could think was *I'm done doing all the cooking, cleaning, and dealing with everyone's drama.*

Relationship boundaries are the art of cultivating connection and integrity.

Insight

Heidi displayed poor boundaries with herself and her family, leaving her emotionally drained and making it impossible for her to enjoy the holiday. Despite having the option to delegate tasks or accept help from family members, she took on the full responsibility of cooking the entire meal. Her desire for control and perfectionism, even at the expense of her own well-being, was a result of her ultra-independent mindset. Someone who thrives on being ultra-independent, like Heidi, can have a coping mask where they avoid being vulnerable. This can stem from past traumas where the person asked for help and their core needs were denied or rejected, so they have learned to solely depend on themselves.

When someone has experienced rejection, they can also adopt people-pleasing tendencies because they have learned to seek their worth by proving to others they are of value through their services. Heidi believed "family is family" even if it meant neglecting herself. For individuals who struggle to set boundaries, holiday festivities can be unbearable, especially when family relationships are not reciprocal. This can make family gatherings a bittersweet experience, where the stress of boundary violations overshadows the joy of coming together.

In the midst of trying to finish the meal on time, the guests arrived earlier than the established meal time. This can make meal prepping quite stressful for a host when guests disregard event etiquette. These situations can be avoided by communicating clear start and end times for events or holidays.

When it came time for the meal, Heidi's brother and second cousin disregarded holiday boundaries when they decided to engage in a political debate. Bringing up controversial topics at a holiday gathering is a sign of poor intellectual boundaries, knowing it may lead to a heated discussion. When the cousins neglected to excuse themselves or refrain from the heated conversation, it impacted the rest of the family, creating greater discontentment for all. If families have ongoing relational patterns that lead to boundary violations, it can create unhealthy generational family cycles at every holiday or celebration for years to come.

Definition of Holiday, Celebration, and Event Boundaries

Holiday, celebration, and event boundaries refer to the standards and guidelines individuals establish to ensure a healthy balance between their personal values and respectful interactions during social gatherings, celebrations, or special occasions. These boundaries help navigate various aspects of occasions, such as guest lists, hosting responsibilities, and interactions with attendees to maintain harmonious relationships.

Planning Details and Delegation

The holidays and celebrations are a joyous time for celebrating with friends and family, but they can also be a time of stress and conflict. One of the biggest sources of tension during holidays or celebrations is not knowing how to establish boundaries with guests. When planning, you may ask yourself, *Who will be invited to the celebration? What kind of traditions will be followed? Who is responsible for cooking or contacting vendors? What type of dress code will be required?*

When setting holiday or celebration boundaries, it is important to keep aligned with your values while simultaneously honoring your guests. This may look like sharing responsibilities with co-hosts during holidays and celebrations without stretching yourself too thin or compromising your personal boundaries. Additionally, delegation can help foster a sense of cooperation and teamwork while maintaining mutually beneficial relationships.

Also, when planning celebrations, it is important to consider food allergies and dietary restrictions. Everyone may have different requirements based on health conditions or preferences around nutritional choices. Guests should not feel like they are a burden or judged for their personal health choices or medical requirements.

Timing considerations can also be vital for planning holidays or celebrations. Many guests may have to travel and will need ample notice to prepare. Depending on the event, the proper notification will vary from a few weeks to a couple of months so guests can book flights, plan road trips, or shop for gifts to prepare in advance. Additionally, it is important to consider setting time limits for arrival, meal time, and departure on the day of the event to prevent guests from overstaying their welcome to maintain your personal space.

On a final note, etiquette and dress codes can also be a requirement for specific celebrations. Some events may be more formal than others, like weddings or cocktail parties, requiring a seating arrangement, electronic usage guidelines, and wardrobe preference for attendance. Following through with the dress code and event etiquette shows respect for the host and upholds the standard of the event. Typically, formal celebrations will specify the dress code requirement and guidelines in advance with an R.S.V.P. for attendance.

Intrusive Guests

Intrusive guests can ruin even the most carefully planned holidays and celebrations. Whether they're coming uninvited or overstaying their welcome, they can quickly turn a pleasant gathering into a catastrophe. One of the most frustrating things about intrusive guests is that they often don't even realize they're being a problem. They may think they're being friendly or helpful when in reality they're making everyone else uncomfortable due to their psychological blind spots.

When there is an obligation to invite ill-mannered guests who have been a part of your life for years, it can be beneficial to have self-awareness of your emotional triggers to set boundaries. Some people can be quite opinionated about how other family members or friends choose to live their lives. These types of guests tend to overstep boundaries by telling others the dos and don'ts of making better decisions from their own beliefs versus accepting others' personal choices. Some common topics they may inquire about or project their viewpoints onto are your relationship status, finances, career, health, politics, religion, or lifestyle choices. Even though an intrusive guest may mean well with their unsolicited advice, it can lead to uncomfortable discussions where you may feel uneasy talking about these specific topics.

The bottom line is every guest will have their own perspective on a particular subject, but how you choose to respond is your choice and responsibility. Setting boundaries with intrusive guests or excusing yourself from difficult conversations will help you feel calmer and more confident at holiday gatherings and celebrations. Also, being aware of how you engage with certain guests who have previously pushed your buttons will be the key to honoring your personal boundaries.

Reframing Holiday Celebrations

If you grew up in a home where family gatherings were emotionally taxing and traumatizing, continuously encountering specific family members for holidays or celebrations can leave you feeling distressed and disrespected. These past events may influence how you choose to interact with family members today or redefine celebrations altogether. If you wish to engage with these family members, mentally preparing in advance what you will say or do if your personal boundaries are breached will help you feel aligned with your values and communicate with confidence. This allows you to effectively manage emotional triggers and implement an actionable plan by setting boundaries with others. You may also find it vital to use emotional regulation techniques or disengage if a conversation becomes an unfavorable exchange.

However, if you find it challenging to reframe holidays or events and still wish to partake in them, there are alternative approaches to consider. Shifting your perspective or creating new traditions can be beneficial to specific situations. Recognizing your threshold for engagement, unhealthy generational patterns, or outdated traditions that no longer resonate with you can bring clarity as you navigate these interpersonal relationships. An individual may also find it more fitting to form new traditions and celebrations, offering opportunities to create positive experiences by giving the holiday or event renewed meaning and purpose.

When setting holiday boundaries, this may include changing locations, the amount of time you spend there, or doing something completely different for the occasion, making it more enjoyable and comfortable for you. There's no right or wrong choice when prioritizing your mental, emotional, and physical health during holidays and celebrations. The quicker you take responsibility for your personal needs, the more pleasure you can experience at holiday family functions and celebrations without feeling trapped by others' opinions, manipulations, or decisions. Holidays are celebrated worldwide in various ways; choosing how you wish to engage on special occasions allows you to reclaim the joy of these moments.

Types of Holiday, Celebration, and Event Boundaries

- Identifying topics of discussion that are mutually respectful
- Knowing your limits for cooking or entertaining responsibilities
- Setting a start and end time for holiday gatherings and celebrations
- Honoring emotional or physical space
- Inviting guests who are respectful and helpful
- Deciding guest capacity based on preferences or event space
- Planning for holiday or celebration travel in advance
- Personalizing celebrations and creating new traditions
- Limiting work hours during holidays or celebrations
- Delegating time with each side of the family
- Establishing gift exchanging guidelines

- Respecting those with dietary restrictions and health conditions
- Honoring proper etiquette and dress code for events
- Refraining from prying or airing family members' private information
- Setting personal limits on food and alcohol consumption
- Including everyone in celebration photos
- Corresponding and sending out invitations on time
- Outsourcing tasks to co-hosts, caterers, florists, etc.

Example of the Boundary Badass Method for Holiday, Celebration, and Event Boundaries

ASAP: Assess with discovery questions, Set a boundary, Agree to a mutual plan, and Proceed with accountability

Step 1: **Assess** *with Discovery Questions*

Boundary Setter: Can you stay an extra hour?

Boundary Receiver: I wasn't planning on it. I need to get home before dark.

Step 2: **Set** *a Boundary*

Boundary Setter: I feel exhausted when left with a huge mess to clean up. I value collaboration. Can we delegate tasks and clean the kitchen together?

Step 3: **Agree** *to a Mutual Plan Using "I" statements and Discovery Questions*

Boundary Receiver: Sure. What would you like help with?

Boundary Setter: Thanks. I can no longer do it all. How about we load the dishwasher first, then wash the pots and pans?

Boundary Receiver: That works. I had no idea this was a concern. I am here to help in any way I can, but I do need to leave by dusk. How about next year we delegate in advance who's responsible for cooking and cleaning the kitchen?

Boundary Setter: That would be great. I think next year, I'll have everyone bring a dish to make it less stressful. And we can all take turns on clean-up duty.

Boundary Receiver: Perfect. I'm glad we had this chat.

Step 4: **Proceed** with Accountability

Boundary Setter: (Next year) I'm planning this year's holiday meal. I'm asking each family member to bring a side dish, appetizer, dessert, or beverage to share. I will handle the mashed potatoes and turkey. What would you like to bring?

Boundary Receiver: We will bring the beverages.

Boundary Setter: Great, I'll check that off the list.

Boundary Receiver: Can we help you with any cleaning after the meal?

Boundary Setter: Yes, let's split up washing and drying the fine china.

Boundary Receiver: Great, I'll be the dryer.

Examples of Discovery Questions and Holiday, Celebration, and Event Boundaries

Discovery Questions:

- Who will be attending this year?
- How come we aren't seeing my family over the holiday?
- Can we make the event black tie?

Holiday, Celebration, and Event Boundaries:

- I feel overwhelmed when there is tension during the holidays and won't make it this year. I value inner peace. How about we connect over a video chat?

- It seems we have different ideas when it comes to allocating time with both of our families over the holidays. I value mutual respect. How can we make time for both of our families?

- It appears we have conflicting perspectives when it comes to the dress code for the event. I value collaboration. How can we find a way to blend our two preferences?

TWENTY THREE

PROFESSIONAL BOUNDARIES

Friday afternoon, Leah walked into her account manager's office and set the paperwork down on his desk. Finley nonchalantly said, "Hey, thanks so much for getting this done on time. I really appreciate it. By the way, what are you up to this weekend?"

Leah politely smiled. "Of course! I never miss a deadline. I plan to relax and have brunch with some friends."

"Well, if you're not too busy, I would like to give you the next big project to glance over and get a head start."

Leah nodded her head. "I am happy to briefly look over it. Can you send the account file?"

Finley said, "Will do. How about we meet Monday morning to discuss it?"

"No problem."

Leah left Finley's office and went back to her desk feeling overwhelmed with another big project. She gathered her belongings and thought, *Why can't I ever catch a break? There goes my weekend.* She tried to stop herself from overthinking, but her brain wasn't shutting out the noise. All she wanted to do was have some downtime before returning to work on Monday. She told herself to take the night off and worry about it on Sunday, as she had plans with her friends. It had been over three weeks since she had seen them.

As Leah and her friends were enjoying brunch, she received a text from Finley.

Hey, I hope you're having a nice Saturday. Did you get a chance to review the client *project I sent? I was hoping to get your quick feedback.*

Leah told her friends that her manager was keeping tabs on her new project. Her friends raised their eyebrows in shock and said, "But it's the weekend."

Finley had never texted her over the weekend before, even if she had an outstanding project. She was beginning to feel like she had no life outside the office. She had been working with him for three years, but this was the first time she felt her work life was bleeding into her personal life. Leah's friends told her to let it go and to enjoy her weekend.

Leah eventually responded back to Finley. *I haven't yet, but it's on my to-do list.*

Finley replied, *Cool. See you at the office on Monday.*

Leah felt a sense of relief that he wasn't mad and hoped it wouldn't be an awkward Monday in the office.

Sunday morning came and she was dreading reviewing the new project. Even though she loved her job, the thought of working over the weekend made her cringe. While clenching her jaw with frustration, she began to review the large file. As she was about halfway through the file, her friends invited her to hike up north for the day. She desperately wanted to go but felt if she didn't have feedback for Finley on Monday, her job would be on the line. This put her in a tough spot.

She was starting to feel undervalued for how much time she dedicated to work outside the office. Out of resentment, she closed her laptop and decided to go hiking instead. Plus, she knew in the back of her mind she wasn't required to work over the weekends.

As Leah and her friends began their hike up the hill, she asked them, "What do you think I should say when I talk to Finley about working weekends?"

One friend said, "I would wait to address it in your quarterly review."

Another friend blurted out loud, "Tell him you would like to maintain a work-life balance or discuss bonuses for the overtime."

Leah graciously responded, "Thanks. I'm annoyed but don't want to lose my job. I despise working weekends. And it wasn't ever part of my job description."

Leah got to the office at her usual time on Monday morning. She had finished reviewing the client's project when Finley came by her office.

Finley said, "How was your weekend?"

"Great! How was yours?"

Finley abruptly cut to the point. "Good times. What's your insight on this new project?"

"It's definitely going to require some extended hours, but it's doable."

Finley responded, "That's good news. Can you carve out some time over the next few weekends? We have a tight deadline with this client, and I want to make it happen."

Leah started fidgeting. She desperately wanted to fire back at him with a no but couldn't and bit her tongue. The whole situation was causing her to perspire through her shirt.

"Sure, I can work some overtime on the weekends. Can you share if every project will be like this going forward?"

Finley looked down at his watch. "I am not sure. Why do you ask?"

Leah's hands began to sweat. "Contractually, weekends were not in my job description. While I respect my job and am very grateful for it, it's definitely creating some personal stress, as there's little downtime."

"You've impressed me over the last six months. What would help you manage the stress better?"

Leah courageously said, "I would like to maintain professional work hours."

Finley looked at Leah without much understanding. "Unfortunately, we have tight deadlines and can't afford to lose our clients. We really value you at our company and hope you continue doing a great job."

Leah texted one of her friends immediately. She felt a pit in her stomach because she was stuck in a hard place of pleasing her account manager and wanting to keep her job, but also feeling disrespected working weekend after weekend. Her friend told her to brush it off until she could start looking for a new job or to address it with human resources. Leah mentally tried to convince herself everything would be okay, but her skin began to itch as she broke out in hives.

Despite her discomfort, she dove headfirst into her new project. She put on headphones and began listening to a podcast to distract herself from the discouraging thoughts. She became highly focused on completing the first milestone for the client's project. Leah hoped if she completed it early, she wouldn't have to work over the weekend.

The next morning, she walked into the office to find a box of her favorite Parisian macarons sitting on her desk. There was a small note attached to the gold box that said *Keep up the great work! ~ Finley*

She was surprised by the nice gesture, but this wasn't going to make up for her working weekends. She knew she was a valuable employee and deserved to either be compensated for her overtime or to maintain her work-life balance. She was starting to question if the company was a good fit for her.

You can't make someone respect you, but you can refuse to be disrespected.

Insight

Leah and Finley's professional relationship can be common in the workplace, as professional boundaries are easily blurred when there is poor leadership and a dismissal of workplace policies. Even though Finley was Leah's manager, he took her strong work ethic for granted by expecting her to work outside professional hours without compensation. This caused Leah an immense amount of distress and left no room for her personal value of a work-life balance.

During their conversations at the office, Leah felt powerless when corresponding with her manager because she wasn't being heard, understood, or valued. Finley tried to deflect from the situation by using a small gift as a way to keep Leah happy. However, this showed his lack of leadership in resolving the workplace issues and maintaining healthy professional boundaries. With Finley ignoring Leah's request, it became a breach of her employment contract.

Instead of Leah setting a professional boundary to maintain self-respect, Leah passively agreed to meet the client's needs and to work diligently rather than negotiate bonuses or specified work hours. While she upheld her work responsibilities, she questioned whether staying at the company was in her best interest.

Organizations that do not have leadership training in place for management can create open invitations for unprofessional conduct like gift giving, denial of overtime pay, or using coercion to meet the demands of the company's growth. Regardless of an individual's professional role, an employee isn't required to work in a culture where they feel threatened, harassed, underpaid, undervalued, or fearful they will lose their job for not complying with demands or requests outside their professional responsibilities.

Definition of Professional Boundaries

Professional boundaries refer to the conduct and communication guidelines that protect each employee's well-being and privacy within the workplace. These guidelines establish workplace policies that promote an ethical standard for creating a healthy company culture among co-workers, c-level executives, colleagues, and clients.

Workplace Culture and Policies

Workplace policies define best practices for employees' and executives' conduct to ensure the company culture is upheld to a professional standard. Policies instill outstanding leadership, guidelines, and values to support a healthy workplace culture while minimizing toxic behaviors amongst team members. Toxic behaviors that are present within professional cultures are power plays, personality complexities, lack of recognition, favoritism, high turnover, ineffective communication, poor work-life balance, insufficient leadership, gossip, lack of growth opportunities, burnout, and workplace exclusion. Having workplace wellness policies can benefit a company's growth while supporting the mental and physical health of employees who are a part of the organization.

Maintaining professional boundaries in the workplace is essential for creating a positive company culture that retains top talent and yields exceptional performance. When employees feel comfortable and respected in a working environment, they are more likely to be productive and engaged in their work. Professional boundaries help to reduce conflict and create trust between employees and their employers. For example, if employees can openly discuss their professional goals or concerns with their manager, they are more likely to feel supported and valued in their role and feel like an asset to the organization. When employees are part of a greater collective, they are more likely to be loyal to their company and work harder to contribute to its success.

Conversely, when there is inappropriate conduct in the workplace, this can be deemed unethical and a violation of professional boundaries. If an employee experiences an unsolicited gesture from another employee, regardless of their role, using assertive communication to address the unwarranted behavior will need to occur immediately. If you stay silent for the sake of others' feelings and opinions or your employment status, then you have stopped honoring the relationship with yourself. It will only perpetuate a feeling of powerlessness and ongoing disrespect in the workplace.

On a final note, it is your responsibility to communicate what feels appropriate based on the company's policies, employment contract, and professional and personal boundaries. Encouraging communication and collaboration supports a healthy work environment while instilling teamwork and feedback for growth.

Leadership Skills

Leadership skills give you an advantage in building valuable connections inside and outside the organization. These skills reflect interpersonal attributes that enable you to connect with co-workers, clientele, colleagues, and C-level management. Most of the time, organizations are looking for employees who can communicate professionally while maintaining the integrity of the company's reputation and mission. For example, this may include negotiating, team development, relationship capital, conflict resolution skills, high-level emotional intelligence, professional boundaries, and most importantly active listening.

A successful leader also knows how to navigate tough situations using critical and creative thinking skills to problem-solve efficiently and effectively. These skills can strengthen the loyalty of customers, increase profitability over time, and improve the health of the company culture. Being adaptable to change or setbacks can show your ability to honor a growth mindset while also being a valuable asset to the company. Every professional relationship will be unique and sometimes challenging, and being able to deal with difficult personalities will require firm boundaries and conflict resolution skills. The more assertive you are and the higher your relationship intelligence, the better equipped you will be to manage and maintain relationships within and outside of an organization in a powerful, productive, and purposeful manner.

Those who struggle with effective leadership skills can have unresolved childhood wounds that reflect their work performance and productivity. These personal limitations can affect leadership skills by impacting trust, delegation, feedback, emotional regulation, and time management. For instance, if a person experienced neglect or abandonment as a child, they may struggle with trusting others and delegating responsibilities to their team members. Or, if a person experienced harsh criticism and high expectations during childhood, they may struggle with being overly critical, expecting perfectionism from their team or themselves, or resorting to procrastination, which can hinder productivity. Overall, these behaviors can lead to self-sabotage because the fear of failure outweighs the risk of success.

Power Imbalances

The workplace can be a stressful environment if there is a toxic work culture. One of the primary sources of stress is power imbalances between employees and their managers. Managers have the authority to make decisions that affect their team, which can often lead to employees feeling like they are voiceless in their work lives. Power plays can take many forms, from subtle put-downs to more overt threats and intimidation. A manager who operates under these terms communicates from a fixed mindset and often has fear-driven thinking patterns. Employees who are expected to obey their bosses without question can lead to a number of problems, including job dissatisfaction, mistreatment, or even quitting altogether. Unfortunately, toxicity is often tolerated or even encouraged in some workplaces, leading to a culture characterized by fear, resentment, increased conflict, and instability. This is not only destructive to morale, but it also has the potential to reduce productivity and result in high turnover.

The best way to prevent power imbalances is to create a culture of mutual respect with healthy boundaries. When employees feel like their voice is being heard and their viewpoints are valued, they are more likely to feel empowered and motivated, and they are even more likely to outperform the company's competitors. By creating a high-value culture with strong leadership, organizations can help prevent power imbalances from hindering their employee satisfaction.

Types of Professional Boundaries

- Valuing time management and deadlines
- Having integrity with roles and responsibilities
- Declining inappropriate favors for financial gain or career advancement
- Refraining from emotional expression that hinders performance
- Addressing tasks outside of work responsibilities or professional hours
- Shutting down inappropriate language, jokes, or gossip
- Disengaging from unwarranted sexual advances or inappropriate conduct
- Securing confidential client information
- Dressing professionally based on company policies
- Knowing personal limits for alcohol consumption at business functions
- Following workplace policies or working from home etiquette
- Setting communication guidelines during business hours
- Requesting additional compensation for overtime or holiday work
- Balancing work and home life
- Respecting personal and physical workspaces
- Negotiating a salary based on professional responsibilities and skill set
- Shutting down power imbalances and workplace mistreatment
- Asking for promotions, bonuses, and salary increases in writing

Example of the Boundary Badass Method for Professional Boundaries

*ASAP: **A**ssess with discovery questions, **S**et a boundary, **A**gree to a mutual plan, and **P**roceed with accountability*

Step 1: **Assess** *with Discovery Questions*

>Boundary Setter: How come I am being asked to work outside of office hours?

>Boundary Receiver: We have a lot of projects right now and tight deadlines to meet.

Step 2: **Set** *a Boundary*

>Boundary Setter: It seems workplace policies are dismissed when faced with an influx of projects. I value work-life balance. How can we effectively manage client projects while adhering to professional office hours?

Step 3: **Agree** *to a Mutual Plan Using "I" statements and Discovery Questions*

>Boundary Receiver: We have deadlines to meet. What do you think would help increase productivity while in the office?

>Boundary Setter: Can we delegate individual responsibilities to team members and set milestones for each client project?

>Boundary Receiver: Sounds like a great idea. I will have my assistant create a spreadsheet for each project.

>Boundary Setter: Okay. Thank you.

Step 4: **Proceed** *with Accountability*

>Boundary Receiver: (Next project) Here is the timeline for the next project. It has a short turnaround. Can you let me know if you and your team members will be able to meet the deadline during office hours this week?

>Boundary Setter: I don't see it being an issue. I will provide an update midweek.

>*(Midweek)*

Boundary Setter: We have met most of the milestones and it looks like we will be finished by Friday at noon.

Boundary Receiver: Great. That will give me two hours for review before it needs to be submitted.

Examples of Discovery Questions and Professional Boundaries

Discovery Questions:

- How come I keep getting pinged with messages?
- What did you mean by that joke?
- How come I have been assigned to accounts outside my territory?

Professional Boundaries:

- It appears we have different communication preferences when using instant messenger. I value constructive communication. Can we establish a response time before sending another message?
- It seems inappropriate when offensive comments are made in the workplace. I value professionalism. How can we agree to keep our communication professional?
- It seems counterproductive when I'm asked to manage client accounts outside my territory. I value productivity. Can we delegate these accounts to the specified team leader?

TWENTY FOUR
ENTREPRENEURIAL BOUNDARIES

Ken was a notable veterinarian in his hometown. He had been born and raised there, so the thought of leaving never crossed his mind. He had purchased the old clinic downtown right after Mr. Leons retired, making it his own veterinary practice.

During his busy work days, Ken often received calls about newborn puppies available for adoption, even though he rarely knew anyone looking to adopt. Nevertheless, he would post the listings in his clinic's waiting room in case his clients were in the market for a new furry friend. Eventually, it sparked his interest to start a virtual adoption agency where families could be matched with dogs anywhere around the globe. One of the agency's perks was to offer families a complimentary first-year check-up with their local vet to help minimize the costs of a new dog.

It was the week before Ken was supposed to present his virtual adoption agency idea to potential investors. He had been working on the concept for over a year and believed the investors would find it appealing since it was for a good cause. He was nervous but also knew it was show time if he was going to get his idea off the ground.

Ken nervously paced the room, eagerly awaiting the arrival of everyone. As soon as they were all seated, he launched into his presentation about his agency to the group of investors. At first, there was a piercing silence, but then the questions began to pour in.

One investor inquired, "I love the idea. But how will we generate profits?"

Ken replied, "I plan on contracting pet brands to advertise on the site and veterinarian clinics who could promote to local adoptees."

Another investor spoke up, "Do you have any brands on board now? And, what are they willing to pay to advertise?"

Ken's throat became scratchy. "We are still in the early launch stage but hope to secure marketing soon. I have a revenue projection and could send that over to you. Regardless, it's for a good cause and we want investors who care about a man's best friend. The dogs are our mission."

An investor sitting in a chair with his arms crossed said, "Right. But we need to understand the profitability margins first."

Ken got defensive when the investors questioned him about the company's profitability and strategy plan. He immediately became enraged and stormed out of the meeting, slamming the door shut. He thought to himself, *Why does every investor only care about money? Doesn't anyone care about the dogs?* While he paced and struggled to contain his emotions, he knew if he said anything else out of anger, it might ruin his chances of getting them to invest. Ken's passionate energy served him well most of the time when caring for animals, but it also became a double-edged sword in business.

About ten minutes later, Ken rejoined the meeting, but everyone was already on their way out the door. Ken was shaken up, fearing he had ruined his idea and lost their investment.

The following morning, Ken showed up at the clinic and was in a bit of a funk. He refused to see any of his clients and made his vet tech handle the appointments. He felt a little down about the response he received from the investors. So, he sulked in his office the rest of the day, fulfilling prescriptions and updating client notes.

While Ken was sitting at his desk, he got a call from his business partner, Layla, who was a part of the new adoption agency. After speaking with the investors, she informed Ken that they were interested in having another meeting, but this time they wanted to see the projected profit margins and business model that would yield a return on their investment. Ken felt a sense of relief that the investors still held some interest, but he also felt the pressure to prove himself after what he thought was a funding rejection.

Although he had reservations about working with the investors, given that he didn't personally know or trust them, Ken realized that he had no other option if he wanted his agency to succeed. Feeling perplexed, Ken demanded Layla do a financial background check on the investors before the next meeting.

Layla told Ken, "Don't worry, let's get to know them at the next meeting on a personal level, as our time and resources are limited."

Ken got frustrated and slammed the medicine vials on the counter. "I said we need background checks. Get them done, or I can't move forward."

Once they arrived at the new meeting, Ken began asking each investor what inspired them about the global adoption agency and if they personally owned dogs. Layla caught wind Ken was interrogating the investors and feared it could potentially turn them off.

Layla pulled Ken to the side. "What are you doing? Please let me handle the investors. I want you to focus on the presentation right now, okay?"

Ken aggressively clenched his fists. "I told you I need to meet them to see if they are trustworthy. Plus, they need to know how many families and dogs we are going to help."

Layla felt stuck. "I don't know why you don't listen to me. One of these days you'll see you are your own worst enemy. There is an art to getting investors on board. This isn't your vet clinic. It is a much bigger project."

"I'm not changing my ways, Layla. These people need to care about dogs, or else I don't care about them."

Layla was frustrated and shook her head. "This is a joint business adventure, and I would appreciate it if you could show some respect for my part. You may understand dogs, but I understand people."

Boundaries allow you to run your company, not let your company run you.

Insight

Ken cherished his role as a successful veterinarian and entrepreneur. However, he struggled with emotional regulation when launching his dog adoption agency. Ken mistakenly interpreted the investors' inquiry about financial prospects as a rejection of his idea, which deeply affected him. Due to his limiting beliefs, Ken resorted to ego-based thinking, adopting an aggressive stance to defend his mission. Ken fled the meeting when he didn't receive an automatic yes from the investors, which activated his flight trauma response.

Apart from abruptly leaving the meeting, Ken neglected to fulfill his responsibilities at the veterinary clinic the following day. This behavior indicated a lack of integrity on Ken's part, which can negatively impact productivity. When an individual is clouded by their own perspective or emotions, more often than not, they will experience ongoing conflict and struggle to set boundaries. Ken's emotional dysregulation caused his feelings to overshadow his value and reputation as a respected business.

Ken's inability to utilize relationship intelligence skills greatly impaired his relationships with the investors, clients, and Layla. As much as he trusted Layla as his business partner, he also wanted to have sole authority on the execution of decisions, lacking a *we* mindset. This showed an inconsideration for Layla's role and impeded their ability to work as a team. Layla also crossed the line when she verbally attacked

Ken and belittled him for his lack of people skills. The absence of clear entrepreneurial boundaries from both sides could have resulted in the dissolution of their partnership.

Ken's distrust in others can stem from unaddressed feelings of betrayal, which can be due to childhood or prior business experiences. Individuals who seek control might project their internal sense of powerlessness onto others as a result of not trusting themselves. If Ken had a trustworthy relationship with himself and embraced a growth mindset, he would have shown trust in the natural progression of his agency's development through investor onboarding. Unfortunately, his actions contributed to an undesirable company culture, posing a potential threat to the overall success of the adoption agency.

Definition of Entrepreneurial Boundaries

Entrepreneurial boundaries are guidelines that sustain the foundational operations of running a thriving business. These limits and policies help protect personal space and time while fostering positive and mutually beneficial relationships within and outside the company for long-term growth.

Client Relations

As an entrepreneur, establishing boundaries with clients is a fundamental aspect of running a company, regardless of the professional industry. Clearly defined boundaries serve to protect both parties, ensuring that they are mutually comfortable with the terms of the agreement for the services or products being purchased. Building strong relationships during the initial onboarding process is crucial for maintaining rapport, respect, and trust, which promotes long-term business growth.

To build a reputable business and foster strong client relationships, it is imperative to provide transparency regarding the commencement and conclusion of services, the specifics and costs associated with purchased goods or services, the procedure for terminating agreements, business hours of operation, and available payment options. Clearly outlining these terms demonstrates your dedication to client satisfaction and the maintenance of a trusting business relationship. Additionally, it shows respect for your time, expertise, personal space, and contractual obligations within the business.

It can be challenging to sustain a strong business structure if operations are entrenched in fear or if there is a lack of assertive communication. Operating from limiting beliefs can lead to loss of clients, inconsistent income, or reduced referrals. If company values and deliverables fall short of integrity, then you are running the risk of devaluing yourself and your business. However, the opposite will happen when you set healthy boundaries. Boundaries support and protect your business's reputation, boost profitability and growth, and strengthen your relationships within and outside the company.

Work-Life-Love Balance

Entrepreneurs tend to work long hours on a continuous cycle as there is a never-ending to-do list. While an individual may be passionate about achieving success or financial freedom, at the same time, it's important to nurture the most important fundamentals of life: relationships. When business is a top priority, the first relationship that usually gets neglected is the one with yourself. This generally can lead to negligence in other personal relationships as well, like family, friends, or romance. Prioritizing work above personal relationships can be extremely detrimental to your health, emotional wellness, and the people you care about the most. If this happens, you are no longer running your company; it is running you.

When it comes to defining work hours and carving out personal time, it will vary for every entrepreneur. Taking time out of one's day to recharge can help a person stay focused and maintain good health. However, if an individual lets their self-care and self-love slip through the cracks, they will likely start to feel overwhelmed and face burnout because they are being pulled in a million different directions. The more an individual is aligned with their values, the better equipped they will be to recognize when they need to take a break to prevent burnout. If one fails to listen to their body's emotional or physiological cues, it can lead to overwhelming amounts of physical and emotional distress and potential illness, which can all be detrimental to the business's success.

As you create a balanced schedule for yourself, keep in mind it can take about an hour a day to implement self-care. Self-care is how you physically care for your body through exercise, nutrition, and hygiene. In conjunction, doing self-love exercises takes about fifteen minutes a day. Self-love is how you mentally and emotionally process experiences to maintain self-worth and achieve emotional regulation. Furthermore, honoring the relationship with yourself is essential to setting healthy boundaries in every facet of your life. An individual's self-worth is not defined by the success of their business or financial wealth but by their internal value.

Additionally, carving out time for a partner, friends, and family is part of creating a work-life-love balance. While you may not see loved ones weekly, spending time with them is necessary for a fulfilling lifestyle. Nurturing connections with loved ones doesn't mean long hours like you put into your business, but it does require consistency, quality time, and communication to maintain the overall health of your relationships.

Company Values

Back in Chapter 4, you defined your relationship values. Similar to your personal and professional values, it is beneficial to establish your company's values to sustain a strong organization. Company values are guiding principles that help your company to become a well-known, respected brand.

When defining a company's values, it's important to recognize they may differ from one's personal relationship values. For example, a business may value time management, teamwork, communication, confidentiality, integrity, growth, and trust to name a few. The company's values will also reflect its mission, vision, and culture. If a company claims to value teamwork but has created a cutthroat work environment, employees will be adversely affected due to the disconnect in the company's values and operations. On the contrary, if a company values integrity, then employees are more likely to be proud to work for the company, given there is alignment between the company's stated values and its actual practices. Ultimately, the company's values play a significant role in shaping the organization's culture.

Business partnerships will also function according to the company's values. This ensures the company's operations meet a greater collective rather than an individual's entrepreneurial goals. If business partners operate on selfishness, greed, competitiveness, or cruelty, creating an environment that keeps the company thriving will be challenging. The partnerships within a business play a key role in relationship capital, financial growth, and the value of the company's reputation.

When it comes to a positive customer experience, a company's values can help attract their ideal clients or customers with similar values, creating synergy. Serving or attracting like-minded people allows for more mutually beneficial relationships and client satisfaction, thus creating consistent revenue streams and meeting the client's needs. A company's values may reflect how problems are solved, the quality of its products or services, and the direct communication and rapport with its customers. People tend to buy from businesses that internally speak to their own values as it feels safer to purchase from a trusted brand they can relate to. At the end of the day, the company's values support the health of the company, as well as one's mental health, when closing out the workday.

Types of Entrepreneurial Boundaries

- Respecting personal and physical space of clients, employees, and business partners
- Giving credit to team members for performance
- Having integrity for deadlines and goals
- Taking responsibility for company errors
- Refraining from disclosing personal information or displaying inappropriate emotions
- Maintaining a healthy self-care and self-love regimen
- Refraining from inappropriate language or gestures
- Working within contractual agreements
- Honoring a company structure and business hours
- Refraining from the exploitation of power over others for personal gain
- Securing confidential client information
- Upholding company values and policies to maintain best practices
- Clarifying employees' roles and responsibilities
- Knowing when to take a break or time off
- Establishing communication platforms and business hours
- Quoting fees of services or goods in writing
- Listing clear payment terms and conditions for services or goods
- Creating work-life-love balance
- Maintaining a calendar for tasks, professional meetings, and personal commitments
- Creating a positive and respectful work culture
- Separating personal and company finances

Example of the Boundary Badass Method for Entrepreneurial Boundaries

*ASAP: **A**ssess with discovery questions, **S**et a boundary, **A**gree to a mutual plan, and **P**roceed with accountability*

Step 1: **Assess** *with Discovery Questions*

Boundary Setter: Can we call a timeout?

Boundary Receiver: How come? I want to get to the bottom of this now.

Step 2: **Set** *a Boundary*

Boundary Setter: It seems unproductive when we communicate in this manner. I value mutual respect. How about we revisit this topic when we can engage more constructively?

Step 3: **Agree** *to a Mutual Plan Using "I" statements and Discovery Questions*

Boundary Receiver: I see your point. I can get carried away sometimes, as my passionate side tends to get the best of me.

Boundary Setter: I understand and want the agency to be a success as well. But we are on a time crunch and aren't getting anywhere by arguing. How about we talk about this tomorrow morning?

Boundary Receiver: How about tomorrow at 9 a.m.?

Boundary Setter: Okay. I'll meet you at the clinic.

Step 4: **Proceed** *with Accountability*

Boundary Setter: (The following morning) I think we will need to secure ten pet brands to launch the agency. Where do you suggest we start?

Boundary Receiver: We are going to have to start reaching out to places. Can you make a list of vendors and brands?

Boundary Setter: Sure, I can start working on this. I know the investors have concerns and we need to eliminate any fears. I can have a list by later today.

Boundary Receiver: Sounds good. I appreciate you taking the lead on this.

Boundary Setter: Let's regroup tomorrow at 11 a.m.

Examples of Discovery Questions and Entrepreneurial Boundaries

Discovery Questions:

- How come you gave the team members a day off?
- How come client information is being openly discussed?
- What additional services were you anticipating?

Entrepreneurial Boundaries:

- It appears we have different perspectives when rewarding our team members. I value collaboration. How about we brainstorm ideas that work for both of us?
- It seems there is a breach in company policies when discussing client information. I value confidentiality. How can we secure our client's information going forward?
- It seems there is a misunderstanding when it comes to our service agreement. I value integrity. Can we view the service agreement together?

TWENTY FIVE

INTELLECTUAL BOUNDARIES

Henry and Emma had been friends for as long as they could remember. Within minutes of conversing at their first law convention, it became evident that they shared a genuine connection. They humorously tried to get under each other's skin until one of them took it too far, which happened more often than not. Many of their colleagues assumed they were brother and sister because of how close the two had grown over the years.

This year's convention was being held in the valley, which was the perfect change of scenery from last year. As Emma began packing her bags for the trip, she called Henry.

Henry answered, "Hey, Emma! How are you?"

Emma enthusiastically smiled. "Great! How are you?"

Henry squinted while looking out the window. "Things are great out here. We go to the beach on the weekends and the kids are growing like weeds. How are things with you?"

"The usual. Running the kids to their weekly activities and being their personal chef. I can't wait to relax by the pool this weekend. This momma needs a break." Emma laughed while getting the evil eye from one of her kids.

"I hear you. You'll definitely get a break this weekend. Well, I got to run and finish packing, but see you tomorrow."

"Looking forward to it."

On the way to the airport, she sent a voice note to Henry saying she would arrive at the hotel around nine o'clock and they should grab breakfast at the cafe next to the hotel. Henry messaged her back confirming he would be there.

While at breakfast, Emma began telling Henry about how the next two days were going to save her sanity. She was worn out and needed some personal time as family and work life kept her on her feet around the clock. Being able to breathe for a few days and not having to attend to anyone's needs but her own felt like a vacation in itself. Whether it was her kids or clients, someone constantly needed something from her so it didn't give her much downtime to recoup from the long days.

Henry sarcastically teased, "Well, I've never known Ms. Emma to not hold down the fort being so self-sufficient and all. How is your law firm doing these days?"

Emma shut down his sarcasm. "Oh Henry, I am human and I have my limits. The firm is slammed. It's good and bad, you know how it goes. But it's been much nicer ever since we started working from home."

Henry paused. "When did you start working from home?"

"About six months ago, and it's been amazing. Everyone is happier and much more productive."

Henry loosened his tie. "I can't imagine being able to trust staff while they are working from home."

Emma responded, "What do you mean? We have hit our highest number of cases this year alone."

"I would never allow my staff to work from home. I'm paying them to work, not watch television," Henry said with a snarky tone.

"Watch television, ha! I told you we've grown, and billable hours are way up. The numbers speak for themselves. Before you shut it down, you should actually try it and get outside your comfort zone for once. You're really starting to become a control freak."

Henry replied, "Not a chance. It sounds like chaos, and I prefer a structured environment where everything is right at my fingertips."

"Have it your way. But this gives me more time with my family and kids. I can be in a meeting one minute and popping dinner in the oven the next. My multi-tasking has reached a whole new level."

Henry replied, "Everyone knows multi-tasking is unfocused work that is never up to par. While it sounds nice now, eventually productivity will decline once everyone gets too comfortable. You will eventually see the shortcomings in your staff. Trust me on this one."

Emma snapped, "Who says, Mr. Know-It-All? I really don't think you should reject the idea until you've actually tried it. You know it might even loosen you up a bit so you can have fun once in a while."

Henry sat back in his chair and crossed his arms. "Oh, Emma. You still don't get it. I like my office and have no plans to ever work from home. I prefer to keep my personal and professional lives separate."

"I prefer not to have to sit in traffic for hours every day. It's lost time that can be spent on my cases. Time is everything. Plus, we have reduced our long-term overhead costs by fifty percent by reducing office space alone. Have you thought about that?"

During their lunch break at the convention, Emma brought up her and Henry's conversation about working from home to their colleagues. With a good mix of lawyers, each had their own perspective. One attorney agreed with Emma and believed working from home made her team more productive. Another attorney mentioned he enjoyed the flexibility of a hybrid model, which provided him with lifestyle balance. And, another attorney supported Henry's perspective stating that he couldn't work from home either because he wouldn't be able to focus.

After hearing everyone's opinion, Emma began searching on the internet for factual evidence that supported the benefits of working from home. She was determined to prove to Henry there were cost benefits for her firm and mental health benefits for her team.

While sitting in her hotel room, she received a text from Henry, *I'm not ecstatic you brought up our conversation in front of our colleagues.*

Emma immediately replied back, *I simply asked a casual question to hear everyone's opinions on the matter. What is the big deal?*

Are you serious? What's the big deal? We may bicker with each other, but I don't find it necessary to involve others in our conversations.

Okay, sensitive Henry.

We communicate to others how we desire to be treated through what we are willing or unwilling to accept.

Insight

Engaging in debates over opposing opinions or beliefs is a common occurrence in everyday life. Whether within personal or professional relationships, people's viewpoints often stem from their upbringing, experiences, values, or expertise, as illustrated in this story. Henry found himself perplexed by Emma's belief that running a law firm from home was sustainable. His conviction on remote work equated to lower productivity, decreased trustworthiness, and a disorganized work environment.

Emma passionately advocated for the benefits of working from home, highlighting increased profits alongside her value of maintaining a healthy work-life-love balance. Henry's inability to consider viewpoints beyond his own and his desire for control over his environment stemmed from his narrow-mindedness on the subject. Emma, feeling unheard when her viewpoint was dismissed, reacted by name-calling, labeling Henry as "Mr. Know-It-All" and "sensitive." This type of behavior is a sign Emma has disconnected from her values and resorted to belittling Henry as a defense mechanism. When someone is in a reactive state, it can undermine the validity of their position and worth, rather than responding with valuable facts that could enhance their position.

Determined to prove her stance, Emma chose to share their debate about workplace environments with their colleagues. Seeking external viewpoints of others on their disagreement could be perceived as triangulation or an attempt to devalue Henry's perspective. Consequently, Henry felt blindsided when Emma brought up their differing opinions in front of their professional circle. This made Henry feel betrayed by Emma, hindering the trust in their connection. Airing personal tensions within a professional atmosphere can jeopardize the professional reputation of either party.

As a result, Emma and Henry realized their friendship lacked intellectual boundaries, leaving both feeling undervalued and creating a disconnect. When limits remain unspoken and an incident occurs, this creates an opportunity to work through differences and set clear boundaries. For Henry, his values of privacy and trust felt compromised, questioning the genuineness of their friendship. From Emma's perspective, she sensed a lack of mutual respect from Henry regarding her viewpoints. Both had neglected to openly discuss the importance of keeping their debate confidential.

When one or both parties resort to insulting each other's character, criticizing viewpoints, or engaging in triangulation, it violates intellectual boundaries that hinder the growth of the relationship. Intellectual debates can foster greater understanding rather than competition – a means of sharing valuable thoughts and insights to broaden perspectives while maintaining the integrity of the relationship.

Definition of Intellectual Boundaries

Intellectual boundaries respect one's thoughts, beliefs, and perspectives while also acknowledging and valuing the viewpoints of others, whether similar or opposing. By setting limits on intellectual topics, individuals can gain awareness of emotionally triggering information, explore new intellectual ideas, and process enlightening information that helps promote individual and relationship growth.

Intellectual Conversations

For years, intellectual conversations have been a part of societal banter, including a wide range of controversial topics such as politics, religion, healthcare, education, social issues, parenting rights, the environment, history, technology, and finance, among others. While each position in these debates may have valid arguments or perspectives, it's important to recognize that some viewpoints might stem from personal projections or biases rooted in life experiences, generational beliefs, or cultural backgrounds. Despite these differences, everyone is entitled to their own viewpoints and thoughts, and judgment should not be displaced merely because someone's perspective conflicts with your own.

If a conversation becomes confrontational, it serves as a signal to respect personal boundaries and to step away from the discussion. This indicates the discussion is no longer about evidence or wisdom but becomes an emotional battle of *me vs. you* mentality. Allowing each individual to emotionally regulate prior to returning to the conversation is crucial for mutual respect. Before exiting the conversation, it is important to communicate to the other person that you need personal space and to suggest a specific time when you can resume the discussion. It is best to resolve relationship conflict within twenty-four to seventy-two hours, if possible.

Ultimately, it's not about winning, being right, belittling others, or saying one perspective is better than the other. Instead, it's about expanding your knowledge, finding a way to understand each other better through active listening, gaining perspective through another lens, and experiencing a deeper self-reflection of your limits. Intellectual conversations can be truly stimulating and enriching when each person feels respected and valued. Furthermore, embracing differences as a necessary part of a healthy discussion can make intellectual conversations a truly worthwhile experience.

Power of Voice

Speaking is a powerful means of activating your authentic inner voice, allowing you to command respect both personally and professionally in your relationships. It encourages you to share your thoughts, ideas, and beliefs, which elevates your ability to be seen as a high-value individual when engaging in intellectual conversations. Your message can influence and inspire those around you when sharing stories, expressing interests, or validating opinions, making an everlasting impact.

Our voice is one of the most valuable assets to help us cultivate genuine connections and initiate greater change through the expansion of our knowledge and understanding. It can break down barriers, bridge the gap between different perspectives, and build trustworthy relationships. Voicing our value creates an emotional experience where we feel supported and appreciated knowing that our words can shape or alter our engagement positively. It can guide healthy decision-making processes and overcome misunderstandings through interpersonal conversations.

When speaking with conviction and clarity, we can use the 5 *C's of Communication* to inspire collaboration and lead conversations toward elevation or resolution. It opens the door for negotiating intense conversations transforming them from confrontational to calm and constructive. This empowers everyone involved to feel comfortable and to vocalize their thoughts or emotions without walking on eggshells, whether with a loved one or a business associate. It inspires intellectual freedom to naturally motivate and persuade those to take action and achieve success without feeling coerced. Everyone's voice adds value to a conversation, as leaving things left unsaid only hinders our development and shuts down communication channels.

As for speakers, our voices can inspire authority and captivate an audience to reach a greater mission amongst the collective. Leaders have the intrinsic ability to bring people together and inspire a movement that elevates everyone around them, as well as their purpose. They have the power to awaken the senses of others through the influence of offering motivational messages or solutions. In return, they instill passion and positive energy in others to help them reach their goals.

Types of Intellectual Boundaries

- Listening without judging or criticizing opposing perspectives
- Choosing topics of discussion appropriate for the environment
- Accepting others do not share your beliefs or values
- Being aware of manipulation tactics that undermine your viewpoint
- Honoring the freedom to voice your own opinions, thoughts, and ideas
- Regulating emotions when discussions become intense
- Respecting the relationship or person despite differences in viewpoints
- Using your voice as a source of value
- Being aware of how others' beliefs may stem from their upbringing
- Finding understanding and value outside of personal perspective
- Excusing yourself from unhealthy conversations
- Honoring your mental and emotional health
- Shutting down insults against your beliefs, thoughts, or ideas
- Utilizing factorial and valuable evidence to support beliefs
- Creating a safe place for open dialogue
- Having an awareness of triggering topics
- Knowing intellectual limits on specific subject matters
- Respecting intellectual property, copyrights, and trademarked content
- Sharing confidential information with trusted sources

Example of the Boundary Badass Method for Intellectual Boundaries

ASAP: Assess with discovery questions, Set a boundary, Agree to a mutual plan, and Proceed with accountability

Step 1: **Assess** *with Discovery Questions*

Boundary Setter: How come you are undermining my opinion about working in an office?

Boundary Receiver: I disagree with it, but I don't believe I said anything wrong.

Step 2: **Set** *a Boundary*

Boundary Setter: It seems we have different opinions when discussing working from home. I value mutual respect. How can we honor our individual preferences for work environments?

Step 3: **Agree** *to a Mutual Plan Using "I" statements and Discovery Questions*

Boundary Receiver: I do respect you as an attorney and friend. Can you share what you found to be offensive?

Boundary Setter: Calling me "Mr. Know-It-All" and "sensitive" while sharing my beliefs about working from home. It seems out of character for you. Where is this coming from?

Boundary Receiver: I am not really sure, but I thought we could tease each other. I'm sorry for offending you. I will be more mindful of my words next time.

Boundary Setter: Thank you. I do value you as a close friend.

Step 4: **Proceed** *with Accountability*

Boundary Setter: (During a phone call weeks later) Hey! I know you have been working from home for the past year. My family is making some adjustments, and I want to pick your brain if you don't mind. I am considering working from home part-time. When are you free to talk?

Boundary Receiver: I have time now. What kind of questions do you have?

Boundary Setter: It's not about me managing my time. I want to be able to trust my staff while I am not at the office. How do you do this?

Boundary Receiver: We have a weekly team call every Monday to report updates on cases. We use a team management software for day-to-day operations and instant messaging for urgent matters. What other questions do you have?

Boundary Setter: Can you send me the applications and programs you use for internal operations?

Boundary Receiver: Yes, I will get it over to you by tomorrow. If any other questions come up, please shoot me a message.

Boundary Setter: Thanks for all your help.

Examples of Discovery Questions and Intellectual Boundaries

Discovery Questions:

- What family traditions do you find offensive?
- How come you are belittling me?
- When can I share my ideas with the team?

Intellectual Boundaries:

- I feel disrespected when I am being stereotyped for my family's traditions. I value open-mindedness. How can we be more understanding of our cultural differences?
- I feel undermined when I am criticized for my viewpoints on the benefits of technology. I value mutual respect. How can we look at technology from multiple perspectives?
- It seems new ideas are consistently overlooked when we have team meetings. I value leadership. What strategies can we implement to ensure innovative ideas are considered before reaching a final decision?

TWENTY SIX

FINANCIAL BOUNDARIES

Mateo had been searching for a talented head engineer for his up-coming skyscraper project. He couldn't afford to compromise on quality, as he had encountered challenges on his last project that cost him a pretty penny. Determined to secure the best in the business, he crossed paths with Quinn, whose exceptional skills and extensive experience immediately impressed Mateo. Mateo hired Quinn right on the spot, trusting he would execute on time and within the allocated budget.

While working together on the project, Mateo and Quinn's friend-ship grew beyond their professional partnership. They spent numerous hours discussing the building's design and sharing their mutual passion for baseball. To celebrate the successful completion of the skyscraper, Mateo and Quinn purchased tickets to the home opener of their favor-ite baseball team. From that day on, they made it their annual tradition.

Two years later, Quinn found himself caught in a downward spiral. He was financially struggling to keep things afloat. There was a huge lull in projects, and every proposal he sent out came back with a declined offer. Quinn was left bewildered and had zero answers. For years, he had put his sweat and tears into his engineering firm, but all of a sud-den, his client base was starting to plummet. The thought of his business dwindling away to nothing terrified him. What scared him even more was the thought of losing his home and work truck. His financial resources were being stretched thin, and he had already defaulted on his monthly truck loan.

With finances being limited, Quinn began to feel a significant amount of stress. He was embarrassed to tell his girlfriend, Blakley, about the amount of debt he was accumulating. Quinn was anxiously feeling stuck and decided to ask Mateo for financial advice. After all, he looked up to him for his business success and as a respectful husband and a father to his family; something Quinn deeply admired and wanted for himself.

Quinn shared with Mateo about his financial situation. "Man, this year has hit me hard. I can't close on new business to save my life."

Mateo raised his eyebrow puzzled. "What's going on?"

"I've never seen it like this in the last ten years. I'm getting outbid like crazy. I hope things turn around soon."

Mateo responded, "Well, I'll definitely refer you if I hear anything. You're okay otherwise?"

"Yes, I'm good. But I'm not sure I can even cover my truck payment this month. I haven't paid for it in the last two months. I'm coming up short and too ashamed to ask Blakely for help." Quinn looked down with self-disgust.

"You need me to help you out? I could loan you the money and you can pay me back when you can."

Quinn's eyes widened with surprise. "You would do that for me? I don't know how I could ever thank you. I literally owe you big time."

Mateo responded, "Well if the tables were turned, I'd hope you would do the same for me."

"Of course, I love you like a brother."

Mateo nonchalantly responded, "Let me know when, and I'll get you the money."

"My payment is past due, so the sooner the better. The bank keeps calling me."

"Okay, I'll get you the funds later this week. We'll meet for lunch or something." Mateo hugged him.

Mateo and Quinn met for lunch a couple of days later, and Mateo gave Quinn the money. Quinn was relieved and couldn't wait to run by the bank and make the payment. Quinn thanked Mateo multiple times and promised to pay him back once he received funds for his next business deal.

A year later, at the baseball home opener, Mateo and Quinn were standing in line to get beverages and snacks when Quinn began telling Mateo how great his year had gone. He was bragging about a huge project he had just closed on. Mateo was happy for him but also a bit perplexed since Quinn still owed him for the truck loan that he gave him a year ago. But he didn't say anything and kept letting Quinn boast about his success because he knew how much he had struggled in the past. Raining on his parade wasn't Mateo's style.

As they headed to their seats, they ran into a few of their other buddies at the game. Everyone was catching up like old times, and then Mateo overheard Quinn bragging again. Mateo was annoyed but knew it was the wrong time to address the issue.

Before they knew it, the game was tied in the seventh inning, and they were all sitting on the edge of their seats to see who would win. Mateo decided to grab one more round of beverages and hotdogs to finish out the game. As he was walking up the stadium stairs, Quinn ran up to join him.

While standing in line, Mateo lost his patience. "Hey man, I'm happy you're doing well this year, but do you mind paying me back for the loan if you have the money?"

"Uh…I guess. I kind of forgot about it."

Mateo angrily raised his voice. "How could you forget when I loaned you a couple of grand?"

"Well, I didn't forget. We haven't seen each other in a long time."

Mateo folded his arms across his chest. "Yeah, but we had a deal you would pay me back when you could. And it's clear you now have the money."

"You're right. I'll get it to you soon."

Boundaries are our lifeline to staying afloat when it feels like everything around us is sinking.

Insight

A lack of financial boundaries can drive a wedge in any relationship. While Mateo and Quinn had built a genuine friendship, they were on different pages regarding the value of financial responsibility. Quinn's lack of reimbursement on the financial loan could have easily destroyed his integrity with Mateo. Mateo inaccurately assumed Quinn had a similar mindset on money, and he quickly learned Quinn had broken his trust. Despite Mateo's relaxed approach to the financial loan, it was just as much his responsibility to initiate a payment plan with Quinn to collect the money he was owed by setting financial boundaries.

Due to Quinn's financial instability, he struggled to maintain a personal budget. He resorted to borrowing from a friend to pay one set of bills while accumulating additional debt elsewhere. Living beyond one's means can quickly become a slippery slope toward poor financial health, as it's only a matter of time before it becomes detrimental to one's livelihood.

When a financial loan goes unpaid, it can tarnish the trust between two individuals, leading to resentment or shattering the relationship altogether. Quinn's lack of financial responsibility could impact Mateo's decision to redefine their relationship from friends to acquaintances or deny him a financial loan in the future. Either situation could greatly affect their friendship and influence any future business partnerships.

When establishing financial boundaries, each individual is responsible for their part and reaching an amicable solution that specifies the terms for reimbursement. Having clarity on financial goals and commitments can prevent future misunderstandings and debts in relationships.

Definition of Financial Boundaries

Financial boundaries refer to personal or professional spending limits, saving, and investing to meet individual needs and lifestyle choices. Financial commitments may also include guidelines around lending, gift giving, debt repayment, or developing a financial plan that supports both responsibilities and relationships.

Financial Etiquette and Goals

Financial etiquette is vital to your relationship with yourself and others. Knowing how or when to make informed financial decisions can greatly impact your mental health. Being financially aware helps you decide when to spend, invest, or save according to your quality of life and goals. Financial planning can help you allocate funds wisely and differentiate between needs and wants. This may entail the development of a monthly or yearly budget and the cultivation of a positive relationship with money to enhance your long-term success.

With any monetary transaction, an emotional component is often tied to the financial commitment or purchase. When emotions are attached to assets or goods, they can weigh heavily on your relationship with yourself and whether or not the purchase hinders or supports your financial goals. Impulsive shopping can often lead to guilt, regret, stress, debt, and even financial bankruptcy. Therefore, emotional regulation is crucial for financial etiquette, ensuring purchases are feasible or beneficial to your long-term financial growth. To keep your financial status in good standing, a financial plan with established boundaries will help sustain accountability and wealth.

When it comes to money talk, openly speaking about personal finances can be seen as taboo in a public setting or in some cultures. Finances are typically private, and discussing them can be frowned upon as poor manners, especially if you do not share an interpersonal relationship with this person. Inquiring about someone's financials or boasting about your own financial success can create an imbalance within interpersonal relationships or sabotage the connection altogether. It is best practice to withhold monetary concerns or goals in a conversation until you have developed a deeper connection and you trust that they have your best interest for confidentiality.

General Financial Taboo Questions:

- What is your annual income?
- How much did you pay for that?
- What is your net worth?
- How much do you invest each year?
- What are your monthly expenses?

Romantic Relationships and Finances

Finances are one of the leading causes of relationship discord and dissolution. It's important for couples to have a monthly check-in to discuss financial planning. Sweeping financial spending differences under the rug can hinder relationship stability. When partners aren't aligned on where to allocate their expenses, or they use salary differences as a power play for purchases, it can create an emotional divide and wreak havoc on the relationship. Salary differences aren't a justification for purchases, as each partner will need to collaborate from a *we* mindset to support the health of the relationship.

Creating a shared and individualized monthly budget can prevent a lot of financial distress and disagreements for couples. Maintaining an open dialogue and firm financial boundaries on responsibilities for bills, entertainment, savings, traveling, or even shopping habits can create a healthy mindset for spending. This can establish good financial health for yourself or the household while preventing overspending, hiding purchases, or splurging on unnecessary habits or items. Financial boundaries aren't meant to feel restrictive; they are meant to support short-term and long-term financial goals out of respect for the relationship while simultaneously honoring the needs of each partner. The more you and your partner are transparent and honest about financial matters, the better off you will be in creating monetary alignment as a couple.

Inner Circle and Finances

Financial competition amongst friends, families, colleagues, or neighbors has been around forever, hence the phrase "keeping up with the Joneses." Individuals may attempt to see who can afford the nicest car, the biggest house, the best watch, the most stylish wardrobe, or who receives the biggest bonus to boost their own ego. When someone tries to financially one-up another person in their inner circle, it can stem from underlying issues with money or personal feelings of inadequacy. Creating competitiveness can also make others feel inadequate through the social pressure of buying items to belong, leading to financial distress.

If an individual chooses to live with a scarcity mindset, they will feel like something is constantly missing or experience dissatisfaction in life or relationships. They feel this burden due to their self-worth being defined by materialism, yearly income, job title, or financial net worth. Adopting a scarcity mindset or feeling like you must keep up with your inner circle financially can ultimately lead to a downward spiral of financial destruction. Eventually, it can erode your mental health, depriving you of happiness while pursuing a social status or chasing after the latest market trends.

Lending financial resources or covering routine expenses for a loved one can create strain on the relationship. Consistently picking up the tab may leave others, including family or friends, with limited respect for you and your financial resources. When it becomes a habit to constantly foot the bill, this can leave an open invitation for others to take advantage of your kindness and resources. While not everyone close to you will share the same financial status, knowing your financial contribution limit will be key to maintaining financial boundaries. This ensures that loved ones will not drain you financially or emotionally.

On the contrary, some individuals may use their financial contributions as a source of power to control the relationship. The financial provider can use their wealth as a means of keeping people at their convenience, dictating the connection, expecting exclusive loyalty, and demanding favors in return. It can create an imbalanced relationship and leave the other person potentially stuck without much say in the relationship if they depend on this person's resources for their livelihood.

Financial Manipulation May Look Like the Following:

- Controlling the relationship through financial resources
- Trying to one-up purchases
- Making others feel guilty for their financial flexibility or limitations
- Pressuring others into grand purchases for status
- Asking for a loan without reimbursement
- Buying one's loyalty for personal gain
- Hiding money or purchases
- Withholding financial resources through coercion
- Sending monetary gifts to secure the relationship

Business Relationships and Finances

Business policies enable a company to operate with ethical standards and financial responsibility to preserve integrity within business relationships. One of the major factors contributing to the decline in a company's financial performance is the quality of its organizational culture, its effectiveness in leadership, and its insufficient commitment to building strong partnerships. Poor relationship management can lead a business to underperform, leaving a company with dissatisfied clients, a tarnished reputation, and limited growth.

The establishment of financial boundaries within the organization is pivotal to sustaining professional relationships with investors, executives, and employees. By proactively fostering these financial boundaries, businesses can lay the groundwork for a stable financial foundation and ensure the longevity of their relationships. A strategic approach involves crafting contractual agreements that define roles and responsibilities for all internal relationships to uphold trust and transparency in regard to dividends, salaries, or bonuses. These comprehensive agreements should outline specific payment terms, deliverable timelines, and the ramifications of non-compliance. Through these well-defined agreements and structured workplace policies, businesses and employees are better equipped to withstand setbacks and make resilient recoveries. When employees feel valued and respected as contributors to the overall growth, they tend to be more engaged, motivated, and committed to achieving the organization's goals.

In addition to the strength of internal relationships, a company's most valuable asset is its network. External relationships are the leading force in driving revenue and increasing the overall bottom line. When initiating a new client relationship, it is paramount to be transparent about financial terms and conditions to avert client dissatisfaction and potential discord. Nurturing these valuable client relationships can also increase your company's revenue stream, as satisfied clients are more inclined to provide client referrals. However, the absence of well-defined financial processes can expose a business to potential risks, including finding itself in the red zone with outstanding balances and losses due to the mismanagement of funds or clientele. When a company has strong internal and external business relationships, it creates a competitive advantage and supports the success of a company.

Compulsive Spending and Impulsive Shopping Habits

Like any unhealthy habit, an obsession with compulsive spending or shopping can also be dysfunctional. Spending recklessly and impulsive buying can destroy an individual's livelihood and closest relationships when there is a lack of financial boundaries. Individuals with a shopping fixation are more likely to place a financial number on their self-worth. Constantly seeking the high of what you can buy next can lead to feeling internally worthless and dependent on the external validation of materialistic items. It becomes an ongoing pattern of averting personal challenges by placing a band-aid over the unresolved emotional wound. Escaping internal dissatisfaction prevents you from healing while depleting your bank account at the expense of your financial health. Attempting to buy your happiness can become a full-time job that will leave you feeling empty time after time. While compulsive spending may alleviate uncomfortable feelings in the moment, it only gives an illusion of control that will leave you numb once the initial high fades.

Unhealthy Spending Habits:

- Obsessing about shopping all the time
- Feeling a sense of extreme elation after a purchase
- Buying retail goods or leisure activities when feeling emotional distress
- Refusing to cut back on spending habits

- Using purchases as rewards but left with guilt
- Spending excessive amounts but still feeling unfulfilled
- Upholding an external image or social status
- Spending outside of financial means
- Searching compulsively for the perfect item
- Purchasing and returning goods repeatedly

Types of Financial Boundaries

- Establishing limits on lending and timelines for reimbursement
- Paying off financial debts in a timely manner
- Spending within financial means
- Saving or investing based on financial goals
- Avoiding competitiveness on purchases
- Refraining from asking others about their financial resources
- Establishing allocation of expenses prior to purchases
- Creating a monthly budget of needs versus wants
- Setting a monthly budgeting meeting with a significant other
- Seeking support for impulsive spending habits or compulsive buying
- Understanding and respecting others' financial means
- Providing transparency for shared financial expenses
- Upholding contractual agreements and payment terms for business
- Honoring the privacy of one's purse, wallet, financial balances, and investments
- Being mindful of credit card spending
- Prioritizing your financial stability before giving to others
- Honoring the agreement terms of a trust, estate, or will

Example of the Boundary Badass Method for Financial Boundaries

ASAP: *Assess with discovery questions,* **Set** *a boundary,* **Agree** *to a mutual plan, and* **Proceed** *with accountability*

Step 1: **Assess** *with Discovery Questions*

> Boundary Setter: How come I haven't received reimbursement?
>
> Boundary Receiver: It totally slipped my mind. I can pay you back, but I don't have the full amount.

Step 2: **Set** *a Boundary*

> Boundary Setter: I feel undervalued when I'm not reimbursed for the money I lent. I value integrity. Can we establish a payment plan?

Step 3: **Agree** *to a Mutual Plan Using "I" statements and Discovery Questions*

> Boundary Receiver: Sure. How about I pay you (x) amount for the next three months?
>
> Boundary Setter: That could work. Can you pay me on the first of each month?
>
> Boundary Receiver: Yes, I can pay you through direct deposit. How does that sound?
>
> Boundary Setter: Yes, that works.
>
> Boundary Receiver: Thank you for being understanding.

Step 4: **Proceed** *with Accountability*

> Boundary Setter: (The following month) Hey, I didn't receive your deposit. When did you send it?
>
> Boundary Receiver: I set up an automatic deposit with my bank. I believe you will have it by the end of the day.
>
> Boundary Setter: Okay. I'll let you know if it doesn't come through.
>
> Boundary Receiver: Great. Can you message me later if it doesn't?

Boundary Setter: Will do.

(The following day)

Boundary Setter: The deposit is not in my account. Can you check with your bank?

Boundary Receiver: Yes, I will call them now.

Boundary Setter: Thank you.

Boundary Receiver: My bank said you'll receive it today. They were closed yesterday for a holiday. Sorry about that.

Boundary Setter: I appreciate you checking.

Examples of Discovery Questions and Financial Boundaries

Discovery Questions:

- How come you expect me to cover the tab every time we go to dinner?
- Can you share how we spent (x) on marketing last month?
- What is wrong with renting an apartment?

Financial Boundaries:

- I feel undervalued when I'm expected to consistently pick up the tab. I value mutual respect. How about we take turns or split it next time?
- It appears we encountered a financial loss when we added the extra marketing expense. I value collaboration. Can we strategize a growth plan and see where we can cut back on expenses?
- I think we have different goals when it comes to our living situations. I value lifestyle freedom. Can we find a way to respect our different preferences?

TWENTY SEVEN
TIME BOUNDARIES

Sunday morning, Paige woke up and went to the kitchen to make matcha lattes for her and her fiancé, Warren. It was their morning ritual to talk about life and worldly news before their week began.

Warren skimmed the headlines. "Did you hear about the heatwave in the West? It's a hundred and fifteen degrees on average."

"Wow, sounds sweltering. By the way, this week is going to be busy. My schedule is jam-packed."

Warren quizzically looked over. "What's going on this week?"

"I have my usual spa clients. Also, I promised Cassandra I would help her out with her dog. Oh, and I'm starting classes."

Warren glanced over his shoulder. "What day are your classes again?"

"Every Monday, Wednesday, and Friday evening from five to eight."

Warren gave a perplexed look. "Basically, I won't see you, and I will be on my own for dinners?"

"Um, yes, unless you want to eat late when class is over." She leaned over and gave him a kiss on the cheek.

"How long is school again? And, how are you going to fit everything in?"

Paige hesitated. "I'm not quite sure. I know it's going to be tough to manage. School is a full year, so it will be an adjustment for sure."

"I think it will be great, but a big time commitment. Do you think you can manage it all?"

"Ha, babe, of course! Are you doubting me?"

Warren replied, "Not at all. I fully support you. I know you tend to become stressed out when you have a lot going on."

Paige shrugged her shoulders. "You're right. I do, but it will pay off."

Warren got up from his chair. "Do you mind picking up the dry cleaning tomorrow on your way home from work since it is near the spa?" He was out of clean dress shirts and desperately needed them for work.

Paige impulsively said, "Yes, I can."

It was the start of a new week, Paige headed to the spa while Warren headed to his office. Once Paige arrived at work, she saw her schedule was fully booked back-to-back with appointments. She loved being busy, as it gave her the opportunity to meet new people. Her dedication to assisting clients in overcoming their skin-related concerns was her true calling. It was what kept her inspired to open her own skincare spa, as she had struggled for many years with her skin complexion.

Before her last appointment of the day, Paige sat down for a ten-minute break. Her longtime client, Olivia, was scheduled for three o'clock but called to say she was running thirty minutes behind. Paige glanced over at the clock and began to fidget. She was worried she wouldn't have enough time to get everything done since she still had to go to the dry cleaners before she went to class at five.

Paige finished Olivia's appointment at 4:45 p.m. and felt stressed about getting to class on time. She quickly gathered her belongings and jumped into her car. As soon as she sat down in class, it dawned on her she had forgotten Warren's dry cleaning. She immediately felt guilty and knew Warren wasn't going to be happy with her.

Once class was over, she called Warren to let him know she would be home shortly and she was famished. When she walked through the front door, she saw he had made dinner for them and thoughtfully left her plate in the oven to stay warm.

While eating dinner at the kitchen island, Warren asked, "How was class?"

"It was intense, but I learned a lot. Thanks for making dinner."

Warren tapped his foot under the counter. "You're welcome. Did you grab my dry cleaning?"

Paige looked down. "Sorry, I ran out of time."

"I asked you yesterday, and you said you could grab it. Now, I have nothing to wear tomorrow for work. You're seriously so careless and only think about yourself and work. I made you dinner and this is how you treat me in return." Warren angrily left the kitchen.

"My client showed up thirty minutes late to her appointment. I had planned to go between my last client and class, but it didn't happen. I was even late to my first class."

"But then you should have never agreed to do it. It's not like this is the first time you have agreed to do something and then don't do it."

Paige yelled across the room, "How come you're getting mad? There was no time. It's not like I make a habit of being late. It rarely happens."

"That's not the point. It's fine. I'll get the shirts tomorrow. I'll have to re-wear my shirt from today."

After dinner, Paige sat on sofa and began going through her to-do list. She and Warren needed to finalize details for their wedding, which was only two months away. Paige asked Warren if he wanted to give welcome bags to the guests and if he had decided on the cake flavor. Warren told Paige it was up to her. Paige sensed Warren was still mad at her for not picking up the dry cleaning because he wasn't offering much help in making decisions for their special day.

Paige was growing frustrated. "You know you could help with making some of these decisions. It isn't just me getting married."

"These are things that are up to you. I care more about what we are eating and the music."

"Okay, fine, but you haven't contacted one vendor or made any decisions. And then you wonder why things are so overwhelming for me. I seriously can't manage it all and feel like I'm going to have a panic attack."

Warren leaned over to rub Paige's back. "Okay, don't freak out. Who do you want me to contact? What do you want me to decide on?"

Paige started to cry. "I don't care at this point. But I'm frustrated with everything going on and you're not helping."

"I'm listening. What is on the wedding to-do list?"

"I want you to take the initiative once in a while instead of putting everything on me to do when we have literally no time left."

Warren sat there in silence for a minute. "You volunteer to do everything so I thought you were fine with it."

Paige snapped, "I'm not fine! I'm trying to attend school, work full-time, and plan a wedding. But if I don't do it, then it won't get done."

"So, now you think I don't do things around here or help out?"

"I have done everything for our wedding. It's like you're blind to the stress it's causing me. I'm over this and going to bed." Paige walked away in tears.

Where we spend our time either enhances or diminishes the quality of our lives.

Insight

Paige, a go-getter, wanted to do it all without feeling like she had to give up something, despite the limited time she had in her schedule. She had big goals in every facet of her life, from going to school, being a great partner, and planning a wedding, but trying to commit to it all at once was proving unsustainable. She felt emotionally depleted and pulled in too many directions by saying yes to everyone and everything rather than honoring her time constraints. Warren was concerned about Paige taking on too many commitments, but it didn't stop him from adding another obligation to her schedule. Paige, being an overachiever, thought she could do it all, but it led to poor time management. When someone is unable to effectively manage their time or schedule, it can often be a sign they are lacking personal boundaries or self-discipline.

In the midst of Paige's commitments, she agreed to pick up Warren's dry cleaning but ran out of time in her day. Unable to preserve integrity with herself and Warren led to an argument between them. Had Paige set a time boundary with her client she could have prevented the disagreement with Warren and honored her existing commitments. Additionally, Warren, aware of Paige's new schedule, showed a lack of consideration when he asked Paige to pick up his dry cleaning. This added more stress to Paige's schedule, leaving no room to breathe between work and school.

When Warren discovered Paige didn't pick up his dry cleaning, he retaliated by throwing it in Paige's face about how he made dinner for her. He became emotionally dysregulated and attacked Paige, stating how careless she was. Couples who have a score-keeping mentality or have unresolved resentments have stepped away from a *we mindset*. When each partner is solely focused on themselves or uses a tit-for-tat approach, the relationship can be disconnected.

As for the wedding planning, a bulk of the responsibility fell on Paige's shoulders, which led to her breaking down from the compounding stress. Warren's lack of collaboration and acknowledgment of the wedding timeline only heightened matters, making last-minute decision-making stressful. Instead of resolving the disconnect for time management, they used accusatory language, like "you" statements, which prevented finding alignment and resolution. With neither honoring time boundaries for life events and weekly schedules, Paige and Warren found themselves taking out their problems on each other.

Definition of Time Boundaries

Time boundaries involve prioritizing responsibilities, effectively managing time to achieve personal and professional goals, and maintaining a work-life-love balance. By establishing time commitments, individuals maintain mutual respect within their relationships while dedicating quality time to their well-being, personal interests, and career growth.

Time Management

Time management is imperative to succeed both personally and professionally while maintaining remarkable relationships. Inefficient prioritization, such as spending too much time on low-priority tasks or overbooking oneself, can hinder productivity and progress toward one's goals. Trying to manage it all without prioritizing daily responsibilities, or asking for help when needed, can lead to being unable to sustain life with integrity.

Ineffectively scheduling appointments and commitments can be a challenge when individuals lack time boundaries. If you find being on time difficult or feel like your day constantly slips away leaving you with a never-ending to-do list, creating a time-blocked calendar can become your trusted confidant. This allows you to grant time between commitments, schedule self-care, and plan for delays or last-minute changes while maintaining personal alignment. Without a time-block schedule, lack of delegation or overcommitting can lead to anxiousness, burnout, or undue stress if tasks are unable to be fulfilled on time. When we fail to properly schedule our commitments it can lead to stunted growth and failed relationships due to inadequate time management.

Procrastination happens when individuals struggle to reach their goals and delay important movement toward a desired outcome. This cognitive process can be due to inefficient time management, paralyzed decision-making, and an inability to self-regulate which can perpetuate a cycle of missed opportunities due to fear of failure or success.

Holding oneself back from reaching fulfillment can stem from having low self-esteem and believing one is unworthy of such success if one achieves their goal. Throughout the procrastination cycle, an individual will stay in their comfort zone to avoid negative emotions or feedback, focus on short-term gratification rather than long-term benefits, and engage in mindless activities deterring them away from their authentic truth and desires.

Time is the most valuable asset and the one thing you can't get back in life, so it's critical to make sure personal choices align best with your values to keep your lifestyle and relationships intact. When it comes to strategizing your time, it can be better managed by setting realistic goals, breaking down tasks into smaller ones, and creating a priority list. Being intentional with your time is vital for time management and making beneficial choices for your life. Knowing where to scale back or increase the time spent in certain areas of your life can help sustain work-life-love balance and prevent strained relationships. The more you are self-aware of your choices and patterns, the better off you will be in transforming habits for effective time management and personal growth.

Time Etiquette

With time etiquette, it's important to be conscious of the start and end times of events. If you are hosting an event, planning a meeting, or making a dinner reservation, being mindful of outside variables and time constraints for those attending is imperative to relationship success. When the timing of events is poorly communicated, it leaves room for delays or people showing up unannounced before the start of the event.

If a person arrives too early or late without open communication, this can convey they have only considered what works for their schedule, except for unavoidable emergencies. It can be a sign of disrespect and poor manners, negatively impacting the individual hosting the event or meeting. These situations can heighten tension or hinder the relationship leading to unnecessary discord. Abiding by the original start time keeps healthy boundaries and embraces mutual respect for all.

Time Etiquette for Events:

- Business Meetings: Arrive 5 minutes early or on time
- Social Gatherings at Homes: Arrive between 5 to 10 minutes late
- Restaurants: Arrive on time, both personally and professionally
- Job Interviews: Arrive 5 to 10 minutes early
- Romantic Dates: Arrive no more than 5 minutes late
- Weddings: Arrive 15 minutes early
- Cocktail Parties: Arrive 15 to 30 minutes after invite time
- Professional Appointments: Arrive on time
- Ticketed Events: Arrive when doors open up until 15 minutes to start time

Authors' note: Time etiquette can vary in different cultures and countries.

Scheduling and Canceling Plans

When planning or scheduling meetings with others, it is best to provide several options. A good rule of thumb is two calendar dates and two time slots. Using a *we mindset* for scheduling joint commitments takes everyone's time into account and honors the relationship for continual growth. If you only offer a single time slot that works for you, it may hinder the ability to meet everyone's needs while creating an impasse. Operating from a *me mindset,* where there's a need for control or power based on your schedule, can push people away from you or hinder the connection. However, if an individual offers multiple time slots that don't align with your schedule, kindly suggest two separate timeframes that work in hopes of aligning on a mutually beneficial time.

Canceling plans can create uneasiness in relationships, especially if it is last minute or impacts the other person's life. On the surface, canceling plans may seem minor, but it can lead to significant inconveniences, disappointments, disrespect, and discord for those involved. Canceling may cause unexpected losses, such as energy from making plans, opportunities, financial investments, experiences, or loss of connection. Good reasons for calling off plans will happen occasionally; however, it's best to be honest and upfront about why you need to cancel. Also, giving ample time when canceling shows courtesy to the others involved, allowing them to reschedule their time. Even though emergencies can arise, it's best to communicate as soon as you know your schedule has altered. Informing others may require apologizing for the inconvenience while offering to reimburse them for any financial commitments involved in the plan. This will best ensure that the relationship stays intact. However, if you make a habit of canceling at the last minute without reason, this may cause the other person to reconsider when making plans with you in the future. Additionally, when needing to cancel plans, it's considerate to offer dates for rescheduling to show you value the relationship.

Types of Time Boundaries

- Being mindful of your commitments and limits
- Taking personal alone time to rejuvenate
- Being responsible for time management
- Having self-awareness of triggers when pressed for time
- Maintaining an organized schedule and calendar
- Establishing a hierarchy of priorities within your schedule
- Being mindful of time spent on electronics
- Making personal time for self-care and self-love practices
- Respecting other people's time

- Breaking down daily tasks and goals with a manageable action plan
- Asking for help from others when time is limited
- Communicating in advance when you need to cancel or reschedule
- Allocating travel time for ticketed events, reservations, or meetings
- Respecting cancellation policies or late fees
- Investing quality time with those who enhance your life
- Taking time off for vacations, celebrations, or bereavement
- Refraining from overcommitting to responsibilities or others
- Honoring time constraints for professional meetings
- Arriving at the appropriate time for scheduled appointments, reservations, or events

Example of the Boundary Badass Method for Time Boundaries

ASAP: Assess with discovery questions, Set a boundary, Agree to a mutual plan, and Proceed with accountability

Step 1: **Assess** *with Discovery Questions*

Boundary Setter: How come you aren't prioritizing our wedding planning?

Boundary Receiver: I didn't know you needed help.

Step 2: **Set** *a Boundary*

Boundary Setter: I feel frustrated when there's minimal effort in planning our wedding. I value mutual partnership. When can we find a time to do it together?

Step 3: **Agree** *to a Mutual Plan Using "I" statements and Discovery Questions*

Boundary Receiver: I understand you have dedicated more time than I have. What does our schedule look like this weekend?

Boundary Setter: Thank you for understanding. How about Saturday or Sunday morning around nine or ten o'clock?

Boundary Receiver: Let's plan for Saturday at nine o'clock over breakfast.

Boundary Setter: Okay. I will put it on our shared calendar.

Boundary Receiver: Cool. I'm happy we can check things off our list.

Step 4: **Proceed** with Accountability

Boundary Setter: (Saturday morning) I'm going to make us matcha lattes. Can you pull up our planning to-do list?

Boundary Receiver: I need to sleep fifteen more minutes.

Boundary Setter: Okay. I'll be in the kitchen.

Boundary Setter: (Fifteen minutes later) Babe! The lattes are ready.

Boundary Receiver: Coming, dear! I am getting my laptop.

Examples of Discovery Questions and Time Boundaries

Discovery Questions:

- Can you space out our client meetings?
- How come you don't want to go to dinner?
- How come you are running late?

Time Boundaries:

- I feel overwhelmed when client meetings are booked back-to-back without breaks. I value personal space. Can we schedule thirty-minute intervals between client appointments?
- I feel stressed when I have too much on my plate. I value lifestyle balance. Can we grab dinner next week instead?
- It seems we have different viewpoints when it comes to being punctual. I value time. How about we find a time that is better suited for both of our schedules?

TWENTY EIGHT
DIGITAL BOUNDARIES

Ainsley had felt like an outsider amongst her peers for as long as she could remember. She had memories of standing in front of the mirror in the sixth grade before heading off to school wondering why she didn't have many friends or look like the women in magazines. She desperately wanted to look like everyone else whom she thought was perfect because in her mind, she wasn't. Ainsley had tried dying her hair, changing her style, and exchanging her glasses for contacts, thinking this would make her likable.

Fast forward thirty years later, Ainsley was still chasing her dream of wanting to be liked, except now it was finally true. Ainsley had become the editor-in-chief of a lifestyle magazine. She knew that if she couldn't be the "it" woman in the magazines, then she would call the shots from behind the scenes.

Ainsley knew the media industry was not for the weak. They lived by the motto: *One day, you are in, and the next day, you are out.* Everyone knew Ainsley took pride in her work and only featured top-notch brands she had developed great relationships with. But, in the back of her mind, she still had doubts about whether her colleagues really liked her or if they just wanted their brand featured on the magazine cover.

Her phone was constantly buzzing with requests from industry friends and professionals, and tonight was no exception. She arrived at the industry event a few minutes ahead of schedule, accompanied by Frankie, her photographer, who was there to capture photos and promote the brand she was representing.

Upon entering the event space, Ainsley was completely amazed by the ambiance. The dimmed, all-black room was illuminated with candlelight, as subdued music played in the background. Frankie began snapping a few photos of Ainsley in her sleek black dress, so she could post them on social media. While Ainsley wasn't on the cover of magazines, she was an icon online within the media industry – a dream of Ainsley's for as long as she could remember.

Ainsley scrolled through the images. "These are awful. Let's turn on the flash and try again."

"Okay, one second." Frankie took ten more images of Ainsley with the flash. "Here, look at these."

"No, these are so blah. I can't post any of them. I'll get ripped to shreds online. Is it the dress or me? Why do I look so washed out?"

Frankie turned her head to get a better look. "I think it's the lighting. Do you want to take photos out front?"

"No, I want the backdrop in my images. The brand is counting on me to post in their dress."

Frankie took fifteen more images of Ainsley in different poses in front of the candlelit ambiance. "Look at these. Do you see any you like?"

Ainsley glanced down. "No. I seriously must have been blind when I left the house in this dress. I look horrendous. But I have no choice but to post, or we may lose advertising from the client. I guess I will settle on this one."

"You look amazing!" Frankie smiled.

Ainsley quickly edited the lighting in the photo as best as she could and posted the image. About halfway through the event, Ainsley excused herself to the ladies' room. She pulled out her phone and couldn't believe the negative comments she was receiving on social media. With thousands of followers, everyone had something to say about her. Her face turned completely white, and she turned to Frankie to ask, "Should I delete it?"

"No. Why would you delete it?"

Ainsley replied, "Because look what they are saying! One person said I look like a trash bag. Another said I'm too old to wear this. Oh look, one nice person says I'm cutting edge. Another said to get a life."

Frankie put on her lipstick. "Those are ridiculous. But I'm shocked you haven't become used to these messages yet. You've been at the top of your game for years. And, you're greatly admired; everyone loves you."

Ainsley looked shocked. "You really think that?"

"Absolutely! I know I look up to you and so does everyone here tonight. These people online are complete strangers. Let's go back to the party."

Ainsley panicked as she scrolled through the messages. Her hands trembled when she read each one. While some of her followers showed support for her success, others clearly wanted to rain on her parade. She knew building her image in the digital world came with some harsh realities, but she hadn't fully grasped just how brutal it could be. After all, her online image was meant to be an avenue for expressing her individuality and lifestyle, not a place for receiving derogatory comments.

She continued trying to block out the chatter of her followers, but the reality was their voices weren't going away. Ainsley had trouble focusing the rest of the evening and ended up dashing out of the event early. She told everyone she had a seven o'clock meeting in the morning. But the truth was, she wanted to go home and take a bubble bath, listen to music, and escape from reality. Not being accepted by others had been her deepest fear since childhood.

The next day, Ainsley headed to work with a fake smile. Sitting at her desk trying to make her embarrassing nightmare disappear, she got a message from a friend about heading to a concert that evening. Ainsley knew dancing to music was exactly what she needed to let loose, so she agreed to go. Rummaging through her closet, she found her favorite jeans and a black top. She looked in the mirror one last time before throwing on her shoes and heading out the door.

While at the concert, Ainsley snapped some photos with her girlfriend. She posted the image of them smiling and dancing then immediately shoved her phone into her back pocket and enjoyed the rest of the concert. Music was her saving grace from stress, and she started feeling free again.

On the way home, Ainsley pulled out her phone and saw thousands of likes on her photo from the concert. It made her smile, and she felt loved again by her fans – that was until she scrolled through the messages.

Ainsley read them out loud. "Look what this person said. 'Do you ever stay home?' And, another 'Wow, you really dressed down tonight.' Or how about this one, 'Did you dye your hair because it looks awful?' And another, 'So cute but so last year.' I seriously can't catch a break lately."

Ainsley's friend replied, "People will always have something to say. Your friends and family are all that matter."

Self-care is unplugging from the rest of the world.

Insight

Ainsley was living her dream of being a lifestyle magazine editor. She was doing exactly what she loved, but it came with the cost of not being accepted by all. Even though she thought she had overcome her worst fears as a teenager, the minute she received harsh criticism from online fans, the self-doubt seeped into her mindset all over again. Ainsley's inner critical voice overshadowed her happiness, both personally and professionally. When a person suffers from low self-esteem, they likely grew up in a home with a highly critical parent or were over-ly pampered. This parent may have emotionally rejected the child for control, solely loved them based on appearance or image, or did every-thing for them, which robbed them of developing their confidence and self-worth. This wreaks havoc on a child's self-esteem and self-image, impacting their adulthood relationships. This led to Ainsley continu-ously searching for external validation as she struggled to find self-ac-ceptance from within.

Her weekly social media posts were required for her career and on-line image as chief editor of a magazine. However, rather than setting digital boundaries for herself, she allowed social media to overpower and infiltrate beliefs about herself. Ainsley placed her self-worth in the hands of her fans and followers instead of accepting herself for who she was outside social media.

When it comes to cyberbullying, learning not to internalize peo-ple's comments or even entertain them as the truth can save someone a lot of emotional distress. Shutting out the online chatter proved chal-lenging for Ainsley because she neglected to operate from her values; instead, she was reacting to her emotional triggers of not feeling good enough. Setting personal limits on the type and amount of information consumed on social media can help create guidelines for a healthy life-style.

Definition of Digital Boundaries

Digital boundaries enable individuals to assess the influence of pos-itive and negative aspects of the digital world on their lives and rela-tionships. They allow for limits to be set on time usage, interactions with apps, text messaging, photo sharing, video calls, and protecting financial privacy during online transactions, as well as managing screen time for television shows and movies.

Digital Privacy

In the digital world of opportunities and convenience, it's imperative to define boundaries that secure your privacy. Protecting your digital life involves adding passwords, activating security features on your devices, utilizing privacy settings on social media, refraining from sharing precise locations, and guarding against potential identity and financial theft.

Having an online presence has become a fundamental part of modern-day life, serving as a platform for connections, professional branding, information sharing, and digital transactions. With an increase in digital footprints, it has also amplified concerns for privacy breaches. The ease of sharing personal information online has inadvertently exposed vulnerabilities in our private lives, such as financial threats, unsolicited spam, location tracking, or unauthorized access to private information. To reduce risk, activating privacy modes and setting passwords empowers you to manage who can access your personal information.

Additionally, your digital privacy choices can significantly influence your real-world relationships. Some may willingly share phone passwords and location details, while others may value their privacy and choose to opt out of providing access to their devices. Determining digital boundaries is a matter for each individual and household, including decisions regarding shared computers, tablets, and passwords among family members. The establishment of such boundaries in a shared living space cultivates healthy relationships by addressing aspects like age-appropriate content, time usage, and mutual respect.

For professionals who utilize electronic devices for work, maintaining clear digital boundaries and protecting personal information is paramount. Storing personal data on shared work devices could unintentionally lead to disclosure within the workplace or accidentally expose sensitive information to unauthorized parties, potentially jeopardizing your career or reputation.

Safeguarding your personal life is crucial for ensuring your privacy, security, and connectivity in the digital world. Maintaining healthy boundaries with family members, limiting personal details with colleagues or employers, and regulating who has access to your online presence and personal information will be your responsibility to protect.

Digital Timeouts

Electronic usage can be valuable and productive, but in today's world, it can also adversely affect your mental health. Sometimes, an individual may be on their phone more than they prefer or get hooked on television marathons, which can become a source of relationship conflict, a distraction from personal goals, or weaken one's self-esteem. When electronic usage takes precedence over being fully present with others or your goals, it may indicate the need to reevaluate one's digital priorities.

Many people, including individuals, couples, and families, discover the benefits of taking timeouts from electronic devices. Boundaries such as refraining from phone usage during meals, implementing the Do Not Disturb function, or setting time limits for screen time can contribute to a healthier relationship with electronics. Establishing timeouts will greatly depend on your personal lifestyle choices and what's best for each individual or relationship dynamic.

For those working independently or within companies utilizing digital communication platforms for performance management, it's best to establish digital boundaries. These boundaries can encompass response times for both urgent and non-urgent matters involving team members, as well as taking timeouts to manage performance and mental health. The constant influx of private messages or chat room interactions from colleagues can disrupt concentration, decrease productivity, and overstimulate the nervous system. By setting digital boundaries, one can support personal time during and after work hours, fostering a harmonious balance between work, life, and love.

Digital Boundaries with Children and Teens

Setting boundaries for children is necessary given the accessibility to digital applications and social media platforms, and technology's impact on child development. Using parental features to protect a child's self-esteem and safety is more important than ever due to a wide range of digital opportunities. It is not difficult for a child or teenager to accidentally click on a site with inappropriate content, predators, or vulgar language that influences the child's behaviors and impairs their safety. Most of the time, when a child ends up on these sites, it's by chance, curiosity, or influence from their inner circle.

Electronics may seem relatively harmless until you notice a child displaying new behaviors, withdrawing from everyday activities, resorting to their room more than usual, showing more signs of secrecy, engaging in unhealthy trends, or exhibiting a diminished interest in school or friends. It may be a sign the child is emotionally struggling with life and needs extra support or real-life engagement outside electronics. Monitoring the use of technology can benefit a child's mental and emotional development, as they are a sponge for learning and interpreting the information they come across on the internet. Constantly comparing themselves to others on digital platforms can lead to questioning their body image, self-esteem, social status, talents, physical athleticism, and identity. Children haven't fully developed their identity during this exploration period, and this can weigh heavily on their belief system and sometimes lead to unfortunate circumstances or choices. Parental involvement and discretion are necessary when setting digital boundaries with children.

Cyberbullying

The surge of online digital platforms has made it easier for people to hide behind screens and engage in cyberbullying. This behavior is not limited to social media but can be found in various online platforms, such as email, private text messages, gaming rooms, and online message boards. Cyberbullying can take various forms, such as harassment, falsified information, defamation of character, stalking, intellectual differences and beliefs, etc. And unfortunately, anyone can become a victim of online intimidation, which is why digital boundaries are a must.

The repercussions of cyberbullying can be detrimental, impacting an individual's self-image and social reputation when exposed online. This impact can have lasting implications on career prospects, educational pursuits, social connections, affiliations with professional groups, and other associations where character evaluation is fundamental to acceptance. In addition to harming an individual's reputation, cyberbullying takes a toll on a person's self-esteem and overall lifestyle. It is crucial to understand that cyberbullies who use disparaging language about another person reveal more about their own character than the victim. Cyberbullies often suffer from low self-esteem and shortcomings that they project onto others to avoid self-reflection. They may make hurtful remarks out of jealousy, envy, anger, instability, low self-worth, or a desire for revenge.

Fortunately, many platforms now actively combat cyberbullying, protecting victims from defamation, abuse, and threatening behavior. While not every hurtful message or comment can be erased, it's essential to cultivate a strong sense of self-worth and establish digital boundaries to protect oneself. This approach prevents the internalization of others' actions and preserves one's emotional and psychological well-being. Ultimately, it's paramount to use digital platforms responsibly, show kindness toward others, and remember that behind every screen is a real person with authentic feelings.

Types of Digital Boundaries

- Establishing digital timeouts to maintain health or relationships
- Restricting notifications, comments, and direct messaging
- Disabling active time stamps or read receipts
- Utilizing the Do Not Disturb feature
- Deleting unnecessary applications
- Unfollowing those on social media who negatively impact your mental health
- Shutting off movies or shows that cause distress or nightmares
- Setting automatic shut-offs on electronics
- Disengaging from cyberbullying and slanderous statements
- Respecting the privacy of individuals' devices
- Ensuring online comments reflect face-to-face communication
- Presenting an authentic persona online
- Setting parental controls for children and teens on usage time, specific apps, and sites
- Asking before tagging someone in a post
- Establishing limits or preferences around text messaging or video chatting
- Adding security features to prevent hacking, tracking, or theft
- Establishing privacy for online banking and investment applications
- Setting passwords to protect private information
- Sharing information, location, and photos with only trusted sources
- Silencing group chats and messenger platforms
- Seeking permission or giving credit when distributing original content

Example of the Boundary Badass Method for Digital Boundaries

ASAP: *Assess with discovery questions,* *Set a boundary,* *Agree to a mutual plan,* and *Proceed with accountability*

Step 1: **Assess** *with Discovery Questions*

> Boundary Setter: How come you keep checking the comments on your posts?
>
> Boundary Receiver: I want to see what everyone is saying.

Step 2: **Set** *a Boundary*

> Boundary Setter: I feel frustrated when we go out and our night revolves around social media. I value quality time. Can we enjoy the night without our phones?

Step 3: **Agree** *to a Mutual Plan Using "I" statements and Discovery Questions*

> Boundary Receiver: Sorry, it's part of my work. But I understand and will try to keep it quick.
>
> Boundary Setter: I know you love your job, but I hardly see you. I was hoping we could just spend time together. Plus, a lot of those comments from followers are rude. How do you deal with it every day?
>
> Boundary Receiver: Oh, it is exhausting day after day! I need to try to check it less for my mental health.
>
> Boundary Setter: Yeah, I love the feature where you can shut off comments.
>
> Boundary Receiver: Maybe I'll try that.

Step 4: **Proceed** *with Accountability*

> Boundary Setter: (Next outing) I am so excited to hang out tonight. How are you?
>
> Boundary Receiver: I am great. It feels like it has been forever since I saw you last. What's new with you?
>
> Boundary Setter: I've been trying to work less. By the way, thank you for suggesting turning off the comment feature. I've tried it

on a few posts, and it has been a huge time saver not to check social media as often. I think it was becoming an addiction.

Boundary Receiver: I'm happy it's helping you.

Examples of Discovery Questions and Digital Boundaries

Discovery Questions:

- What movie did you pick?
- How come I received several emails about the same issue?
- Can you please shut off your alarm?

Digital Boundaries:

- I feel uncomfortable when we have to watch thriller films because they give me nightmares. I value collaboration. What can we watch instead that we both will enjoy?
- I think it's disruptive when I receive multiple emails on the same subject matter. I value productivity. How can we streamline communication?
- I feel annoyed when the alarm keeps going off and I'm trying to sleep. I value mutual respect. How can we be mindful of each other's sleep schedules?

CLOSING THOUGHTS

Now that you have embarked on a journey of setting boundaries, you have learned the techniques to authentically express yourself, define your limits, meet your needs, and ultimately elevate the quality of your life and relationships. By voicing your value, you can sustain self-respect without the fear of others' reactions or feeling powerless. Your inner strength will illuminate an entirely new perspective on what defines healthy relationships and how powerful you truly are. Setting boundaries grants you the confidence to assert your worth when encountering challenges or evolving your connections, thus paving the way for long-lasting relationship success.

The BOUNDARY BADASS METHOD serves as a valuable communication skill that fosters clarity, connection, and conflict resolution in all relationships. By defining your standards on what you're willing and unwilling to accept, you prioritize your well-being across all facets of life, both personally and professionally. Boundaries are indispensable for cultivating inner peace, authentic self-expression, personal freedom, and relationship alignment. We hope that this book inspires you to live a fulfilling life – one in which you feel heard, understood, respected, and valued. Establishing healthy boundaries liberates you from powerlessness and transforms you into a BOUNDARY BADASS.

References

1. Ainsworth, M. D. S., Blehar, M. C., Waters, E., and Wall, S. (1978). *Patterns of Attachment: A Psychological Study of the Strange Situation*. New Jersey: Lawrence Erlbaum Associates.

2. Archer, Dale. (2017). "The Danger of Manipulative Love-Bombing in a Relationship". https://www.psychologytoday.com/intl/blog/reading-between-the-headlines/201703/the-danger-of-manipulative-love-bombing-in-a-relationship.

3. Asper, Kathrin. (1992). *Inner Child in Dreams*. C. G. Jung Foundation Books Series. Boulder, CO: Shambhala.

4. Baumrind D. (1967) "Child Care Practices Anteceding Three Patterns of Preschool Behavior." *Genet Psychol Monogr.*;75 (1):43-88. https://pubmed.ncbi.nlm.nih.gov/6032134/

5. Bourbeau, L. (2002). *Heal Your Wounds and Find Your True Self: Finally a Book That Explains Why It's So Hard Being Yourself*. Silver Lake, WI: Lotus Press.

6. Bourne, J. E. (1995). *The Anxiety and Phobia Workbook*. New Harbinger Publications, Inc.

7. Bowen, M. (1993). *Family Therapy in Clinical Practice*. 1st Ed. Lanham, MD: Jason Aronson, Inc.

8. Bowlby, J. (1969). *Attachment and Loss*. (OKS Print.) New York: Basic Books.

9. Bowlby, J. (1988). *A Secure Base: Parent-Child Attachment and Healthy Human Development*. New York: Basic Books.

10. Bradshaw, John. (1990). *Homecoming: Reclaiming and Championing Your Inner Child*. 1st. Ed. New York, NY: Bantam.

11. Carlson, J. and Englar-Carlson, M. (2017). *Adlerian Psychotherapy (Theories of Psychotherapy Series)*. Washington, DC: American Psychological Association.

12. Clance, Pauline. (1985). *The Impostor Phenomenon: Overcoming the Fear That Haunts Your Success*. Atlanta, GA: Peachtree Publishers Ltd.

13. Carnes, P. (2019). *The Betrayal Bond: Breaking Free of Exploitive Relationships*. Revised Ed. Deerfield Beach, FL: Health Communications, Inc.

14. Dana, D. and Porges, S. (2018). *The Polyvagal Theory in Therapy: Engaging the Rhythm of Regulation*. New York: W. W. Norton & Co.

15. Darwin, Charles. (2009). *The Expression of the Emotions in Man and Animals*. London, UK: Penguin Books.

16. Dreikurs, Rudolf and Stolz Vicki (1991). *Children: The Challenge: The Classic Work on Improving Parent-Child Relations--Intelligent, Humane & Eminently Practical*. New York, NY. Plume.

17. Dweck, Carol S. (2007). *Mindset: The New Psychology of Success*. New York, NY: Random House Publishing Group.

18. Erikson, E. H. (1950). *Childhood and Society*. New York: W. W. Norton & Co.

19. Frankl, Viktor (2006). *Man's Search for Meaning*. Boston, MA. Beacon Press.

20. Firestone, R., Firestone, L., and Catlett, J. (2002). *Conquer Your Critical Inner Voice: A Revolutionary Program to Counter Negative Thoughts and Live Free from Imagined Limitations*. Oakland, California: New Harbinger Publications.

21. Goleman, Daniel. (2005). *Emotional Intelligence: Why It Can Matter More Than IQ*. 10th Ed. New York, NY: Random House Publishing Group.

22. Goleman, D., Boyatzis, R. E., and McKee, A. (2013). *Primal Leadership: Unleashing the Power of Emotional Intelligence*. Brighton, MA: Harvard Business Review Press

23. Gordon, Thomas. (2000). *Parent Effectiveness Training: The Proven Program for Raising Responsible Children*. 1st Ed. Chatsworth, CA: Harmony

24. Gottman, J., and Silver, N. (2015). *The Seven Principles of Making a Marriage Work*. Revised Ed. Chatsworth, CA: Harmony.

25. Gottman, J., and Declaire, J. (1998). *Raising an Emotionally Intelligent Child: The Heart of Parenting*. 3rd Ed. New York: Simon & Schuster.

26. Gottsman, Diane. "The Etiquette Rules of Being on Time." The Muse, 20 June 2020, https://www.themuse.com/advice/the-etiquette-rules-of-being-on-time.

27. Hall, Edward.T. (1965). *The Silent Language*. 5th Ed. Greenwich, CT: Fawcett Premier.

28. Hall, E. T. (1966). *The Hidden Dimension*. New York: Anchor Books.

29. Jurkovic, G. (2015). *Lost Childhoods*. 1ˢᵗ Ed. New York: Routledge.

30. Li, Pamela. (2023). "4 Types of Parenting Styles and Their Effects on Children." https://www.parentingforbrain.com/4-baumrind-parenting-styles/#baumrind

31. Luft Joseph (1969). *Of Human Interaction*. Palo Alto, CA: National Press Books.

32. Maccoby E. E., and Martin J. A. (1983). Socialization in the Context of the Family: Parent-Child Interaction. In P. H. Mussen, & E. M. Hetherington (Eds.), *Handbook of Child Psychology*: (Vol 4.) Socialization, Personality, and Social Development. (1-101). New York: Wiley.

33. Main, M., and Solomon, J. (1986) Discovery of a New, Insecure-Disorganized/Disoriented Attachment Pattern. In T. B. Brazelton & M. Yogman (Eds), *Affective Development in Infancy*, pp. 95-124. Norwood, NJ: Ablex.

34. McKee, Maralee. "The Best Time to Arrive at Business and Social Events." The Etiquette School of America, https://www.etiquetteschoolofamerica.com/the-best-time-to-arrive-at-business-and-social-events/

35. Mehrabian, Albert. (1972). *Silent Messages*. Belmont, CA: Wadsworth Publishing Company.

36. Mehrabian, A. (2017). *Nonverbal Communication*. New Brunswick: Aldine Transaction.

37. Minuchin, Salvador. (2012). *Families and Family Therapy*. Cambridge, MA: Harvard University Press.

38. Porges, Stephen W. (2011). *The Polyvagal Theory: Neurophysiological Foundations of Emotions, Attachment, Communication, and Self-Regulation*. 1ˢᵗ Ed. New York: W. W. Norton & Co.

39. Pronin, E.; Lin, D. Y.; Ross, L. (2002). The Bias Blind Spot: Perceptions of Bias in Self Versus Others. *Personality and Social Psychology Bulletin*. 28 (3): 369–381

40. Rogers, Carl. R. (2004). *On Becoming a Person: A Therapist's View of Psychotherapy*. New Ed. London, UK: Constable & Robinson Ltd.

41. Rogers, C., and Farson, R. (2015). *Active Listening*. Connecticut: Martino Publishing.

42. Roseberg, Morris (2015). *Society and the Adolescent Self-Image*. Princeton, NJ: Princeton University Press.

43. Schneiderman, I., Zagoory-Sharon, O., Leckman, J. F., and Feldman, R. (2012, January 26). Oxytocin During the Initial Stages of Romantic Attachment: Relations to Couples' Interactive Reciprocity. *Psychoneuroendocrinology* 37(8), 1,277-1,285 Retrieved from http://www.ncbi.nlm.nih.gov/pmc/articles/PMC3936960/

44. Stone, H. and Stone, S. (1993). *Embracing Your Inner Critic: Turning Self-Criticism into a Creative Asset.* San Francisco, CA: HarperOne.

45. Titelman, P. (2008). *Triangles: Bowen Family Systems Theory Perspectives.* 1st Ed. Philadelphia, PA: Haworth Press.

46. Vygotsky L. S. (1987). *Thinking and Speech. The collected works of Lev Vygotsky (Vol. 1).* New York, NY: Plenum Press.

47. Walker, P. (2013). *Complex PTSD: From Surviving to Thriving: A Guide and Map for Recovering from Childhood Trauma.* California: CreateSpace Independent Publishing.

48. White, B. A., and Porterfield, S. P. (2013). *Endocrine and Reproductive Physiology.* Oxford, UK: Elsevier Health Sciences.

Index

Resources

Visit
https://www.boundarybadass.com
or
https://www.janandjillian.com
for more valuable resources on relationships, boundaries, and conflict resolution.